REVOLUTION
___

Volume 4

BLACK DEMOCRACY

BLACK DEMOCRACY

The Story of Haiti

H. P. DAVIS

Routledge
Taylor & Francis Group

LONDON AND NEW YORK

First published in Great Britain in 1929 by George Allen & Unwin

This edition first published in 2022
by Routledge
4 Park Square, Milton Park, Abingdon, Oxon OX14 4RN

and by Routledge
605 Third Avenue, New York, NY 10158

Routledge is an imprint of the Taylor & Francis Group, an informa business

© 1928 H.P. Davis

All rights reserved. No part of this book may be reprinted or reproduced or utilised in any form or by any electronic, mechanical, or other means, now known or hereafter invented, including photocopying and recording, or in any information storage or retrieval system, without permission in writing from the publishers.

Trademark notice: Product or corporate names may be trademarks or registered trademarks, and are used only for identification and explanation without intent to infringe.

British Library Cataloguing in Publication Data
A catalogue record for this book is available from the British Library

ISBN: 978-1-032-12623-4 (Set)
ISBN: 978-1-003-26095-0 (Set) (ebk)
ISBN: 978-1-032-18724-2 (Volume 4) (hbk)
ISBN: 978-1-032-18726-6 (Volume 4) (pbk)
ISBN: 978-1-003-25592-5 (Volume 4) (ebk)

DOI: 10.4324/9781003255925

Publisher's Note
The publisher has gone to great lengths to ensure the quality of this reprint but points out that some imperfections in the original copies may be apparent.

Disclaimer
The publisher has made every effort to trace copyright holders and would welcome correspondence from those they have been unable to trace.

BLACK DEMOCRACY

THE STORY *of* HAITI

By H. P. DAVIS

Copyright, 1928, by
THE DIAL PRESS, INC.

MANUFACTURED IN THE UNITED STATES OF AMERICA
BY THE VAIL-BALLOU PRESS, INC., BINGHAMTON, N. Y.

CONTENTS

PART I

	PAGE
INTRODUCTION	3
CHAPTER I THE SPANIARDS	8

Discovery of Hispaniola—Second expedition of Columbus—Extermination of the aborigines—Inauguration of the slave trade—Progress and decline of the Spanish colony.

CHAPTER II THE FRENCH COLONY OF ST.-DOMINGUE ... 16

The *boucaniers*—Origin of the French colony—Rapid and prosperous development—Inception of the mulatto caste—Social and political conditions on the eve of the Revolution—Political conditions in France reflected in the colony—Declaration of the "Rights of Man"—Whites, mulattoes, and blacks.

CHAPTER III THE REVOLUTION ... 36

Uprising of the Blacks—Failure of the first French commission—The second commission—Emancipation of the slaves—Desperate condition of the colony—The British expedition—Toussaint l'Ouverture—The third commission—Strife between blacks and mulattoes—Toussaint in supreme power.

CHAPTER IV "FIRST OF THE BLACKS" ... 58

Napoleon Bonaparte and Toussaint—The Leclerc expedition—Toussaint defeated—Ravages of yellow fever—Death of Leclerc—Defection of black and mulatto leaders—The surrender of Rochambeau and triumph of the blacks.

CHAPTER V DESSALINES, DICTATOR AND EMPEROR ... 87

Proclamation of freedom—Problems of reconstruction—Declaration of independence—Dessalines governor-general—He is crowned emperor—Death of Dessalines.

CONTENTS

CHAPTER VI CHRISTOPHE AND PÉTION . . 99

The black *vs.* the mulatto—First constitution of the Republic—Christophe elected president—He declines to serve—The North and South divided—Civil War—Christophe creates his own "State of Haiti" in the North—Pétion elected president of the Republic of Haiti—Christophe crowned king of the "State of Haiti"—Separation of the South—War between the two states—France attempts to regain her lost colony—Death of Pétion—Boyer succeeds him—Revolution against Christophe—His tragic death.

CHAPTER VII THE HAITIAN REPUBLIC FROM 1818 TO 1908 . . 114

The North and South united under Boyer—The Spanish port consolidated with the Republic of Haiti—Foreign relations—Negotiations with France for recognition of the Republic—Boyer forced to accept a most humiliating compact—Revolt of the people—Death of Boyer—Four presidents in four years—Solouque elected president—He creates the second empire—His extraordinary reign of over eleven years—Failure to reconquer Santo Domingo—He is deposed—President Geffrard serves ably for nine years—Concordat with Holy See—Attempts at settlement in Haiti by American Negroes—Revolt suppressed—British gun-boat sunk—Cap Haitien fired on by British—Salnave enters Cap Haitien—Geffrard resigns—Salnave as president—He is deposed and executed—Miserable condition of the "Republic"—Domingue's disgraceful administration—Canal—Rivalry between Liberal and National parties—Canal resigns and is succeeded by Salomon, who serves nine years—Resigns—Légitime serves one year and six months—He resigns and is succeeded by Hippolyte, who serves creditably for nine years—Simon Sam serves for six years—Resigns—Death of Admiral Killick—Nord Alexis elected—His courageous devotion to his office—The consolidation scandal—Revolution puts Simon in office.

PART II

FOREWORD 141

CHAPTER I THE REVOLUTIONARY PERIOD, 1908–1915 143

Reorganization of the National Bank—Cacos put Leconte in power—Haiti's first civilian president—Approaching bank-

CONTENTS

ruptcy—First steps towards American intervention—Salvaging $500,000—Admiral Caperton personally conducts a revolution—American commissioners fail to negotiate a treaty.

CHAPTER II THE AMERICAN INTERVENTION 161

Situation on the night of July 26th—Massacre in the national prison—Murder of President Sam—Inception of the American occupation—German aspirations—Preparing for the presidential election—Senator Dartiguenave elected.

CHAPTER III THE HAITIAN-AMERICAN TREATY 180

Negotiations for the treaty—The custom houses seized—American insistence on the treaty—Winning over the Haitian legislature—The treaty—Breaking the insurrection in the North—Embarrassment of the Dartiguenave Government—The treaty extended to 1936.

CHAPTER IV THE OCCUPATION . . . 194

The treaty officials—The *gendarmerie*—Finance and customs control—Public works and public health—Handicap of treaty officials—Protocol of 1919—First dissolution of the Haitian legislature—Struggle over the new constitution—The second dissolution—The constitutional "plebiscite"—Provisions of the constitution—Shall the white man own Haitian land?

CHAPTER V THE CACO UPRISING . . . 216

The *corvée*—How the *corvée* came to be abused—The caco outbreak—The attack on Port-au-Prince—Charges against the marines—The Naval Court of Inquiry—The Senate inquiry.

CHAPTER VI NATIONAL ELECTIONS . . 240

The myth of "representative government"—The Council of State as a reasonable concession—First election by the Council of State—President Borno's defence of the *status quo*—President Borno's re-election—The thorny problem of the constitutional amendments—The "freedom of the press"—Reorganization of the judiciary.

CONTENTS

CHAPTER VII HAITI TO-DAY—WHAT IS
                BEING DONE 265
  The handicap of divided authority—The treaty officials—A civilian commissioner suggested—Process of financial reorganization—Public works—Public health—The *gendarmerie*—Department of Agriculture—*Service Technique*—Character and policy of the treaty officials.

CHAPTER VIII WHAT SHOULD BE DONE 290
  Three possible policies—Problem of the *élite*—The peasant class—Our duty to the Haitian people.

NOTES 303

EXHIBITS 338

BIBLIOGRAPHY 359

ILLUSTRATIONS

	FACING PAGE
A *Boucan* (*left*)	17
A *Boucanier* (*right*)	17
French Colonial Aqueduct and Sugar Mill (*above*)	24
French Colonial Bridge (*below*)	24
Toussaint l'Ouverture, "First of the Blacks"	58
Citadel of King Christophe from the Air	99
Ruins of Sans-Souci from the Air	110
The Citadel of King Christophe	111
The Coronation Ceremony, April 18, 1852	121
Faustin the First, Emperor of Haiti	122
The Empress Adelina	123
Statue of Dessalines (*above*)	143
Old and New Cathedrals in Port-au-Prince (*below*)	143
Note found on the Body of General Charles Oscar Etienne, July 28, 1927	163
President Dartiguenave, His Cabinet, and Officers of the *Gendarmerie*	180
A Crack Troop of the Old Army	194
Haitian Peasants Typical of the Class from Which the Cacos Were Recruited	219
A Peasant (*left*)	224
A Caco (*right*)	224
Louis Borno, President of the Republic of Haiti	240

ILLUSTRATIONS

	FACING PAGE
Place d'Indépendance, Port-au-Prince	266
Peasant Women Going to Market	267
New Palace of Finance	272
Telephone and Telegraph Building (*above*)	273
New School Building (*below*)	273
A Ward, General Hospital in Port-au-Prince (*above*)	276
A Rural Clinic (*below*)	276
New *Gendarmerie* Head-quarters, Port-au-Prince (*above*)	277
Review of *Gendarmerie,* National Palace (*below*)	277
Gendarme Rifle Team Which Won Second Place at Olympic Games (*above*)	282
American Marines, *Gendarmerie* Head-quarters Staff (*below*)	282
Rural Farm School (*above*)	283
Boys' Industrial School (*below*)	283
National Palace, Port-au-Prince (*above*)	288
Champ de Mars, Port-au-Prince (*below*)	288
A Residence in Port-au-Prince (*above*)	289
Dock at Port-au-Prince (*below*)	289
Royal Bank of Canada and Banque Nationale (*above*)	292
Street in Port-au-Prince (*below*)	292
Typical Peasant Home (*above*)	293
Haitian Peasants (*below*)	293
Haitian Market (*above*)	294
Petit Commerce (*below*)	294

MAPS

République d'Haiti	(*frontispiece*)

ILLUSTRATIONS

	FACING PAGE
Map of the Island of Tortuga in 1650	17
Cap François (Cap Haitien), Charlevoix, 1733	22
Economic Map of the Colony of St.-Domingue in 1791	23

EXHIBITS

		PAGE
A	RULERS OF FREE HAITI, 1804 TO 1928	338
B	THE HAITIAN-AMERICAN TREATY (1915) (Full Text)	340
C	ADDITIONAL ACT (1917) (Full Text)	346
D	CONSTITUTION OF 1918 (Some Provisions)	347
E	MÉMOIRE OF THE UNION PATRIOTIQUE D'HAÏTI (May, 1921—Conclusions)	348
F	REPORT OF DR. CARL KELSEY TO THE AMERICAN ACADEMY OF POLITICAL AND SOCIAL SCIENCE (March, 1922—Extracts)	350
G	"THE SEIZURE OF HAITI BY THE UNITED STATES" Foreign Policy Association of New York (Extracts)	352
H	"OCCUPIED HAITI" Report of Committee of Six—Woman's International League for Peace and Freedom (Conclusions)	354
I	COUNCIL OF STATE (Extracts from *Dictionnaire de Législation Administrative*)	357

PART ONE

INTRODUCTION

WHEN the average American hears of Haiti, if he does not confuse it with the island of Tahiti—thousands of miles away in the Pacific—he thinks of a small, unimportant West Indian country productive of revolutions, surcharged postage stamps, and newspaper discussions of the American intervention or perhaps of alleged atrocities by the United States Marines. Of the difficult and complicated problems involved in the task which the United States has assumed in Haiti, or of the steps so far taken towards its accomplishment, reports published in the United States have been so conflicting as to bewilder the average reader. Of the Haitians themselves, their background, or present condition, the American people generally have no conception.

Frederick Douglass, the great Negro orator, once said something to the effect that in measuring the progress of a race or people one must consider not only the heights to which the race has attained, but the depths from which it sprang. To reach any understanding of conditions in Haiti to-day, it is necessary to realize something of the fascinating and tragic history of the island now divided between the black republic and the mulatto (Dominican) republic.

No country in the world, civilized or uncivilized, has had within the same space of time a more dramatic or more distressing history.

When Columbus landed on the island which he named Hispaniola, he was welcomed by a primitive people estimated to number a million souls. Fifteen years later this people had been reduced by cruel exploitation to 60,000. Scarcity of labour resulting from their swift extermination led to the importation of Negroes from Africa, and thus was initiated the slave trade which was profoundly to affect the political and economic future of the Americas. The Spanish adventurers were essentially seekers for gold, and the natural resources of Hispaniola remained practically neglected until the settlement by the French in the eastern part of the island in the middle of the fifteenth century.

Though the French developed, in the eastern part of this island, the richest colony in the world, they, like the Spanish, lost their potentially most valuable colonial possession through disregard of the first principles of humanity and expediency. Just complaints of the French colonists against the home government (which was infinitely more tyrannical than that of England over her American colonies) were finally aggravated to the breaking point by the Jacobin colonial policy of the Estates-General, which threatened to deprive them of their chief possessions, the slaves. Dissension between the colonists and the home government, then in the throes of the French Revolution, was seized upon by the mulatto caste as affording an opportunity to better their condition, but armed attempts to obtain recognition of their rights were unsuccessful. Finally the great mass of the blacks, realizing their strength, rose against their masters. They ravaged the island with fire and sword, drove out the whites, and finally Dessalines, "the Tiger," standing on the beach at Gonaives, tore the tricolour of France into three pieces. Dramatically hurling the white portion into the sea, he united the red and blue and created the flag of independent Haiti.

The history of the Haitian struggle for independence is as dramatic as that of any nation in the world. The three great black leaders, Toussaint l'Ouverture, Jean Jacques Dessalines, and Henri Christophe, had all served the

INTRODUCTION

whites in various capacities, from that of slaves to general officers in the Army of France in St.-Domingue. The mulatto Pétion, first president of the Republic of Haiti, was a graduate of a French military school. The influence of the despotic government under which they had lived and the French ideals inherited from their former masters may be traced in the careers and policies of the early leaders and of all the subsequent rulers of independent Haiti. Even today the French influence predominates. The official language is French, as is also the culture of the small class which constitutes the *élite* of Haiti.

The history of the Spanish part of this island, of the French colonial period, and of the Haitian struggle for independence has been written in Spanish, French, German, and English. A great number of books, pamphlets, and articles have been published on the Haitian Republic and on the American intervention. Nothing, however, is available to the general reader which might enable him to trace the history of the Haitian people from the discovery of Hispaniola by Columbus to the present time.

After a long residence in the black republic and a careful study of its history, including material not ordinarily available, the author ventures to present this story of Haiti. A study of the available historical material discloses such marked discrepancies, and such conflicting opinions as to the more prominent figures in the struggle for freedom and the early history of the Haitians as a free people, that accurate analysis of the principal characters and events of this most amazing drama is now impossible.

In treating of this period, the writer has attempted only to review the more important aspects of the careers of the individuals who freed the country from France and created the black republic. To others more ably equipped is left the fascinating task of dramatizing this extraordinary story. For readers who may wish additional detailed information,

BLACK DEMOCRACY

an appendix and brief bibliography have been added to this volume.

The story of Haiti may be roughly divided into six periods: the pre-Columbian or aboriginal period, the period of Spanish discovery and settlement, the period of French colonization and development, the period of internal strife ending in emancipation of the slaves, the inauguration and turbulent history of the black republic, and, finally, Haiti and the American intervention.

It is the story of the second-largest and one of the most fertile of the islands of the Caribbean Sea, the first land colonized by Europeans in the Western World, and for years the seat of Spanish rule in the Americas. The island was discovered by Columbus and visited by Pizarro, Ponce de Leon, Cortez, and Velasquez. It was attacked by Drake, and the blood of the buccaneers survives in the mulatto aristocracy. For many years it contributed vast sums to the wealth of the kingdom of France and was the source of over a third of French commerce. It is of extraordinary natural beauty, which might almost have inspired Rousseau's dreams of the ideal primitive state of nature. We will borrow the words of Washington Irving to describe the land to which Columbus gave the name of Hispaniola:

"In the transparent atmosphere of the tropics, objects are descried at a great distance and the purity of the air and serenity of the deep blue sky give a magical effect to the scenery. Under these advantages the beautiful island of Haiti revealed itself to the eye as they approached. Its mountains were higher and more rocky than those of the other islands; but the rocks rose from among rich forests. The mountains swept down the luxurious plains and green savannahs; while the appearance of the cultivated fields, of numerous fires at night and columns of smoke by day, showed it to be populous. It rose before them in all the

INTRODUCTION

splendour of tropical vegetation, one of the most beautiful islands in the world and doomed to be one of the most unfortunate."

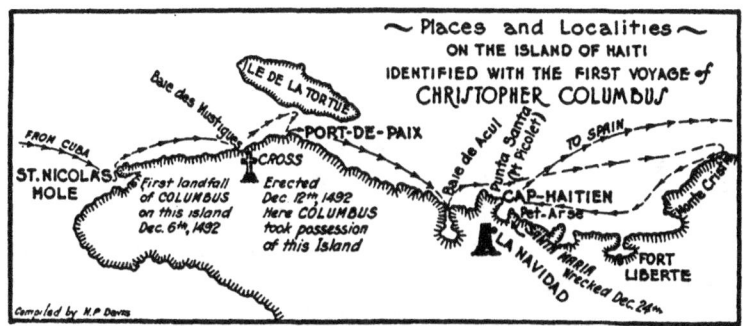

~ Localities in Haiti Identified with the First Voyage of Columbus ~

CHAPTER I

THE SPANIARDS

ON December 6, 1492, Columbus sighted the island of Haiti, and that evening entered the harbour of Mole St. Nicholas. Leaving the Mole on the following day and skirting the north coast, he landed at the Baie des Moustiques and, on the 12th of December, erected a cross at the entrance of this harbour and with great ceremony took possession in the name of his sovereigns of the island, to which he gave the name Hispaniola. Columbus, in a report to Ferdinand and Isabella, said of the aborigines: "So lovable, so tractable, so peaceable are these people that I swear to your Majesties there is not in the world a better nation nor a better land. They love their neighbours as themselves; and their discourse is ever sweet and gentle, and accompanied with a smile; and though it is true that they are naked, yet their manners are decorous and praiseworthy." The fact that there exists to-day not one pure-blooded descendant of this race is eloquent testimony to the unfortunate subsequent history of these "so lovable and tractable" people.

While cruising along the coast, Columbus encountered a large canoe manned by Indians, who invited him to visit their cacique, Guacanaguari, who later was to play an important part in the relations between the Conquistadores and the natives of Hispaniola. It was while attempting to locate the village of this chief that Columbus was wrecked in his flagship, the *Santa Maria*. Cacique Guacanaguari came at once to the rescue, and by his aid the vessel was unloaded and the cargo and stores safely deposited on

THE SPANIARDS

the shore. No civilized people could have observed more scrupulously the rights of ownership than did these savages. Merchandise of all descriptions, beads, hawks' bells, looking-glasses, and showy trifles of all kinds were strewn on the beach, together with the more practical essentials brought by the Spaniards. Nothing was touched; the Indians in no way took advantage of the misfortunes of the white strangers.

The *Pinta* had become separated from the fleet before the landing at Mole St. Nicholas, and the loss of the *Santa Maria* left the Admiral with only the *Niña*, a small and far from seaworthy ship totally incapable of accommodating all the Spanish adventurers. In this predicament Columbus determined to return to Spain, report his discoveries, and fit out a new expedition to take possession of the New World. The natives, who lived in deadly fear of periodical incursions of wild bands of nomad Caribs, gladly assented to the proposal that a number of the Spanish mariners should be left to protect them.

The kindly attitude of the Indians and the indolent and easy life which they had lived since the wreck of the *Santa Maria* so appealed to the Spaniards that Columbus had no difficulty in securing volunteers to remain on the island. From the wreck of the *Santa Maria* a tower named La Navidad was constructed, and fortified with the guns taken from the wreck. Having garrisoned this tower with thirty-eight men, Columbus sailed for Spain to report his discoveries.

It was a most romantic age, and nowhere in Europe was the adventurous spirit more prevalent than in Spain. The wars with the Moors being over, the grandees and soldiers of Spain, tired of peaceful monotony, were eager to accept any exploit which promised aggrandizement or gain. The visionary reports of Columbus and the extravagant accounts of his followers, whose vague recollections were by now but confused dreams, were accepted and exaggerated by the people until the most extraordinary fancies were entertained with respect to the New World. Hidalgos of high rank fresh from the romantic wars of Granada, and ecclesiastics eager to convert the heathen, joined with adventurers who were seeking only a chance to make their fortunes. Altogether it is probable that not less than fifteen hundred souls took passage with Columbus in the three large ships and fourteen caravels which sailed from the Bay of Cadiz, September 25, 1493.

Two months later this fleet arrived off the coast of Hispaniola and anchored in the harbour of Monte Cristi. Spanish sailors, ranging the coast, found on the green bank of a small stream the bodies of a man and a boy. The former had a cord of Spanish grass about his neck, and his arms were extended and tied to a stake in the form of a cross. Their bodies were so badly decayed that it was impossible to tell whether they were Indians or Europeans. But Columbus's worst doubts were confirmed on the following day, when, at some distance, two other bodies were found, one of which, having a beard, was undoubtedly the corpse of a white man.

The natives had from the beginning been friendly to the Spaniards. They had allowed the garrison of La Navidad to choose wives from their number, and had gladly indicated to them the streams in which could be found the yellow metal they sought so eagerly. But the Spaniards had appropriated so many of their wives and daughters, and had conducted themselves with such brutal licence, that the natives had finally risen and, led by Caonabo, a chief of Carib birth, massacred the entire garrison.

When met by Columbus on his return from Spain, the natives showed every evidence of friendship, but the discovery of the massacre at La Navidad naturally led to distrust of the Indians and provoked the Spanish to reprisals which

THE SPANIARDS

soon led to open hostilities, and finally to ruthless slaughter of the weaker people. On the return of the Admiral from a voyage of discovery in the south and west, he found the most deplorable conditions existing in the colony.

Bartholomew Columbus, who had been left in charge, had neither the strength of character nor the prestige necessary to control this band of restless adventurers, most of whom were soldiers of fortune fresh from the Moorish wars, and many of noble birth. The principal officers had not come to create a colony, but to seek gold and precious stones. The adventure they sought failed to materialize and they bitterly resented being subordinate to the Columbus brothers, to whom they considered themselves greatly superior. Expeditions into the interior resulted in the finding of some gold, and the plants and seeds brought from the mother country produced an abundant harvest. Columbus had, however, been unfortunate in the selection of a site for his capital; the unhealthy location of Isabella and the exposure to the heat and humidity, to which the Spaniards were unaccustomed, as well as the labour attending the building of the new town, resulted in sickness and discontent among the adventurers, who had anticipated a far different and less laborious life. Many openly disregarded the Admiral's instructions in their treatment of the natives, and some of the influential grandees became disgusted with conditions and returned to Spain bearing evil reports of the new colony. Their departure deprived the colony of many of the most responsible leaders, and the licentious conduct of their fellows had destroyed all hope of friendly relations with the Indians.

In 1500 Bobadilla, who had been sent to investigate complaints against the administration of Hispaniola, arrived while Columbus was absent on another voyage of discovery. He assumed absolute command of the colony, and on the return of the Admiral arrested him and sent him in chains to Spain. Although the Spanish crown disavowed the action of Bobadilla and appointed Ovando in his place, Columbus was deprived of his authority and never regained either his title or the share of the revenues which had been promised him.

Ovando arrived in April, 1502, with considerable reinforcements and stores. He was a harsh but thoroughly competent soldier who had served with distinction against the Moors, and in spite of a record of atrocious cruelty his administration was marked by a period of prosperous development which, though it lasted only a short time, resulted in a decided growth in the importance and wealth of the colony.

Forty thousand natives of the Bahamas were imported by Governor-General Ovando on the shallow pretext that they would thus secure the benefits of the Christian religion, but in reality to replace the rapidly disappearing islanders. Notwithstanding this accession to their numbers, and strict injunctions from Spain that the natives should be treated with kindness, the Indian population was rapidly exterminated.

Sugar-cane, imported from the Canaries in 1506, was particularly adapted to the soil and climate and soon became an important product. Within a few years after its introduction, the cultivation of cane and extraction of sugar were the chief source of wealth of the colony.

Ovando was succeeded by Don Diego Columbus, son of the Admiral. The new Governor being accompanied by his wife, daughter of the famous Duke of Alva, and by a large number of distinguished and wealthy Spaniards, life in the colony assumed a far more brilliant aspect under his administration and the city of Santo Domingo, then the capital of the Spanish possessions in the New World, reached the height of its prosperity.

THE SPANIARDS

But the rapidly increasing expenses of the colony and the insatiable demands of the home government so spurred the development of the sugar industry and the search for gold, both of which were dependent upon manual labour, that the condition of the Indians became increasingly desperate.

The natives were apportioned among the Spanish grandees according to the rank of the latter, and in this virtual state of slavery, the Indians, totally unaccustomed to sustained labour, died like flies. Although the census of 1508 had estimated the Indian population at 60,000, the enumeration made in 1514 showed that only 14,000 survived.

Father Las Casas was sent by Queen Isabella to stop the cruelty of the Spaniards to her "dearly beloved Indian subjects." He became known as "the protector of the Indians," and through his zeal for these unfortunates, this worthy father seems to have been responsible for the importation of slaves from Africa. It is a matter of record that as early as 1510 Africans were imported to provide labour for the mines and sugar plantations. As this latter industry developed, the need for labour became a vital consideration and Negroes were imported in increasing numbers. By 1518 Emperor Charles V had confirmed the legal status of the slave trade. Under a royal grant it was permissible to import not more than 4,000 Africans each year; yet, as it is known that in 1522 the slaves were numerous enough to attempt a formidable rebellion, it seems probable that many more than the number permitted by the royal grants were annually imported.

Charles V greatly enlarged the powers of "the Royal and Supreme Council of the Indies" which had been created by Ferdinand in 1511. This body became supreme in the affairs of the colonies; but Spain never made constructive attempts to develop industries in her colonies, and the council, although it exercised all civil and ecclesiastical functions, did little to promote actual production, and Santo Domingo became a financial burden to the mother country.

In spite of this, Spain jealously guarded her Western possessions from settlement and permitted restricted trade with them to Spanish ships sailing only from the port of Seville. In 1560 not a twentieth of the commodities exported to America were of Spanish manufacture, yet all this merchandise had to be deposited in warehouses of the *Casa de Contracion,* which also received all shipments from the Western world.

The profits of this huge brokerage naturally remained in the pockets of Spanish merchants, and the colonists welcomed the more profitable though illegal trade with other nations. This trade gradually assumed such proportions that Spain organized a fleet of *guardia costa,* or guard ships, to prevent foreign vessels from touching at Spanish possessions. Queen Elizabeth of England realized that this monopoly of trade was one of the chief sources of Spain's power, and privately encouraged English adventurers to challenge her supremacy in the New World.

In 1586 Drake attacked and partly destroyed Santo Domingo City, exacting a ransom of $30,000. Within the next few years British and French raiders had so demoralized the trade of Hispaniola (Santo Domingo) that in 1606 the Court of Madrid arbitrarily closed all ports of the island excepting only Santo Domingo City. This completed the destruction of the once prosperous commerce between Hispaniola and Spain.

The Spaniards had come to Hispaniola for gold, and on gold Columbus had depended to finance his vast schemes for a colonial empire. He had been deluded by the quantities of the metal first procured from the Indians. Later, mineralogists sent from Spain returned with astonishingly optimistic accounts of vast stores of mineral wealth, and

THE SPANIARDS

discoveries of great deposits of gold were daily expected.

As a matter of fact, no workable deposits of gold "in place" have ever been found on the island, and while placer gold is still washed from some of the rivers in Santo Domingo, it soon became evident that the river deposits were the accumulation of centuries and were not to be counted on for continuous production, and many of the adventurers quitted the colony in disgust.

Although sugar had become an extremely profitable export, cultivation of cane and the mechanical processes of producing sugar were not attractive occupations to men of the character of the Spanish adventurers. The most enterprising and ambitious, fired by exaggerated accounts of gold discoveries on the mainland of America, departed for new and more promising countries.

In 1788 the total population of the Spanish colony of Santo Domingo, including about 15,000 slaves, did not exceed 120,000. The colour line had by this time become loosely drawn and intermarriage between whites and mulattoes a common practice, and it is probable that less than one-half the free population were of pure blood. Agriculture had become neglected and little was left of the once flourishing colony but the city of Santo Domingo and a dwindling population of herdsmen in the interior.

CHAPTER II

THE FRENCH COLONY OF ST.-DOMINGUE

WHILE the Spanish colony in the eastern part of the island was losing its importance and failing to realize any of its glowing promises, the French had succeeded in gaining a foothold on the western part. In defiance of the pretensions of Spain to the sole ownership of the New World, English and French adventurers had in 1625 taken possession of St. Christopher, a small island of the Leeward group, where they established ports of call and refitting stations for ships engaged in the "prohibited" trade in the Spanish Main.

In 1629 a Spanish fleet attacked and destroyed these settlements. Some of the survivors, after a dangerous voyage in open boats, found refuge on Tortuga, a small unoccupied island off the north coast of Santo Domingo. Here they were later joined by a number of Dutch who had been similarly expelled from Santa Cruz. This was the nucleus of the French settlements on the island of Santo Domingo.

For some years French, English, and Dutch, all refugees from Spanish oppression, lived in harmony on Tortuga. Their time was chiefly occupied in hunting the wild cattle which roamed in great herds on the adjacent island of Santo Domingo, and in cultivating food crops and tobacco on Tortuga, where, because of its rugged shore and isolated position, they fondly hoped they could live unmolested. These, the original permanent white settlers on territory now incorporated in the Haitian Republic, became known as *boucaniers* from their habit of curing their meat over

FRENCH COLONY OF ST.-DOMINGUE

small fires of green wood on spits which were called by the Indians *boucans*.

The Abbé Raynal thus describes these people: "The dress of these barbarians consisted of a shirt dipped in the blood of the animals they killed in hunting; a pair of drawers dirtier than the shirt and made in the shape of a brewer's apron; a girdle made of leather, on which a very short sabre was hung, and some knives; a hat without any rim, except a flap before, in order to take hold of it; and shoes without stockings. Their ambition was satisfied if they could but provide themselves with a gun that carried balls of an ounce weight, and with a pack of about five-and-twenty or thirty dogs." The *boucaniers* spent their life in hunting wild bulls, of which there were great numbers on the island, since the Spaniards had brought them. The best parts of these animals, when seasoned with pimento and orange juice, were the most common food of their destroyers, who had forgotten the use of bread and who had nothing but water to drink. The hides of these animals were conveyed to several ports and bought by the navigators.

The original settlers on Tortuga were not pirates, privateers, or filibusters, but contented themselves with hunting and the cultivation of their little gardens. It was only after the Spanish had repeatedly attacked them that any reprisals for their original misfortunes were attempted. In 1638 an expedition, secretly fitted out by the Spanish governor of Santo Domingo, choosing a time when the majority of the hunters were absent, landed on Tortuga, killed the men, women, and children who had remained at home, and burned their houses. Survivors who had taken refuge in the hills and those who had been hunting on the mainland had already set about rebuilding when an Englishman named Willis, with three hundred followers expelled by the Spanish from the island of Nevis, arrived at Tortuga. The English now greatly outnumbered the French

~ *Above:* Map of the Island of Tortuga in 1650 ~
~ *Left:* A Boucan ~
~ *Right:* A Boucanier ~

and Dutch, and Willis, a man of unusual force, was unanimously chosen chief.

These inoffensive settlers were continually harassed by the Spaniards. They had to fight or die, so they organized a society called the "Brethren of the Coast" and in their long boats attacked Spanish vessels *en route* between Spain and her West Indian colonies. The men of Tortuga so engaged were called freebooters, filibusters, or *boucaniers*, and although some of them continued to hunt cattle on the mainland, the occupation from which this latter name was derived, *boucanier* soon became synonymous with "pirate," and for many years the "Spanish Main" from the Leeward Islands to the coast of Central America lived in dread of these bloodthirsty adventurers.

Under the energetic rule of Willis the prosperity of the colony rapidly increased, but it was not long before jealousy and racial prejudices resulted in bitter enmity between the English and French, and seizing some real or fancied violation of the code of the "Brethren of the Coast" as an excuse, Willis and his companions fell upon the French inhabitants, murdered part of them in cold blood, and expelled the rest. A few of the survivors reached the island of St. Christopher, where the Chevalier de Poincy was governor of the re-established French colony, now the principal French settlement in the West Indies. De Poincy, who was at that time contemplating the establishment of a French colony on the island of Santo Domingo, dispatched his second in command, Captain Le Vasseur, with a strong expedition to found a settlement on the mainland and to take possession of Tortuga Island.

It was in 1641 that Le Vasseur landed on Santo Domingo and established a settlement which he called Port Margot, and from which he attacked Willis and his following, and expelled the English from Tortuga. In 1652 the Chevalier Fontenay was sent by the French West India Company

FRENCH COLONY OF ST.-DOMINGUE

to supersede Le Vasseur. Fontenay, finding that Le Vasseur had been killed in a quarrel with one of his officers, took possession of the island and the settlements on the mainland in the name of the Company. As first governor of Tortuga, whose authority was directly derived from the French Crown, Fontenay governed the island until 1654, when the French were again expelled by the Spanish.

The *boucaniers* who survived this attack scattered over the north coast of the island of Santo Domingo and, in defiance of the Spaniards, engaged in their old occupation of hunting wild cattle until 1656, when an expedition organized by the French West India Company and supported by the *boucaniers* drove the Spaniards from Tortuga.

In 1665 Bertrand d'Ogeron, an ex-captain of marines, who had served many years in the West Indies, was appointed by the Company governor of the French on Tortuga and the French settlements on the island of Santo Domingo. He proved to be a most efficient and energetic officer, and under his administration these settlements attracted colonists from other islands, and later received large numbers of emigrants from France. Gradually increasing in wealth and importance under the rule of d'Ogeron, settlements spread along the coasts and even into the valleys in the interior.

The *boucaniers* had brought few women to Tortuga, and in default of white women many of these adventurers took as mistresses, in some instances even as wives, Negresses purchased from traders or abducted from Spanish or English settlements. These unions were responsible for the inception of the mulatto caste as a community, and for many years a majority of the children born here were of mixed white and Negro blood. D'Ogeron, thoroughly convinced of the value of the colony, made every effort to encourage immigration from France. He arranged for the shipment of a cargo very attractive to the *boucanier* benedicts of his colony, consisting of fifty young female "orphans" whose previous condition is indicated by the fact that they were sold at auction to the highest bidder, as well as by the following illuminating paragraph from their matrimonial contract: "I take thee without knowing, or caring to know, who thou art. If anybody from whence thou comest would have had thee, thou wouldst not have come in quest of me. But no matter; I do not desire thee to give me an account of thy past conduct, because I have no right to be offended at it at the time when thou wast at liberty to live either ill or well according to thy own pleasure, and because I shall have no reason to be ashamed of anything thou wast guilty of when thou didst not belong to me. Give me only thy word for the future; I acquit thee of the past." Then, striking his hand on the barrel of his gun, the bridegroom added: "This will revenge me of thy breach of faith; if thou shouldst prove false, this will surely be true to my aim."

Tortuga and the settlements on the mainland were held in defiance of Spain for over forty years after the French West India Company appointed Fontenay first governor. It was during this period that the "Brethren of the Coast," *boucaniers,* or filibusters, as they were indiscriminately called, developed from a band of desperate fugitives employing only home-made, and far from seaworthy, "longboats" to a powerful organization feared by every ship that sailed the Spanish Main. Primarily they were French, English, or Dutch, but the society included Portuguese, Spanish, and men of other nations who, after joining the brotherhood, put aside all differences of race, religion, and social status. Though ruthless and unprincipled, they remained loyal to the brotherhood and were generally honest among themselves. Romance has glorified many of their deeds which were, in fact, dastardly crimes; and there is small doubt that the whole lot were arrant, unscrupulous knaves, with little to commend them save their reckless

FRENCH COLONY OF ST.-DOMINGUE

courage. Among their leaders were such men as Francis L'Ollonais (Lolobais), Peter the Great (Pierre le Grand), Mansvelt, Michael le Basque, John Davies, De Graaf, Roch (Rock) Brasiliano, and Henry Morgan, who, following a career of piracy, became lieutenant governor of Jamaica and was knighted by the British Crown.

At first the factors of the French West India Company attempted to curb the activities of the brotherhood, but, finding this impracticable, became partners in their enterprises and shared in the ill-gotten gains. For a time Cayona, the principal town on Tortuga Island, was the most notorious and dissolute, but one of the most prosperous, of the communities in the West Indies.

Spain had not yet recognized the right of the French in Santo Domingo, and the development of the colony had been seriously retarded by continual conflict with the Spanish. In 1617 d'Ogeron organized a force of four hundred men under the famous filibuster Delisle, who captured the Spanish town of Santiago de los Caballeros and exacted a substantial ransom.

For the purpose of inducing the French government to send a sufficient force to conquer and occupy Spanish Santo Domingo, d'Ogeron returned to France. Unfortunately for his plans, which, owing to the pitiably weak state of the neglected Spanish colony, would undoubtedly have been successful, he died shortly after his arrival. He was succeeded by his nephew, M. de Pouancey, under whom the colony continued to prosper. At this time a French settlement at Samana was removed to Cap Français (Cap Haitien), which became the centre of an increasingly prosperous agricultural community.[1] Flourishing plantations of cotton and indigo were established, and in spite of a highly restrictive government monopoly, tobacco was one of the chief products.

In 1664, commissioners were sent from France to establish courts and regulate the administration of justice, and for some years the colonists enjoyed peace and plenty. But the declaration of war between France and Spain in 1689 brought them again face to face with disaster. The French raid on Santiago de los Caballeros was revenged by the Spanish Admiral Don Ognacio Coro, who defeated the French in a great battle, killing the governor and sacking Cap Français and other towns.

The arrival of refugees from St. Christopher, which had again been attacked by the Spanish, helped to re-establish the colony, and du Cussy, who had meantime been appointed governor, by his excellent administration gave a new lease of life to the demoralized settlements. But this prosperity was of short duration, for in 1694 both Cap Français and Port-de-Paix were captured and destroyed by combined English and Spanish forces. Under the active direction of du Cussy, and aided by the arrival of a large party of immigrants from St. Croix, these towns were rebuilt and the growth of the French settlements resumed.

The Treaty of Ryswick, signed in 1697, recognized for the first time the right of the French to the western part of the island of Santo Domingo. Under the energetic and intelligent administration of the French, settlements in their part of the island had always prospered, and now, freed from the danger of raids by the Spanish, farms and plantations rapidly multiplied. The success attending the cultivation of indigo encouraged the establishment of large estates, while the increased importation of African slaves made possible the cultivation of sugar-cane on a much greater scale than had hitherto been attempted. Cocoa planted by d'Ogeron in 1665 had been grown successfully until destroyed by some unknown blight in 1716. Replanted in 1736, this crop became one of the most important sources of revenue, and French St.-Domingue for many years furnished the greater part of the world's supply of chocolate.

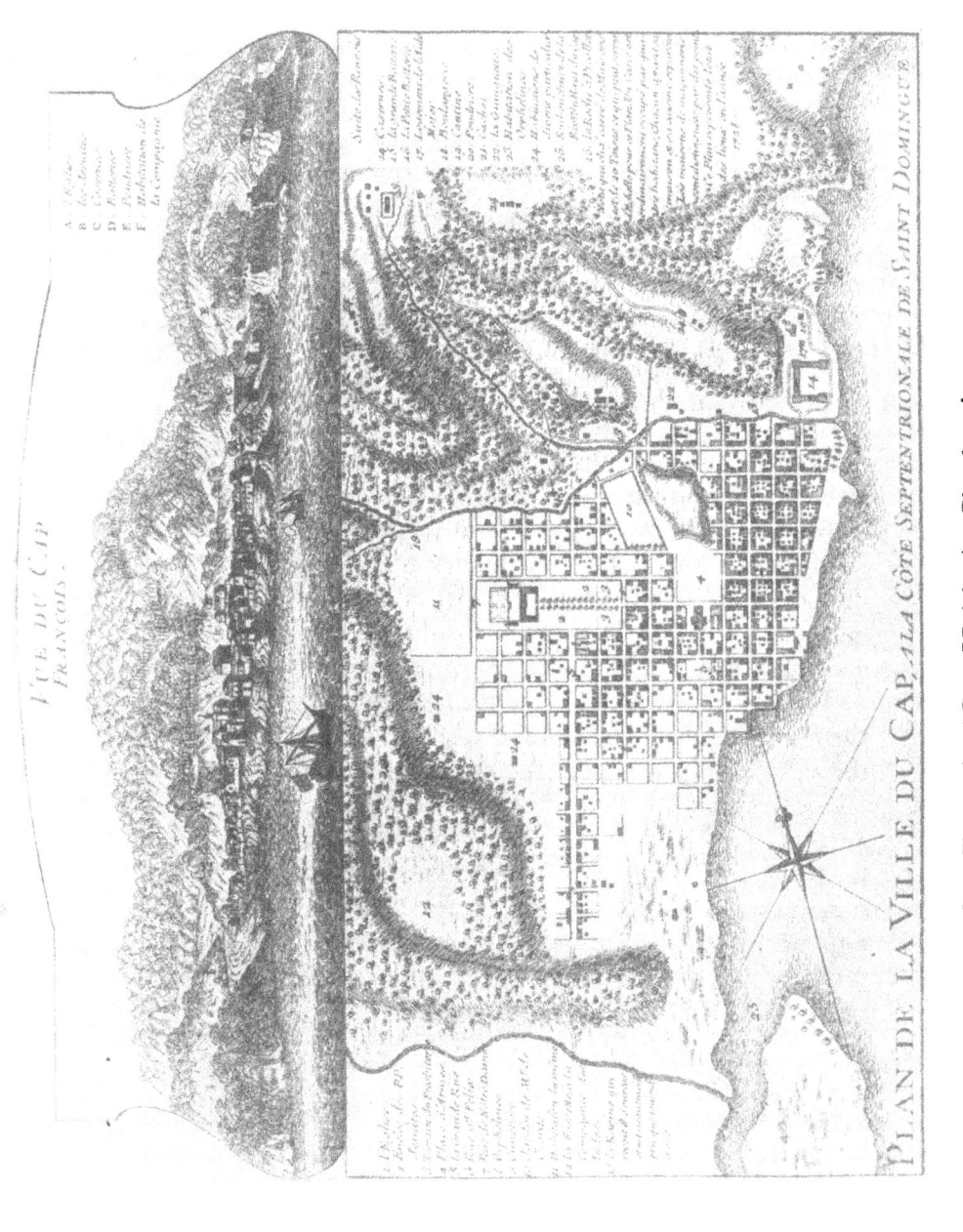

Cap François (Cap Haitien), Charlevoix, 1733

FRENCH COLONY OF ST.-DOMINGUE

In 1728, 50,000 Negro slaves were employed on the various plantations. In 1754 the population was estimated at 190,000, including 14,000 whites, 4,000 mulattoes, and 172,000 Negroes. Sugar estates to the number of 599, and 3,379 indigo plantations, were in operation. The great prosperity of the large planters and their easy and luxurious lives, made possible by ideal climatic conditions and myriads of slaves, had tended to demoralize the colonists to such an extent that as early as 1760 social conditions in the colony were the subject of a special investigation. A report made by a commissioner of the French government that year included the following: "It arises from the too intimate intercourse of the whites and blacks, the criminal intercourse that most of the masters have with their women slaves. A legal wife, seeing the intercourse of her husband with her servant, in the absence of the husband has her punished severely. If the master is not married, and that is mostly the case (marriage not being popular, and libertinage more tolerated), the inconstancy natural to the men of this climate makes them change or multiply their concubines, from which arise innumerable jealousies and distinctions; and in the first, as in the second case, are the causes of taking vengeance now upon the fortunes of the master, in poisoning his Negroes, or taking his life, or that of his wife, or even of their children."

From the middle of the eighteenth century to the French Revolution was a period of increasing and unexampled prosperity, French St.-Domingue being counted the richest colonial possession in the world.

Reference to the map will show that this astonishingly productive colony, which then supplied not only France, but half of Europe, with sugar and cocoa, occupied only a small portion of the island, the greater part still remaining in possession of Spain. This map also shows that by far the greater portion of the area held by France was exceedingly

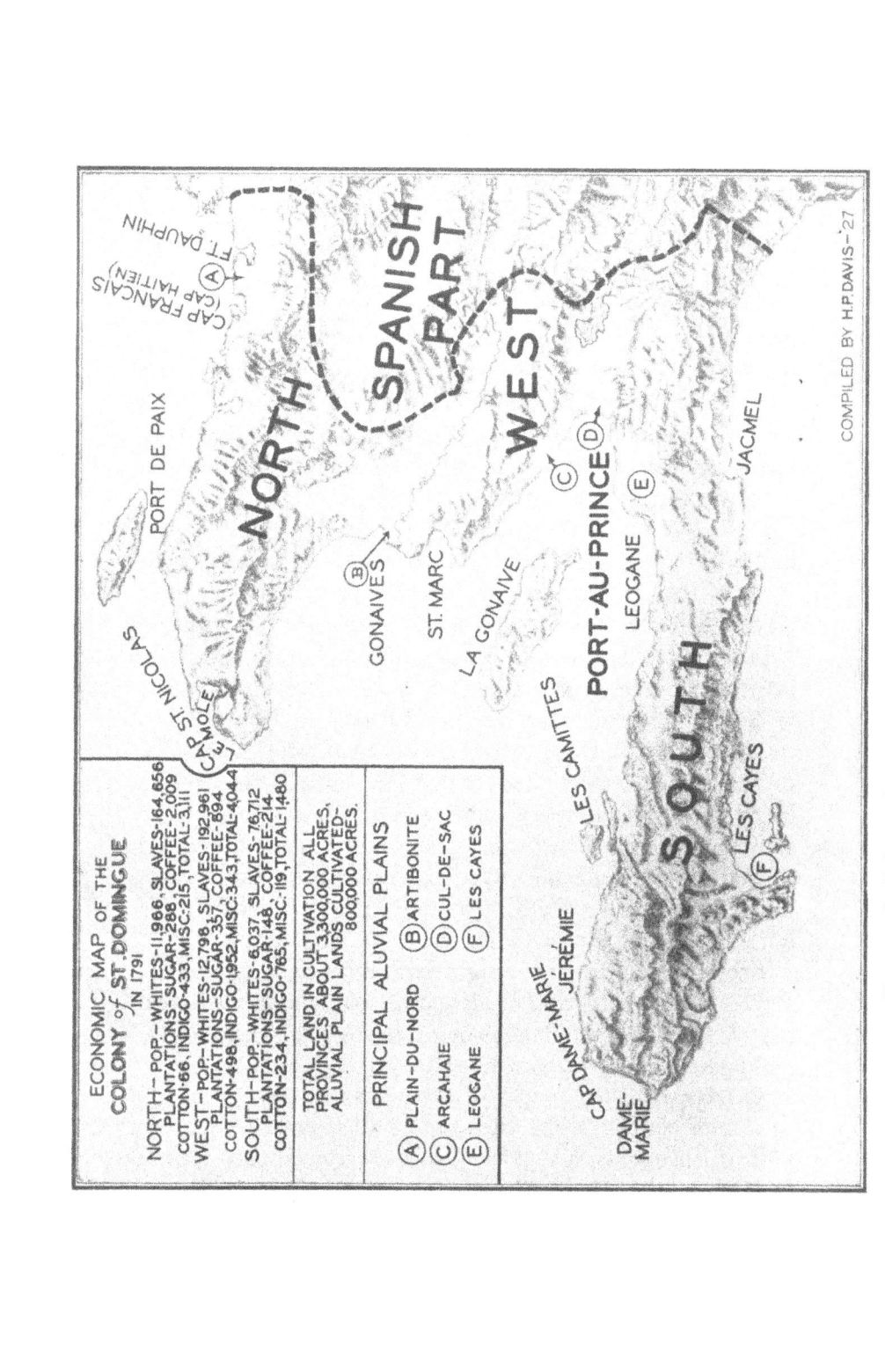

Economic Map of the Colony of St.-Domingue in 1791

mountainous. Each of the two long peninsulas is a spur of great mountain ranges, and the boundary line between French and Spanish possessions followed the crest of high mountains. The comparatively narrow strip lying between the boundary and the sea is frequently cut by towering mountains arising precipitously from the water's edge.

Coffee and some indigo were grown most successfully in the mountain districts, but the bulk of the wealth of the colony was produced from the marvellously rich alluvial soil of the great Plaine-du-Nord, lying east and south of Cap Français, the plain of the Artibonite formed by the river of that name, the Cul-de-Sac near Port-au-Prince, and lesser alluvial plains in the south and west.

The Plaine-du-Nord and the Cul-de-Sac were crossed in every direction by splendid roads and covered with magnificent habitations, ruins of which still testify to their former luxury. Fields of cane stretched in every direction, bounded by well-kept hedges, and long avenues of royal palms gave shady approach to the houses surrounded by beautiful gardens. Many of the planters spent half the year in Paris, where "rich as a Creole" had become a common expression.

At the latter end of this period the population was estimated at 536,000, consisting of 32,000 whites, exclusive of the troops and seafaring people; 24,000 freedmen, and 480,000 slaves. As it was to the interest of the planters to minimize the number of their slaves in order to avoid the head tax, children and those too old to be of productive value were omitted, and it is certain that the number of Negroes was greatly in excess of the official estimates.[2]

Although 1785 to 1791 were years of discord and threatened disaster, the material prosperity of the colony is shown by the fact that there were over three thousand indigo plantations, an equal number growing coffee, nearly eight hundred great estates devoted to the production of sugar, and

~ *Above:* French Colonial Aqueduct and Sugar Mill ~
~ *Below:* French Colonial Bridge ~

FRENCH COLONY OF ST.-DOMINGUE

an equal number of cotton plantations. Cocoa was still a valuable crop, while among the lesser industries were included rum distilleries, lime kilns, brickyards, potteries, and tanneries. Approximately two million, five hundred thousand acres of land were in cultivation, almost half a million Negroes were employed in the various establishments, and the commerce of the colony with the mother country comprised over a third of the total foreign trade of France.

The exports from Haiti in 1791 included:

Sugar	177,230,000 lbs.
Coffee	73,944,000 "
Cotton	6,820,000 "
Indigo	1,009,000 "
Molasses	29,000 "
Dyewoods	6,788,634 "

The value of these products at the present market values would exceed $50,000,000. The total value of the establishments, lands, slaves, and livestock was estimated at $193,500,000.

Bountifully endowed by Nature with every advantage of soil and climate, abundantly supplied with the cheapest and, under the conditions, the most effective labour, firmly established in the production of crops for which a ready and liberal market existed in Europe, the planters seemed to possess everything necessary to promote happiness and prosperity. Nevertheless, in the ignorant, semi-civilized mass of black slaves and the more enlightened mulattoes and free Negroes, two danger spots existed, to some extent realized but generally ignored by the white proprietors.[3]

The downfall of white supremacy in French St.-Domingue and the establishment of the Haitian Republic resulted from causes far less simple than is generally realized. It would be difficult to imagine political or social conditions more complicated than those existing in this colony at the period immediately preceding the expulsion of the whites. The different elements constituting the population included "whites" born in the colony, known as "Creoles"; French-born bureaucrats, landowners, or poor whites; mulattoes, both freedmen and slaves; and the Negro slaves, who exceeded in numbers the combined white and "coloured" population by almost ten to one.

Prior to the beginning of the eighteenth century, tobacco, cocoa, and indigo cultivation, while profitable, was conducted on a comparatively small scale, and labour requirements were met by a few slaves and the whites, either Creole or indentured European servants. The success which attended the cultivation of sugar caused vital changes in political and social conditions through the establishment of great estates, which employed hundreds or even thousands of Negro slaves. As their fortunes increased, a considerable number of the Creole landowners acquired the habit of spending much of their time and most of their money in France. Intermarriages between powerful French houses and the wealthy Creole families tended to strengthen the social ties between the colonies and the mother country.

It has been estimated that up to the end of the eighteenth century the equivalent of over three hundred million dollars had been invested in St.-Domingue. France had a great stake in the country, and the representatives of this invested capital exerted a powerful political influence.

The taxes and duties exacted from the colony became a most important source of revenue to the French government, and the commerce with St.-Domingue, particularly the slave trade, employed a large percentage of the merchant-marine of France. Bureaucrats who were sent over to administer the increasingly important financial affairs of the colony naturally associated with the French landowners and great merchants, and gradually there grew up a strong party which neither understood nor sympathized with the Creole population.

The colony of St.-Domingue was ruled by a governor-general and an intendant, both appointed by and responsible to the Minister of Marine who administered all French colonial possessions. The authority of these two officials was never strictly defined, and the balance of power depended on the character of the men who held these offices or on the terms of the special commission under which they were appointed. Nominally the governor was the representative of the Crown, the head of the military, and supreme in the external affairs of the colony. The administration of civil and judicial affairs was in the hands of the intendant, who collected all taxes, duties, and revenues, and regulated the finances.

The so-called colonial assembly which made and regulated all laws, customs duties, and taxes was composed of the governor-general, the intendant, the attorney-general, the commander of the navy, the chief officers of the militia, and the presidents of the provincial councils, all of whom were officers of the Crown, and not one a representative of, or necessarily in sympathy with, the colonists. Neither the white colonists nor the free mulattoes had any voice in the colony's government, while the blacks, numbering more than nine-tenths of the population, were almost all slaves.[4]

Disputes resulting from divided authority and the antagonism between the subordinates of the two departments tended to emphasize the harsh and arbitrary administration of the laws, of which the colonists justly complained. The colonial judiciary had been superseded by lawyers from France who conducted judicial affairs with the tedious and intricate detail for which French jurisprudence has always been noted. Under the arbitrarily enforced colonial policy, the colony was compelled to buy only from France and to sell its products only to France. These products could be shipped only on French ships. Manufacturing plants were prohibited in the island.

In the exceedingly complex society of St.-Domingue no party was satisfied with the existing conditions. Not only was the white society divided by educational or financial qualifications, but the "Europeans," as the resident French were called, had little in common with the Creole whites. The only policy in which all classes of whites were united was in the absolutely irrevocable determination to draw the colour line, to keep clearly and definitely to the established principle that the mulattoes were in fact Negroes, and that no consideration of shade or wealth could alter or minimize this fundamental fact. The white men who occasionally married mulattoes were not only ostracized by their white associates but deprived of their civil rights and prohibited from holding office or any official position of trust.

The small planters, merchants, and superior white employees of the estates, both European and Creole, formed a respectable class, but they had no political power and received little consideration from the officials or from the wealthy planters.

The poor whites of the town, generally a dissolute collection of adventurers, were ready at all times to serve any interest which promised personal gain. But the most disturbing and potentially dangerous element in the population were the mulattoes, who, notwithstanding stringent laws prohibiting intercourse between the planters and their slaves, had increased in such numbers that in 1719 they constituted not less than five per cent of the population.

A considerable number of the "people of colour," as the mulattoes called themselves, had received their freedom and, in many cases, valuable land grants. In the later colonial days the planters often treated the children of their coloured mistresses with great liberality, and many of these

FRENCH COLONY OF ST.-DOMINGUE

people, some of whom were almost white in appearance, were very wealthy. In 1789 it was estimated that the mulattoes possessed at least ten per cent of the productive land and owned over 50,000 slaves. Many of them had been educated in France, where they were not discriminated against. Indeed there was at this time in France a large and growing party actively engaged in securing for them political equality with the whites. In the colony they had practically no civil rights, were prohibited from practising any of the learned professions, and denied the right to wear European dress. In churches, theatres, and public conveyances, special places were assigned to them. The poor whites, jealous of the wealth of the mulatto landowners, lost no opportunity to insult and humiliate them.

Until the establishment of the Estates-General in France, the attitude of the colonists toward the mulattoes had never been seriously questioned by the home government, which had apparently realized that to maintain the established status of the whites in the colonies the complete subjection of the coloured people, as well as the Negroes, was absolutely essential. The prosperity of St.-Domingue was founded on the production of sugar, which in turn depended on slave labour. Therefore slavery was the basis of both the economic and social life of the colony.

Although the colonists had many legitimate reasons for dissatisfaction with the home government, the fundamental cause of the break between France and St.-Domingue, which led finally to the loss of the colony, was the attempt of the Jacobin government of France to impose laws and regulations which controverted the prescribed status of the mulattoes.

In September, 1788, a committee claiming the title of "Commissioners of St.-Domingue" presented to the Minister of Marine a petition asking for colonial representation in the French Estates-General which was to be convened at Paris in May, 1789. This movement had the support of wealthy planters and merchants of St.-Domingue, and in France of an even more influential party which included some of the richest of the absentee owners of colonial estates. But the colonists were far from united in their attitude toward participation in the Estates-General. The official class naturally preferred that conditions should remain as they were, and a considerable number of planters, fearing the effect on the institution of slavery of an open discussion of the affairs of the colony, strongly opposed participation in French political assemblies. In this same year a society entitled *Amis des Noirs* (Friends of the Blacks) had begun an active campaign for the freedom of the Negroes, an outgrowth of the movement for the abolition of slavery which had started in England and spread rapidly to France.

The "reforms" demanded by the proprietors in St.-Domingue all tended toward establishing the supremacy of the planter class, and did not in any manner benefit the majority of the white citizens. In spite of much opposition, the colonial assemblies met in September, elected thirty-seven deputies, drew up a statement of grievances, and made demands for certain specific reforms in colonial administration. In France the efforts of the colonial committee resulted in the very effect which conservative planters had most feared. The *Amis des Noirs* were both active and powerful, and many of the planters, formerly in favour of representation in the home government, had come to realize the dangers of their program.

In 1789 the Estates-General was convened in Paris, and in June admitted six of the thirty-seven delegates sent by the assemblies of St.-Domingue. The interest of the French public in colonial affairs had now been aroused. The white planters had committed a fatal mistake in demanding representation; for the immediate effect of their action was

FRENCH COLONY OF ST.-DOMINGUE

to stir up the *Amis des Noirs,* who asked political rights for the mulattoes. They also urged the abolition of slavery. What would have been the fate of St.-Domingue if the colonial situation had not been submitted to the Estates-General is uncertain, but the declaration of the "Rights of Man" promulgated in August was a fatal blow to the supremacy of the whites in the colonies.

Conditions in France made the appeals of the mulattoes for political liberty exceedingly difficult to combat. In October, 1789, the president of the National Assembly, which had then superseded the Estates-General, responding to a petition of the mulattoes for the fulfilment of the recently promulgated recognition of the rights of all men to citizenship, said: "Not a single part of the nation shall ask in vain for its rights from the assembly of the representatives of the French people."

This danger the colonists of all parties were quick to realize, and, too late, the opposing factions among the whites united to uphold the institution of slavery and save themselves from ruin. The plan of the colonials was simple but effective. Their chief aims were to remove colonial affairs from consideration of the National Assembly of France and to assure the continuation of the supremacy of the planter class. A proposed colonial assembly assured both these conclusions. Membership was limited by qualifications which guaranteed control by the planters, and the independence from the National Assembly of France was provided by making the colonies accountable only to the Crown. Under the authority of the Minister of Marine, orders to this effect were sent to St.-Domingue, and for the moment the threatened danger seemed averted.

In March, 1790, the committee on colonies laid before the Assembly a draft of a decree most satisfactory to the wealthy colonials. The harsh provisions of the *pacte colonial,* which had placed great burdens on the colonial proprietors, were either nullified or amended, and the planter class was assured of support in its position regarding the mulattoes. A clause in the decree, most destructive to the hopes of the "people of colour," read: "While the National Assembly considers the colonies part of the French Empire, and while it desires to see them enjoy the fruits of the happy regeneration which has just taken place, it has, notwithstanding, never intended to comprehend the interior government of the colonies in the constitution decreed for the kingdom, or subject them to laws incompatible with their local establishments. They therefore authorize the inhabitants of each colony to signify to the National Assembly their sentiments." This was, of course, a terrible blow to the mulattoes and their supporters, and immediate steps were taken, both in France and in the colonies, to secure the revocation of this decree.

The position of the National Assembly, which had so recently promulgated the doctrine of the "Rights of Man," was extraordinary. After vainly endeavouring to draw up instructions which would uphold their decree of March 8th and at the same time conform to the declaration of the "Rights of Man," they compromised on a miserable evasion, so ambiguous that debates in the Chamber failed to elucidate the most vitally important provision—the question of the rights of the mulattoes to citizenship. The "Instructions" finally passed by the Assembly included a clause which apparently established the rights of the mulattoes to the franchise, but which left the whole matter open to construction by the local authorities.

Meanwhile affairs in the colony were going from bad to worse. An uprising of the mulattoes in the valley of the Artibonite, while quickly suppressed, was followed by others in various parts of the island. So far active rebellion had been averted, but all classes were greatly excited and only a spark was needed to set the colony in flames.

FRENCH COLONY OF ST.-DOMINGUE

The mulattoes had come to see that their hope for the present lay in supporting the authorities. Among the Creole whites the better element was becoming alarmed at the revolutionary attitude of the lower classes and therefore was less openly hostile to the government. On the convocation of a new colonial assembly at St.-Marc, on April 15, 1790, it was at once evident that the turbulent element had control of the convention. Without attempting to settle impending questions of vital importance, this colonial assembly proceeded to arrogate to itself supreme authority, excluding the French National Assembly from all power in colonial affairs, and recognizing no authority save that of the king of France. The great planters and merchants of the North were strongly opposed to granting such sweeping powers to the colonial assembly and, recalling their representatives, allied themselves with the governor.

A letter from Governor Peynier to La Luzerne, French Minister of Marine, discloses the complicated and dangerous condition which had already resulted from the acts of the National Assembly: "The colony is at this moment in the greatest agitation. Two parties divide it. The one, entirely devoted to the General Assembly, demands its continuation; the other seeks its dissolution. This latter party is the more numerous, and contains the most intelligent and responsible citizens; nevertheless I very much doubt whether it will be successful. For the other party is made up of the discontented, the declaimers against pretended despotism, and the mass of working men and artisans, who are persuaded that their opponents are composed solely of those persons wishing to maintain abuses."

The Provisional Assembly of the North, meeting at Cap Français, refused to endorse the action of the Colonial Assembly and united with the faction which supported the home government. The immediate effect of this action was a declaration by the colonial assembly nullifying the trade laws, and branding the members of the Provisional Assembly of the North as traitors.

The mulattoes, taking advantage of the dissensions among the colonial whites, and encouraged by their supporters in France, had during the interval been actively engaged in propaganda of their own designed to obtain political and social recognition for the "coloured people." Raymond, a mulatto leader, very active in France on behalf of his brethren in the colony, wrote urging the "people of colour" not to oppose the popular colonial assemblies, for, he said, in such bodies the mulattoes would in the end outvote the whites and dominate the colony. Thus inspired and encouraged by the *Amis des Noirs,* Vincent Ogé, a young mulatto who had been educated in France, returned to St.-Domingue, determined to establish the claims of the mulattoes to citizenship. Ogé was deluded by promises of aid which never materialized, and, relying on them, attempted almost single-handed to inaugurate a rebellion in the stronghold of the colonial aristocracy, Cap Français. This gallant but pitiful attempt established him as one of the great mulatto martyrs; for the small band of men recruited by him and his friend Chavanne was easily defeated, the two leaders and some of their associates being put to death on March 12, 1791. These executions, carried out with barbarous cruelty, added fury to the discontent among the mulattoes, who immediately began organizing in secret in all parts of the island.

The ambiguity of the decree of March 8, 1789, and the confusion resulting from the vacillation of the French National Assembly left the legal status of the mulattoes in doubt until May 15, 1791, when the National Assembly finally decided that the men of mixed blood born of free parents should be admitted to the colonial assemblies. This decree excited the white colonists to violent protestations, and the governor himself went so far as to pronounce the

FRENCH COLONY OF ST.-DOMINGUE

suspension of the operation of the law. The resulting confusion intensified the already serious animosity between the races and was at least indirectly responsible for the atrocities which within a few months devastated the colony and horrified the civilized world.

CHAPTER III

THE REVOLUTION

ON the night of August 14, 1791, at a meeting masked under the guise of a Voodoo ceremony, Boukmann, Biassou, and Jean-François, three leaders of the blacks, adopted definite plans for an uprising against the whites. Six days later, led by Boukmann, the slaves of the Turpin plantation, near Cap Français, indiscriminately massacred every white man, woman, or child upon whom they could lay their hands. This inaugurated a general insurrection, and within a few weeks the magnificent plantations of the Plaine-du-Nord were in ruins and the white population either murdered or cooped up in the larger towns.

Accounts of this period of Haitian history, whether written by sympathizers of the blacks or supporters of the French, vie with each other in the recitation of almost incredible ferocities. In fiendish cruelty there seems to have been little to choose between the whites and blacks. The French burned captured Negroes alive, broke them on the wheel, or buried them to their necks in sand and poured melted wax into their ears. These atrocities were paralleled by equally revolting exhibitions of black savagery.

Fortunately for historical accuracy, Bryan Edwards, distinguished British historian, who arrived at Cap Français shortly after the initial revolt and while the Northern plain was still in flames, has left an impartial first-hand account of scenes the horrors of which, he says, "imagination cannot adequately conceive nor pen describe." "To detail the various conflicts, skirmishes, massacres, and slaughter which

THE REVOLUTION

this exterminating war produced, were to offer a disgusting and frightful picture. A combination of horrors wherein we should behold cruelties unexampled in the annals of mankind; human blood poured forth in torrents, the earth blackened with ashes, the air tainted with pestilence. It is computed that, within two months after the revolt began, upwards of two thousand whites had been massacred, one hundred and eighty sugar plantations and about nine hundred coffee, cotton, and indigo settlements had been destroyed (the buildings had been destroyed by fire); and twelve hundred families reduced from opulence to abject destitution. Of the insurgents, it was recorded that upwards of ten thousand had perished by the sword or famine and some hundreds by the hand of the executioner, many of these on the wheel."

Jean-François, who had become the acknowledged leader of the blacks, assumed the absurd title of "Grand Admiral of France" and, with Biassou, Boukmann, and Jean Jannot, completely controlled the insurgent Negroes of the North. The country was in a state of unutterable confusion, the people being divided not only as to colour and race, but by conflicting political ideas. The Negroes, who outnumbered the combined whites and mulattoes by not less than eight to one, had to some extent begun to realize their strength, but they were as yet unorganized and had no well-defined plans for the abolition of slavery.

The mulattoes, lacking organization and able leadership, were in no position successfully to assert their claims, but they opposed granting freedom to the slaves and had as yet no idea of admitting the blacks to the privileges for which they themselves were contending. The whites, engaged in factional quarrels, were united only in a determination to suppress the revolt of the slaves and in a refusal to recognize the decree of the French National Assembly, which gave certain political rights to the mulattoes.

BLACK DEMOCRACY

Although this decree gave political equality to only a small percentage of the mulattoes, it was generally realized that if it went into effect the cause for which the "people of colour" and their supporters in France were contending was morally won. The defiance of the National Assembly by the colonists was held by the mulattoes to be rebellion against the home government. Assured by their leaders of the support of an element then very powerful in France, they had, even before the blacks rose in the North, determined to obtain their rights by force.

This movement, organized in the western provinces, where many of the mulattoes were wealthy proprietors and slave-owners, was soon strengthened by the adherence of a number of white proprietors who were alarmed by the revolt of the blacks. These whites, many of whom had commanded mulattoes in the colonial national guard, counted on being able to guide this movement and preferred to recognize the claims of the "people of colour" rather than face a conflict with both blacks and mulattoes. Such was the condition in the colony when, on September 26, 1791, civil commissioners appointed by the National Assembly of France to restore peace in St.-Domingue arrived at Cap Français.

The sending of this first civil commission to St.-Domingue reflected the futility which characterized the acts of the French Assembly in connexion with colonial affairs in general and those of St.-Domingue in particular. This commission, which had been appointed early in the summer, did not leave France until the fall, and the delay had a most important bearing on subsequent events.

Appointed at the time of the decree of May 15th, the members of the commission, while heartily in favour of granting political equality to the mulattoes, were opposed to the destruction of the institution of slavery. Before their sailing, however, the National Assembly had reversed its

THE REVOLUTION

point of view, but, for some obscure reason, had failed to change the personnel of the commission. The commissioners were therefore in the anomalous position of supporting principles directly opposed to their original instructions, and were further handicapped by the vagueness of these instructions and by indefinite authority and lack of means to enforce it. They were, moreover, men of no distinction and little ability, and as no news of the insurrection had reached France before their departure, they were stunned and horrified by the awful situation presented to them on their arrival at Cap Français.

The coming of the commission and the announcement that a large military force would be dispatched from France to restore order, so greatly disheartened the insurgent blacks that a few days later Jean-François, the leader of the revolt, sent a letter to the commissioners, suggesting negotiations for peace.

The commission replied with a proclamation of general amnesty and pardon to all who would lay down their arms and return to their former places. This was satisfactory neither to the white planters, who refused to contemplate a free pardon to the rebels who had murdered their relatives and destroyed their homes, nor to the blacks, who pointed out that, more than one hundred thousand men being in arms, their leaders were dependent on the general will. They proposed that if peace was to be restored the commissioners must emancipate from slavery several hundred of the more prominent blacks, explaining that with all the more influential leaders working to this end it might be arranged, although, they admitted, it would be dangerous. "For," they said, "false principles will make the slaves very obstinate; they will say they have been betrayed and the result may be fatal."

The failure of the commissioners to provide any acceptable remedy for the situation led to contempt and open defiance of their authority, and the order to disarm the "men of colour" resulted in driving large numbers of mulattoes into the camps of the insurgent blacks. The hopelessly involved conditions so discouraged the commissioners that they left the colony, two of them sailing for France, and the third proceeding to Spanish Santo Domingo.

In France the Jacobin party was now in the ascendancy. Urged by the society of *Amis des Noirs,* it took active steps to carry out an anti-slavery program. In April, 1792, the National Assembly reaffirmed the right of the freedmen to a share in the colonial government, and appointed three new commissioners, who were instructed to recognize but two classes, freedmen, regardless of colour, and slaves. The assembly also provided six thousand troops to establish the commissioners' authority.

The personnel of the new commission reflected the conditions then prevailing in France. Danton and all advocates of moderation were losing ground, and the only moderate appointed to the commission, Ailhaud, became disgusted with his associates soon after his arrival in St.-Domingue and returned to France. The other commissioners were a notorious Jacobin, Sonthonax, and one Polverel, who was only a degree less objectionable.

It would have been difficult to find men more obviously unfitted for the task of restoring tranquillity in the distracted colony. Their pronounced and open hostility to the "aristocratic class," their excesses, dishonesty, and petty quarrels so antagonized the colonial proprietors that effective co-operation was hopeless. The commissioners had declared, on their arrival, that they had no intention of making any change in the colonial government, yet one of their first acts was the dissolution of the colonial assembly and the arbitrary removal of Governor Blanchelande. His successor proved an unsatisfactory tool, so he too was re-

THE REVOLUTION

moved, as was a *commission intermédiaire* instituted by the commissioners soon after their arrival.

In May, 1793, M. Galbaud was sent from France as governor. He was a man of proved ability and an experienced soldier. He had, however, married a Creole heiress, and through his wife was proprietor of a coffee estate in St.-Domingue. On his refusal to become a tool of the commissioners, he was indicted by them under an old law prohibiting colonial proprietors from holding office, and was ordered to return to France. Galbaud fully realized that the program of the commissioners could lead to nothing but complete disaster; but he also knew that resistance would result in civil war between the white troops on whom he could depend and the mulatto soldiers who had been brought from the South by Sonthonax, so in spite of the prayers of the white population that he remain, he decided to accept his dismissal.

The commissioners at this time had ordered a wholesale deportation of the whites who had opposed them, and the fleet in the harbour was crowded with people who had been condemned to exile or who were abandoning the colony in despair. As the ships were about to sail, a quarrel between mulatto soldiers and French sailors on shore-leave precipitated a general conflict, during which Galbaud landed at the head of a strong force of sailors. The regular troops, garrisoning the harbour fortifications, offered no resistance to this landing, but the soldiers of the French national guard, who were still faithful to the commissioners, sided with the mulattoes and there began a furious struggle in which the citizens joined, the white inhabitants supporting Galbaud and his sailors. The mortality was frightful, but the discipline of Galbaud's troops prevailed and the commissioners and their allies were forced from the city. That night the commissioners, realizing that unaided they were powerless to regain the city, resorted to the revolting expedient of inducing the blacks of the plains to come to their aid by offers of liberty and complete freedom to plunder.

On the following morning over fifteen thousand fanatic blacks entered the city and Galbaud, unable to contend against such overwhelming odds, retired to his ships and set sail for the United States, taking with him thousands of despairing refugees and leaving the town in flames, with hundreds of dead and dying in the streets and on the quays. For two days and nights the whites who had taken refuge in the hills watched the flames consume the richest and most beautiful city of the French colonial empire, while the commissioners stood by and refused to allow any interruption of the sacking of the town.

The destruction of Cap Français and the responsibility of the commissioners for this terrible disaster were interpreted by the whites of St.-Domingue as the end of French supremacy in the colony. From every port ships crowded with refugees sailed for the United States, Europe, or other West Indian islands, while the Spanish border posts received streams of terrified and destitute whites, many of whom, abandoning all their possessions, had escaped only with their lives.

Since early in May, 1793, a small number of Spanish troops had been conducting ineffective operations on the eastern border of the French colony. The atrocious action of the commissioners in deliberately turning over Cap Français to the hordes of blacks had so disgusted the French troops that thousands of the French regulars and national guard deserted and joined the Spanish, as did many of the black leaders. These included Jean-François, Toussaint, and Biassou, who received high military rank in the army of Spain. Thus reinforced, the Spanish began a strong offensive, and by the end of July they were seriously threatening the northern part of the French colony.

THE REVOLUTION

In July, Sonthonax, in a characteristic message to the French Convention, reported the general exodus of the white population and the desertion of thousands of his white troops to the Spanish. "Without ships, without money, without a month's supply," he wrote, "still we do not despair of the safety of the *patrie,* we ask no troops, no ships, no sailors; it is with the real inhabitants of this country, the Africans, that we will save to France the possession of St.-Domingue."

Sonthonax, when this report was written, had already issued a proclamation giving freedom to all Negro warriors who would fight for the Republic under the civil commissioners, and had promised liberty to all who would enrol themselves in the forces of the Republic.

On the 28th of August, 1793, he formally proclaimed the freedom of the slave population of the northern provinces.

Polverel, then at Port-au-Prince, although angry and alarmed at this totally unauthorized and radical proceeding, was forced to follow suit and immediately proclaimed the freedom of the slaves in the South and West.

Thus the miserable policy of the commissioners had culminated in the very result which they, on their arrival, had pledged themselves to prevent. They had utterly destroyed the influence and prestige of the whites by elevating to positions of authority the mulattoes, and now they completely alienated the "people of colour" by pandering to the blacks.

Lasalle, the governor-general at this time, reported to France that "he found himself surrounded by epaulettes of all grades worn by slaves of the day before," and stated that a black ex-slave had been recently appointed by the commissioners to the office of inspector-general of the colony.

These procedures, and especially the emancipation of the slaves, which was known to have been done without authority from France, failed completely in their purpose.

BLACK DEMOCRACY

The black leaders, on whom Sonthonax now depended, distrusted him, and thousands of Negroes who had enlisted in the army of the commissioners at the time of the looting of Cap Français, finding nothing left to plunder, vanished to the hills or joined the Spanish army, which at least served a king.

Even Mocaya, one of the first of the black chiefs to swear allegiance to the French Republic, deserted and sent to Sonthonax a most astonishing letter in which he said: "I am the subject of three kings—the king of the Congo, lord of all the blacks, the king of France, who represents my father, the king of Spain, who represents my mother. These three kings are descended from those who, led by a star, went to adore the Man-God. If I passed into the service of the Republic, I should perhaps be forced to make war upon my brothers, the subjects of these three kings to whom I have sworn fidelity."

Jean-François, Biassou, and their followers now regularly enlisted in the Spanish service, refused to recognize the authority of the commissioners, stating that since the beginning of the world they had obeyed the will of a king. Having lost the king of France, they would obey the king of Spain, who, they said, had constantly rewarded and assisted them. They further declared that they would not recognize the commissioners until France had enthroned a king.

Notwithstanding the troubles of the past few years, a certain amount of cultivation had continued; but now the blacks became completely insubordinate and, in spite of regulations which gave to them one-fourth of the products of their labour, they abandoned the plantations and spent their time in idleness and debauchery.

Ever since the first massacres of the planters of the Plaine-du-Nord in 1791, refugees from St.-Domingue had been beseeching the British government to send a force to take possession of the island, preferring the rule of a for-

THE REVOLUTION

eign country to the loss of their possessions and the surrender to the blacks which they even then foresaw.

This feeling had been greatly intensified by the results of the outrageous conduct of the civil commissioners, and in 1793 an association of proprietors of the South and West entered into a treaty with the British governor of Jamaica. It was stipulated that St.-Domingue should be occupied by the British forces on condition that the French colonists assisted in subduing the insurgent Negroes and in restoring order in the colony.

The governor of Jamaica was instructed to send an expedition to St.-Domingue and accept the submission of those inhabitants who solicited the protection of the British government. This expedition was received with great enthusiasm, and the British quickly took possession of the South with the exception of the important town of Aux Cayes, which was held for the commissioners by the mulatto general Rigaud. Two months later the garrison of the great fortress at Mole St. Nicholas, composed of Irish battalions and national guards in the service of the French Republic, surrendered to the British. These troops, disgusted with the conduct of the commissioners, had for some time been insubordinate, and on the appearance of an English ship of war they capitulated without firing a shot.

Thus the commissioners not only lost the strongest military post in the island, a vast store of supplies, and over three thousand of their few remaining white troops, but suffered an irreparable blow to their prestige, which led to further disasters.

The mulattoes of Port-au-Prince, while enraged at the emancipation of the slaves, which they as bitterly opposed as did the whites, had been kept in some sort of restraint by Commissioner Polverel and a few faithful and able mulatto leaders. The successes of the British, however, filled the mulattoes with dread that they would be deprived of their hard-won privileges, and many of the mulatto strongholds openly revolted against the commissioners, till nothing was left to the latter but Port-au-Prince, hemmed in by British forces and a shattered republican army under General Laveaux in the North.

In October Laveaux reported that in addition to the extreme danger of foreign enemies he had to face a desperate lack of supplies and equipment, miserable hospital conditions, and a dangerous sickness among his few remaining soldiers. It was evident also that the Negro troops were discontented and about to demand that they should be led by one of their own colour.

Laveaux wrote, in the latter part of October: "We are in a country where, by the course of events, the white man is detested. The guilty have fled, it is true; but the hatred toward the whites, borne by the Africans, is not in the least assuaged thereby, and who can force these new citizens to do their duty, once they have abjured it? Will they respect the handful of white troops which yet remains?"

France was now in the throes of the Terror, and hatred of the aristocrats blinded any intelligent consideration of the desperate state of the French colonies.

In February, 1794, three deputies from St.-Domingue, a black and two mulattoes, were received with enthusiasm by the National Convention, and a decree was promulgated declaring slavery abolished in all the colonies and that all men, without distinction of colour, domiciled in the colonies were French citizens. This decree completed the alienation of the mulattoes in the colony, who thus saw themselves deprived of their slaves and forced to contemplate the equality of the "savage Africans" whom they feared and despised.

In May the British captured Port-au-Prince, and the commissioners with their few remaining troops sought ref-

THE REVOLUTION

uge with General Rigaud, who by his military skill and his influence with the mulattoes still maintained an army in the South. A month later Sonthonax and Polverel sailed for France to answer to the Convention for their atrocious mismanagement of the mission which had been entrusted to them.

— Areas Occupied by Spanish and British in 1794 —

Except for a small area still held by Rigaud, the South and West were now in the hands of the British, and in the North General Laveaux was barely maintaining his hold on Port-de-Paix, the one important post remaining to the armies of the Republic. At this critical moment there appeared on the scene a man who, suddenly emerging from obscurity, was destined to complete the emancipation of the blacks and expel both French and English from the island.

BLACK DEMOCRACY

Toussaint l'Ouverture, the outstanding character in Haitian history of whom not only Haitians but all Negroes may well be proud, was born near Cap Français, on the Breda plantation, a slave of slave parents. In a country where this degrading institution was the fundamental basis of economic life and where slaves were treated with less consideration than were beasts of burden, this extraordinary man developed qualities of leadership and political sagacity unparalleled in the annals of his race.

In his youth Toussaint attracted the attention of the plantation manager by his intelligence and received an opportunity to acquire the rudiments of an education. Whether or not he was identified with the first revolt of the slaves is uncertain. It is known, however, that he had refrained from joining the insurgents until after his master had been forced to take refuge in Cap Français, and that on joining Jean-François he was given the somewhat extraordinary title of "Physician to the Armies of the King." He was rapidly promoted, and served as aide-de-camp both to Biassou and to Jean-François.

In the spring of 1794, when the position of the commissioners was most desperate and just prior to their departure for France, Toussaint had reached a position of high rank in the Spanish army. He was no longer subordinate to Jean-François, but the independent commander of over four thousand well-trained troops. He had, through his prestige among the blacks, attracted to his command the most influential of the Negro chiefs and had also succeeded in securing the services, as drillmasters, of many of the French regulars who had deserted to the Spanish at the time of the destruction of Cap Français.

In August, 1793, Sonthonax announced the emancipation of the slaves, and at the same time Toussaint, from a camp in the hills of Spanish Santo Domingo, issued the following proclamation:

THE REVOLUTION

In Camp Trivel, August 29, 1793.
BROTHERS AND FRIENDS:

I am Toussaint l'Ouverture; my name is perhaps known to you. I have undertaken to avenge your wrongs. It is my desire that liberty and equality shall reign in St.-Domingue. I am striving to this end. Come and unite with us, brothers, and combat with us for the same cause.

Your very humble and obedient servant,
TOUSSAINT L'OUVERTURE,
General for the Public Welfare.

After the departure of the commissioners in April, 1794, General Laveaux was defending Port-de-Paix against almost overwhelming odds. He seized every opportunity to gain adherents to the French cause, and secretly negotiated with Toussaint, who readily fell in with the plans of the French general and agreed to desert the Spanish service on condition that he be given high rank in the French army. This proposal was eagerly accepted by Laveaux, who agreed to confer on Toussaint the rank of *général de brigade*.

Toussaint deserted the Spanish army, as agreed, under circumstances which are cited by his critics as proof of their contention that he was a "cunning hypocrite." He had been completely trusted by the Spanish, had received the command of a host of blacks, and was treated with the utmost consideration by his immediate superior, the Marquis de Hermonia, who is quoted as having said: "God Himself could not actuate a spirit more pure." Yet Toussaint deserted, taking with him all the blacks under his command and using them to overthrow the Spanish troops whom he encountered while marching to join General Laveaux.

It is useless to deny that in this change of allegiance and in several of his later actions Toussaint used methods which may be termed hypocritical; but it cannot be questioned that he held a sincere conviction that he was destined to be the saviour of his people and to free them from slavery. It seems probable that to the mind of this ex-slave any means to that end were justified. The continual treacheries of those against whom he fought were scarcely calculated to inspire him to acts of chivalry.

At this time Toussaint was about fifty years old, a rather unimpressive black man who appears singularly unheroic in contemporary portraits that survive. But his extraordinary force and energy impressed all with whom he came in contact. The officer of the French army in St.-Domingue described him thus: "He has a fine eye, and his glances are rapid and penetrating; extremely sober of habit, his activity in the prosecution of his enterprises is incessant. He is an excellent horseman and travels on occasion with inconceivable rapidity, arriving at the end of his journey alone or almost unattended, his aides-de-camp and domestics being unable to follow him in journeys often extending to fifty or sixty leagues."

Toussaint's defection threw the Spanish operations into complete disorder and resulted in the surrender of all the important Spanish posts in French St.-Domingue. Through his influence the blacks were won over to the French cause and by his military skill reduced to order and discipline. Within a few weeks the North was again held by France, and Toussaint, the author of these victories, stood in high favour with General-in-Chief Laveaux.

Learning from unsuccessful attacks on the British that his soldiers were ineffective against trained troops, Toussaint with his characteristic energy organized a number of regiments which, under the instructions of French soldiers and the strict discipline of their Negro commander, soon attained a remarkable degree of efficiency. In 1795 peace between France and Spain ended the Spanish operations against the French in St.-Domingue and, Jean-François

THE REVOLUTION

having retired to Spain, Toussaint was left without a serious rival for the supreme leadership of the blacks.

During March of the following year the citizens of Cap Français rebelled against General Laveaux and imprisoned him, and the municipality of Cap Français installed the mulatto general Villatte in his place. This high-handed proceeding was protested against by some of the black officers, who notified Toussaint of Laveaux's predicament. Nothing could have better suited the plans of Toussaint than this opportunity to place Laveaux under further obligations to him. He hastened to the Cape with 10,000 soldiers, liberated Laveaux, and restored him to power.

At this time the appointment of Laveaux as governor-general of the colony arrived from France, and his first official act was to name Toussaint his chief aide with the title of lieutenant-governor. "This is the black," said Laveaux, "who was foretold by Abbé Raynal as destined to avenge the injuries of his race." Laveaux described Toussaint as the saviour of the whites and the hope of the blacks, and expressed his determination to be guided by Toussaint's advice in his administration.

There is no doubt that the influence of Toussaint immediately benefited the condition of the blacks. Order was restored and the cultivation of the soil resumed throughout the North. But from this moment the influence of the whites in the colonies rapidly declined and the power of Toussaint steadily increased.

The Directory of France, in May, 1796, sent a new commission to supervise the reorganization of the colony. Incredible as it may seem, this commission was headed by the notorious Sonthonax, whose wretched policy had been the principal cause of the failure of the second commission. Prior to Sonthonax's departure from St.-Domingue in 1794, he had conceived strong feelings of enmity against the mulattoes; and he returned with the full intention of destroying their influence. As General Laveaux was fully in accord with this policy, Sonthonax had no difficulty in inaugurating a program the object of which was to use the blacks against the mulattoes and thus restore the whites to supremacy.

The new commission, after appointing Toussaint a major-general of the army of France and confirming the mulatto leader Rigaud as a brigadier-general, resorted to the reprehensible measure of sowing dissension between the blacks and the mulattoes. Major-General Rochambeau, who had accompanied the commission, did not hesitate to express his disapproval of this policy and was sent back to France. This left but three major-generals in the colony: Laveaux, commander-in-chief; Desfourneaux, and Toussaint l'Ouverture. Desfourneaux was already in disfavour, and Toussaint realized that if he could get rid of Laveaux he would in all probability become commander-in-chief of the French forces in St.-Domingue.

Sonthonax's policies had utterly failed and he was at odds with all the whites, including his fellow commissioners. But he still hoped to control the colony through Toussaint, whom he was treating with the utmost courtesy and heaping with grossest flattery. Commissioner Geraud, being distrusted by Sonthonax, was hounded out of the colony. Leblanc died, it was said by poison, and the mulatto commissioner, Raymond, considered by Toussaint and Sonthonax too weak to be dangerous, was bullied into complete submission.

Both Toussaint and Sonthonax desired to remove General Laveaux, the former because the general stood between him and the chief military rank and because he was becoming too popular with the Negro chiefs, and the latter because Laveaux was the one influential white man, except himself, left in the colony. Together they resorted to a clever trick.

THE REVOLUTION

The Republic of France had assigned a number of seats in the National Assembly to the colony, and to one of these seats the two wily plotters decided that Laveaux should be elevated. An election was held at Cap Français, and as the black general in command threatened to burn the city if Laveaux was not chosen, he was "elected" by a large majority and sailed for France. This left the way open for the appointment of Toussaint as commander-in-chief of the French forces in the colony, and the clever black, now invested with the highest military authority, proceeded to eliminate Sonthonax by exactly the same method they had already used to remove Laveaux.

Toussaint had heartily supported Sonthonax in his policy of eliminating the influential whites from the colony, and Sonthonax apparently did not realize that he had been playing into the hands of the crafty black leader until he suddenly found himself "elected" deputy to the French Assembly. In spite of his energetic resistance, he was forced to sail for France on August 20, 1797.

The French Directory grew alarmed at the arbitrary actions of Toussaint, but having no military force at their disposal, they were obliged to content themselves with sending General Hédouville to St.-Domingue with instructions to re-establish the authority of France. A few days after Hédouville's arrival the British were compelled by Toussaint to evacuate Port-au-Prince, and in October, 1798, they surrendered their last stand at Mole St. Nicholas to the triumphant black general.

Nothing now stood between Toussaint and absolute power but the presence of Hédouville and the remnant of the mulatto party led by Rigaud, who was still in command of the French forces in the South. Hédouville, with the intention of weakening Toussaint's influence by playing Rigaud against the more powerful black, called the two generals to a conference at Cap Français. This conference not only was a complete failure, but gave to Toussaint an opening of which he was not slow to take advantage. He deliberately circulated rumours that the French commissioner was planning the destruction of the Negro leaders and the re-establishment of slavery. This shrewd move started a general uprising among the blacks of the Plaine-du-Nord and the renewal of destruction and carnage such as had inaugurated the first slave revolt.

As Toussaint had foreseen, Hédouville, powerless to quell these disorders, appealed to him for assistance. The uprising in the North had spread. The district around Cap Français was in utter disorder, with the situation each day becoming more acute, when Toussaint suddenly appeared among the rebellious Negroes and advanced with them on Cap Français. Word that Toussaint was leading a host to capture *le Cap* resulted in the desertion of a majority of its defenders, and Hédouville, finding himself without an army, embarked for France, leaving Toussaint completely master of the situation.

After Hédouville's departure the Negroes at once resumed their peaceful occupations. The "revolt" subsided as quickly as it had commenced. Toussaint, now in control of the North and West and, except for Rigaud, unopposed ruler of St.-Domingue, resorted to one of those spectacular plays of which he seems to have been a past master. Calling together the people of Cap Français, he announced that, having accomplished the salvation of his race, he would retire to private life. As he had taken care to surround the assemblage with picked troops, he was, as he anticipated, immediately besieged by representatives of all classes of society, begging him to reconsider, and under the "pressure" of this universal demand he consented again to assume the leadership.

Fearing the effect in France of his arbitrary expulsion of

THE REVOLUTION

Hédouville, Toussaint invited the return of Roume, a member of the first French commission who had been residing in Santo Domingo. Subsequent conference between Roume, Toussaint, Rigaud, and other leaders resulted in temporary peace, but jealousy of Toussaint's power and the disinclination of the mulattoes to serve under a black led to fresh disorders which ended with complete defeat of the mulattoes and the expulsion of Rigaud, Pétion, and a number of other mulatto officers, who sailed for France.

In August, 1800, Toussaint, having thus broken the power of Rigaud, decided on a general subjection of the mulattoes. For this purpose he appointed Dessalines governor of the South, with general orders for the "pacification" of the country. Dessalines did not disappoint his master. Backed by overwhelming masses of Negro troops, this ferocious "tiger" traversed the districts of the South and slowly and methodically weeded out the mulatto population. Men, women, and children were systematically done to death, generally after excruciating tortures. It is estimated that not less than ten thousand persons were killed in this campaign. Reproached for this barbarity, Toussaint remarked: "I told Dessalines to prune the tree, not to uproot it."

Now in absolute control of French St.-Domingue, General Toussaint determined to unite the whole island under his rule and, basing his action on the treaty between France and Spain which ceded Santo Domingo to the former country, dispatched an army to take possession of the Spanish colony. His personal prestige was so great that little resistance was offered. On assuming the government of the entire island, he promptly promulgated a constitution which was a model of justice and moderation, and so effectively administered affairs that it is interesting to speculate what the possible development of the Haitian people might have been had Toussaint been left unmolested in his autocratic rule, or even if France had been willing to confirm him as governor of the colony.

Toussaint was fully conversant with the situation and the natural wealth of the island. He knew how his race could endure forced labour and realized that, could he but wring sufficient wealth from these two factors, he might hold the loyalty of the Negro leaders. To this end he turned the whole power of his extraordinary energy. Ten years of war had already assembled the strong men of the Negro race in the ranks of his army, and this army was wholly subservient to its leader's will. The entire country was scoured by Toussaint's troops, the Negroes being herded from their vagabond life back to work such as they had never known under the old régime. In spite of their "emancipation," the black cultivators found themselves once more slaves—slaves of a military state. The colony was divided into districts, each under a general, and at least Dessalines, captain-general of the South and West, showed himself eminently successful in his stewardship. He patrolled his districts like a king of Dahomey, sentencing shirkers or insubordinate blacks to be buried alive or sawn between two planks. When slavery was abolished in 1793, the blacks had refused to work. Production had practically ceased; but under the new régime prosperity returned immediately.

Toussaint consistently maintained his policy of encouraging the return of the whites who had been expelled during the revolution. In this he displayed his political and administrative sagacity. On the reconstruction of the great productive agricultural system, which had been completely destroyed, rested Toussaint's main hope of perpetuating his power. In addition to the rehabilitation of the plantations which would result, Toussaint could also count on the potential value of those *émigrés* as hostages in case the French tried to regain the colony, and also on the fact that

THE REVOLUTION

the sight of their former masters bowing in submission to him would add greatly to his prestige with his black followers. The estates of many of the former proprietors were restored to them, and they were provided with black labourers who, notwithstanding the nominal freedom, were forced to toil under a system whereby the "cultivators" worked the plantations for a share of the crops.

His authority now established and recognized throughout the whole island, Toussaint promulgated, in the autumn of 1801, a constitution and confirmed his title as governor-general for life with the power to name his successor. This season found St.-Domingue in quiet submission, and economic conditions throughout the island rapidly improved. The more influential and intelligent Haitians, imitating their former masters, lived in luxury, and churches and theatres were reopened. The country had entered on a promising period of reconstruction.

Such was the state of St.-Domingue when cessation of hostilities in Europe allowed Bonaparte, now First Consul, to turn his attention to the Western World.

CHAPTER IV

"FIRST OF THE BLACKS"

> "Toussaint, the most unhappy Man of Men!
> Whether the whistling Rustic tend his plough
> Within thy hearing, or thy head be now
> Pillow'd in some deep dungeon's earless den,
> O miserable Chieftain! where and when
> Wilt thou find patience? Yet die not: do thou
> Wear rather in thy bonds a cheerful brow:
> Though fallen thyself, never to ride again,
> Live, and take comfort. Thou hast left behind
> Powers that will work for thee: air, earth, and skies.
> There's not a breathing of the common wind
> That will forget thee: thou hast great allies;
> Thy friends are exultations, agonies,
> And love, and Man's unconquerable mind."
> —*Wordsworth.*

IN France a white man had risen by some inevitable process of selection from the chaos of revolution. He had brought order to a distracted people, built powerful armies, and by a combination of craftiness and courage become the most powerful man in Europe. Now he turned his eyes toward the Western World, where, on an island, a French possession, a black man, an ex-slave, had through possession of like talents attained a comparable position of power.

That these two should come into conflict was, under the circumstances, inevitable, and the Frenchman's advantage seemed so great that any resistance appeared futile. Napoleon did defeat Toussaint, and sent him to die in a French

~ Toussaint l'Ouverture, "First of the Blacks" ~

"FIRST OF THE BLACKS"

prison. But in a struggle of intense dramatic interest the armies built by the black man, aided by disease, ultimately destroyed all hope of French dominion in the Western Hemisphere.

Peace with England lifted the ban from the movement of French ships in the Caribbean Sea and enabled Napoleon to turn his attention to the recovery of the colonies and the creation of a French colonial empire. In the fall of 1800 Bonaparte had secured a treaty with Carlos IV whereby Spain agreed to cede Louisiana, and though this compact was not consummated until 1802,[1] Bonaparte's policy of colonial expansion included the development of the province of Louisiana, and the recovery of St.-Domingue, the logical base for French operations in the West Indies, was of double importance. At the moment, St.-Domingue was completely dominated by Toussaint; the situation in Guadeloupe was precarious and Martinique was in the hands of the English. It was obvious that French supremacy must be restored in St.-Domingue before any plans for the development of a French colonial empire in the Americas could be effected.

Bonaparte's advices from St.-Domingue were most conflicting. Vincent and Roume, each of whom was familiar with conditions in the colony, wrote that Toussaint was the one man who could save St.-Domingue for France, and advised a conciliatory policy, while General Hédouville, who had been expelled from the island and was then in the United States, took a diametrically opposite view and pointed out that Toussaint had already assumed the independence of St.-Domingue and that the "First of the Blacks," as it was reported Toussaint had styled himself, must be eliminated. In this the ruined colonial planters and the mulattoes who had been expelled from the colony, having nothing to lose and everything to gain, strongly agreed.

Toussaint had saved St.-Domingue from the British, had

brought about peace among the conflicting elements, and was making rapid progress in restoring prosperity. But from all reports it was evident that the authority of France had been destroyed, and it was extremely doubtful whether the black chief would agree to any terms that Bonaparte was prepared to offer. Therefore an expedition was planned which, though ostensibly peaceful, would be prepared to take the colony by force should any resistance be offered by Toussaint.

Of this expedition Mme. Junot, Bonaparte's close friend and an intimate of his sister Pauline and her husband General Leclerc, wrote: "The expedition to St.-Domingue encountered plenty of approbation and plenty of censure. The censurers alleged that it was folly to oppose the entire population of a distant colony whose savage disposition refused all quarter to their adversaries, thus exposing our troops to the double perils of a murderous warfare and a no less murderous climate. They were grieved to see so fine an army dispatched to America before the remnant of that which the deserts of Africa had nearly engulfed was restored to us. They contended that in spite of his profound ambition, in spite even of his cruelty, it was necessary to guarantee to Toussaint l'Ouverture the government for life which had been conferred upon him by the colonists. He had very distinguished military talents, a political address, or rather an ingenious cunning which had saved St.-Domingue from the English yoke and, above all, from its own passions. They were therefore of opinion that the First Consul should leave Toussaint l'Ouverture at liberty still to call himself, if he so pleased, the 'First of the Blacks,' and that he should be acknowledged governor of St.-Domingue, subject to the dominion of France—terms to which he would most willingly have agreed. But the First Consul justly observed that Toussaint was a hypocrite who, while protesting his devotion to the Consular government, was meditating the liberation of the French Antilles from the authority of the Republic."

In December, 1801, fifty-four vessels, twenty-six of which were ships of war, sailed with twenty thousand veteran troops, most of them from the army of the Rhine. This expedition was commanded by General Leclerc, who was accompanied by his ambitious and beautiful wife Pauline. General Rochambeau,[2] General Kerverseau, and General Boudet held subordinate commands, while Rigaud, Pétion, and Villatte, all mulattoes who had been expelled from St.-Domingue, received minor military rank.

Bonaparte, apparently with the hope of securing his object by peaceful means if possible, also sent with this expedition the two sons of Toussaint who had been for some years in school in France. These two boys, Placide and Isaac, were accompanied by their tutor and were entrusted with the delivery of a letter from Bonaparte to their father, written in the most friendly and conciliatory tone.

In January, 1802, the fleet arrived at Samana Bay, a fine harbour at the eastern extremity of St.-Domingue, where it separated into four divisions. General Kerverseau was dispatched with a division to Santo Domingo City, General Boudet to Port-au-Prince, and General Rochambeau to Manzanilla Bay on the north coast just east of Fort Dauphin (Fort Liberty). Leclerc, with the main body of the troops, proceeded to Cap Français (Cap Haitien).

It is most difficult to ascertain what information Toussaint had of the nature and design of this expedition. It is affirmed that he had expected only such ships and troops as might naturally be sent on a peaceful mission from the mother country to an obedient colony. But, on the other hand, it is probable that he was to some extent aware of the hostile designs of Bonaparte, and of this there could no longer be any question after the proceedings of Rochambeau, who was the first of the commanders to effect a landing.

As a matter of fact, Leclerc had been instructed by Bonaparte to divide the conquest of St.-Domingue into three periods. In the first, lasting from fifteen to twenty days, Leclerc should occupy the coast towns and organize his forces; in the second, a quick converging movement from several points should break organized resistance; in the third, mobile flying columns should hunt down the scattered Negro bands in the woods and mountains. Thereupon the colony should be reconstructed along lines analogous to those of the Old Régime, though chattel slavery was not to be restored. This program Napoleon tersely summed up in the following words:

> Never will the French nation give chains to men whom it has once recognized as free. Therefore all blacks shall live at St.-Domingue as those in Guadeloupe to-day.
>
> Your conduct will vary with the three periods above mentioned.
>
> In the first period you will disarm only the rebel blacks. In the third you will disarm all.
>
> In the first period you will not be exacting; you will treat with Toussaint, you will promise him everything he asks, in order that you may get possession of the principal points and establish yourself in the country.
>
> As soon as you have done this, you will become more exacting. You will order him to reply categorically to your proclamation and to my letter. You will charge him to come to Le Cap.
>
> In your interviews with Moyse, Dessalines, and Toussaint's other generals, you will treat them well.
>
> Win over Christophe, Clervaux, Maurepas, and all the other black leaders favourable to the whites. In the first period confirm them in their rank and office. In the last period send them all to France, with their rank if they have behaved well.
>
> All Toussaint's principal agents, white or coloured,

"FIRST OF THE BLACKS"

should in the first period be indiscriminately showered with attentions and confirmed in their posts; in the last period, all sent to France; with their rank if they have behaved well during the second; prisoners if they have acted ill.

All blacks in office should during the first period be flattered, well treated, but undermined in authority and power. Toussaint, Moyse, and Dessalines should be well treated during the first period; sent to France in the last, in arrest or with rank according to their conduct.

Raymond has lost the Government's confidence; at the beginning of the second period you will seize him and send him to France as a criminal.

If the last period lasts fifteen days, all is well; if longer, you will have been fooled.

Toussaint should not be held to have submitted until he shall have come to Le Cap or Port-au-Prince in the midst of the French army, to swear fidelity to the Republic. On that very day, without scandal or injury but with honour and consideration, he must be put on board a frigate and sent to France. At the same time, if possible, arrest Moyse and Dessalines; if possible hunt them down; and then send to France all the white partisans of Toussaint, all the blacks in office suspected of disaffection. Declare Moyse and Dessalines traitors and enemies of the French people. Start the troops and give them no rest until you have their heads and have scattered and disarmed their partisans.

If after the first fifteen or twenty days it has been impossible to get Toussaint, proclaim that within a specified time he shall be declared a traitor, and after that period begin a war to the death.

A few thousand Negroes wandering in the mountains should not prevent· the Captain-General from regarding the second period as ended and from promptly beginning the third. Then has come the moment to assure the colony to France for ever. And, on the same day, at every point of the colony, you will arrest all suspects in office whatever their colour and at the same moment embark all the black generals no matter what their conduct, patriotism, or past services; giving them, however, their rank and assuring them of good treatment in France.

All the whites who have served under Toussaint and covered themselves with crimes in the tragic scenes of St.-Domingue shall be sent directly to Guiana.

All the blacks who have behaved well, but whose rank forbids them to remain longer on the island, shall be sent to Brest.

All the blacks or mulattoes who have acted badly, whatever their rank, shall be sent to the Mediterranean and landed at Corsica.

If Toussaint, Dessalines, or Moyse is taken in arms, they shall be passed before a court martial and shot as rebels within twenty-four hours.

No matter what happens, we think that during the third period you should disarm all the Negroes, whatever their party, and set them to work.

All those who have signed Constitution 24 should in the third period be sent to France; some as prisoners, others at liberty as having been constrained.

White women who have prostituted themselves to Negroes, whatever their rank, shall be sent to Europe.

You will take the regimental flags from the National Guard, give out new ones, and reorganize it. You will reorganize the *gendarmerie*. Suffer no black above the rank of captain to remain on the island. . . .

The Captain-General shall allow no temporizing with the principles of these instructions; and any person talking about the rights of those blacks who have shed so much white blood shall under some pretext or other be sent to France, whatever his rank in the service.

Whatever Toussaint's plans may have been, it is extremely doubtful whether he had any idea of submitting to a forcible attempt to eliminate him from power in St.-Domingue. His position was apparently a very strong one. His armies included over twenty thousand regular troops well armed and disciplined and under officers whom he believed to be loyal. Christophe, with five thousand men, with

"FIRST OF THE BLACKS"

head-quarters at Cap Français, held the north. At Port-de-Paix was General Maurepas with a strong body of seasoned troops. Dessalines, the terror of the mulattoes, commanded the south and west with eleven thousand picked troops; and in Spanish Santo Domingo, where Paul l'Ouverture, brother of Toussaint, was governor, four thousand soldiers garrisoned the principal towns under the command of General Clervaux, a mulatto chief of great ability. In addition to these regular troops, Negro irregulars all through the interior had gradually been armed and to some extent organized.

If time had been available to co-ordinate these forces and to plan a united resistance, the program outlined by Bonaparte must have failed in the beginning. But the French acted promptly and boldly and with the most astonishing success. On the second of February, General Rochambeau [2] arrived off Fort Dauphin and, without the formality of presenting his credentials or any attempt to summon the commander of the port, landed his troops on the beach and opened fire on the Negroes there assembled, killing and wounding a great number of innocent bystanders.

On the following day the main body of the troops under Leclerc arrived off Cap Français, where immediate preparations were made to effect a landing. Christophe, the black general in command of the city, on the approach of the French ships, sent his port captain to inform the chief officer of the fleet that, Toussaint, the general-in-chief, being absent in the interior, no disembarkment of a military force would be permitted. He further stated that if a landing were attempted before the receipt of a reply to a message he had sent to Toussaint, the town would be burnt.

In reply, Leclerc sent the following letter:

BLACK DEMOCRACY

LIBERTY AND EQUALITY

*Army of St.-Domingue
Head-quarters on board the* Ocean,
13th Pluviôse, 10th year of the Republic.

The General-in-Chief of the Army of St.-Domingue, Captain-General of the Colony, to the General of Brigade, Christophe, Commandant at Cap Français.

I learn with indignation, Citizen-General, that you refuse to receive the French squadron and the French army that I command, under the pretext that you have received no orders from the Governor-General.

France has concluded a peace with England, and its government sends to St.-Domingue forces capable of subduing the rebels; at least, if any are to be found in St.-Domingue. As to you, General, I confess it will grieve me to account you among them.

I give you notice that if you have not in the course of this day surrendered the forts Picolet and Belair, with all the batteries on the coast, to-morrow, at daybreak, fifteen thousand troops shall be disembarked.

Four thousand men are, at this moment, landing at Fort-Liberté; eight thousand more at Port Republicain.

Herewith you will receive my proclamation, which expresses the intentions of the French government; but recollect, whatever individual esteem your conduct in the colony may have inspired me with, I hold you responsible for what may happen.

I salute you.
Leclerc.

To this Christophe immediately replied:

*Head-quarters at Cap Français, 13th Pluviôse,
Year 10.*

Henri Christophe, General of the Brigade, Commandant of the *arrondissement* of Cap, to the General-in-Chief, Leclerc.

Your aide-de-camp, General, has delivered to me your letter of this day. I have the honour to inform you that I could not deliver up the forts and post confided to my command without previous orders from the Governor-General, Toussaint l'Ouverture, my immediate chief, from whom I hold the powers with which I am invested. I am fully persuaded that I have to do with Frenchmen and that you are the chief of the armament called the expedition; but I wait the orders of the Governor, to whom I have dispatched one of my aides-de-camp, to apprise him of your arrival and that of the French army, and cannot permit you to land until I have received his answer. If you put in force your threats of hostility, I shall make the resistance which becomes a general officer; and, should the chance of war be yours, you shall not enter Cap Français till it be reduced to ashes. Nay, even in the ruins will I renew the combat.

You say that the French Government has sent to St.-Domingue forces capable of subduing the rebels, if any such be found; it is your coming, and the hostile intentions you manifest, that alone could create them among a peaceable people, in perfect submission to France. The very mention of rebellion is an argument for our resistance.

As to the troops which you say are this moment landing, I consider them so many pieces of card which the least breath of wind will dissipate.

How can you hold me responsible for the event? You are not my chief; I know you not and can therefore make no account to you till you are recognized by Governor Toussaint.

For the loss of your esteem, General, I assure you that I desire not to earn it at the price that you set upon it, since to purchase it I must be guilty of breach of duty.

I have the honour to salute you.

H. Christophe.

On the following day a deputation of terrified inhabitants from the town presented a petition to Leclerc, begging him to await word from Toussaint and pointing out that any attempt to land would be followed by a general massacre of the whites and the complete destruction of the city by fire. Leclerc refused, however, to make any promise and suggested the public reading of a proclamation of the First Consul, copies of which had been distributed in the city. This proclamation, which is here reproduced, was written in the same insidious style which characterized all subsequent letters and orders of Bonaparte and his agents to Toussaint.

> INHABITANTS OF SAINT-DOMINGUE: Whatever your origin or your colour, you are all French; you are all free and all equal before God and before the Republic.
> France, like St.-Domingue, has been a prey to factions, torn by civil commotions and by foreign wars. But all has changed, all nations have embraced the French and have sworn to them peace and amity; the French people, too, have embraced each other and have sworn to be all friends and brothers of Europe.
> The Government sends you Captain-General Leclerc; he brings with him numerous forces for protecting you against your enemies and against the enemies of the Republic. If it be said to you these forces are destined to ravish from you your liberty, answer the Republic will not suffer it to be taken from us.
> Rally round the Captain-General; he brings you peace and plenty; whoever shall dare to separate himself from the Captain-General will be a traitor to his country, and the indignation of the Republic will devour him, as the fire devours your dried canes.
> Done at Paris, etc. The First Consul, BONAPARTE,
> The Secretary of State, H. B. Maret.

Leclerc did not wait the reply of Toussaint to Christophe's message, but on receipt of assurances that Rochambeau had landed and could be counted on for co-operation, he prepared to attack Cap Français. Christophe, fully realizing the hopelessness of making any effective defence, gave orders to burn the city, and in the evening, when Leclerc came within sight of the town, he beheld it in flames.

The scenes which followed are thus described in an interview with an American ship captain published in the *Colum-*

"FIRST OF THE BLACKS"

bia Sentinel (Boston, Mass.), March 15, 1802: "Fire and faggots lighted up the flames in many parts at the same time and the place, during the night, exhibited a scene of horror and destruction beyond the power of description and equalled only by the dreadful fate it experienced in the year '92. Many massacres took place and the brutal rage of the Negroes spared neither age nor sex, not of their own colour, except Americans, only one of whom (Mr. Lancaster of Charleston) was killed. Those that escaped the sword were preserved to witness more horrid sensations, being dragged by the Negroes (who evacuated the town during the fire and after the demolition of the forts) to their strong places in the mountains, to serve as hostages or to glut their fury. On the morning of the 5th, of 2,000 houses, 59 only had escaped the ravages of the flames and their tenants, except a wretched few on board the American shipping, were nowhere to be seen. Sugars and other property either rolled in liquid fire along the streets, or mounted in cloudy volumes to the skies. All the plantations of the extensive and once flourishing plain around the Cape for many miles exhibited the same tremendous appearance."

Christophe, after starting this conflagration in his own home, retired to the hills to await the coming of Toussaint.

On the same day that Leclerc landed at Cap Français, General Boudet had with little difficulty captured Port-au-Prince. This success was immediately followed by the surrender of La Plume, the commander of the south, who had been one of the first of the western leaders to put his followers under the direction of Toussaint. His defection gave the French the whole department of the south, and within a few days word was received that the Spanish area, where Paul l'Ouverture, brother of Toussaint, was in command, had surrendered. Thus, within ten days after their arrival, the French had succeeded in carrying out the first part of the program laid down by Bonaparte. They had gained possession of all the important coast towns and commercial centres and of the principal agricultural districts, and had succeeded in alienating many of Toussaint's black and mulatto generals, particularly those of the south and west.

Toussaint was, however, in the field and still supported by such powerful leaders as Dessalines, Christophe, and Maurepas. Fresh troops were daily expected from France, and pending their arrival Leclerc determined to try to secure the submission of Toussaint by diplomatic negotiations. To this end he sent Toussaint's sons accompanied by their tutor, with messages to the black leader. The boys had been instructed to point out to their father the hopelessness of opposition to Bonaparte and to assure him that, even yet, high honours awaited him if he would agree to submit to the orders of the First Consul. While expressing their feeling that this peaceful message should have preceded hostilities, they undertook the mission and a few days later met their father at Ennery, one of his plantations in the mountains.

The tutor, Coisnon, who was a trusted agent of the French Directoire, strongly urged the futility of opposition and enlarged on the consequences that would result from further hostile measures. He guaranteed the sincerity of Bonaparte's assurances of friendship and presented a letter from the First Consul, teeming with friendly expressions: "We have made known to your children and to their preceptors," Bonaparte wrote, "the sentiments by which we are animated. . . . Assist with your counsel, your influence, and your talents the Captain-General. What can you desire? Freedom of the blacks? You know that in all the countries in which we have been we have given it to the people who had it not. Do you desire consideration, honours, fortune? It is not after the services you have rendered, services you still can render, and with the personal estimation we have for you that you should be doubtful with respect to your consideration, your fortune, and the honours that await you."

In replying to these appeals, Toussaint very reasonably reproached Leclerc for withholding the letter over three months and having preceded its delivery by hostile acts which made it very difficult for him to accept the assurances of the peaceful object of the expedition and the sincerity of friendly feelings towards himself. He concluded by saying that he required time to consider his final decision.

Leclerc wrote again, asking Toussaint to come to Cap Français for a conference and giving his word that if the black chief would submit he would be appointed first lieutenant to the captain-general of the colony. Toussaint's delays in accepting these conditions convinced Leclerc that the black chief was seeking to gain time to prepare his armies, and now having over nine thousand veteran French troops available for active service, as well as a host of well-armed and fairly disciplined blacks and mulattoes, he determined to complete the work so satisfactorily begun and on the 17th of February he proclaimed Toussaint an outlaw and launched an intensive campaign well worthy of a general of Napoleon.

The end of February saw the French in full possession of the principal towns and, notwithstanding the desperate courage of such leaders as Dessalines, Christophe, and Maurepas, the greater part of the insurgent blacks had been driven into the mountains. The following letter from Dessalines to Toussaint, which fell into the hands of General Boudet, showed, however, that the blacks were still defiant: "Nothing is hopeless, Citizen-General," wrote Dessalines, "if you can but deprive the invaders of the resources of Port Republican [Port-au-Prince]. Try to burn that place by every means of force and guile. . . . Watch for the moment when the garrison is weakened by expeditions into the plains and then try to surprise and capture that town behind them. Do not forget that while we are waiting that rainy season which should rid us of our enemies, our resources are destruction and fire. . . . Ambush the roads, throw dead men and horses into the springs. Destroy all, burn all, so that those who come here to force us back into slavery may have ever before their eyes the image of that hell which they desire."

At the end of February Maurepas, who had for months been heroically defending Port-de-Paix, became finally convinced of the hopelessness of his position and opened negotiations with the French. He was granted very favourable terms. He and his officers retained their rank and, together with two thousand regular Negro troops, were taken into the French service. This opened the way for a final attack on Toussaint's main position in the hills surrounding the Artibonite Valley, where he had slipped through the French lines and was holding the fortress of Crète-à-Pierrot.

Leclerc realized the immediate necessity for the capture of this important post. Toussaint had again aroused the Negroes of the north, and Leclerc's communications were seriously threatened. Four desperate assaults by the finest of the French troops, in which over fifteen hundred French soldiers lost their lives, were repulsed by the Haitians with desperate courage. But the lines steadily closed in about the besieged fortress, and after three days of continuous bombardment the defenders, being without provisions, abandoned their position and, losing over half their numbers, heroically cut a way through the French battalions.

Much desperate fighting followed, but the surrender of Maurepas and the loss of Crète-à-Pierrot completed the demoralization of the blacks, and a few days later Christophe, having secured the promise of a pardon and military

"FIRST OF THE BLACKS"

rank in the French service, surrendered with twelve hundred regular troops who, as usual, passively followed their chief into the French service. On the first of May, Toussaint and Dessalines surrendered, Dessalines joining the French with the rank of general and Toussaint retiring to his estate at Ennery.

Three months after the landing of the French the prime object of the expedition had been accomplished, but the explicit program outlined by Bonaparte had not been fulfilled. The leaders of the blacks had not been deported; in fact, except for Toussaint, most of the men who survived had been taken into the French service; and while organized resistance had been ended, the blacks had not yet been disarmed. Leclerc had fought well and had shown astonishing energy and perseverance, but the campaign had cost him more than half his army. He had now about seven thousand colonial troops in the pay of France, including mulatto and "free Negro" corps and the black insurgents who had surrendered to him. The former were fairly trustworthy, but the black regiments were still officered by their old leaders and it was certain that any attempt to deport their chiefs would result in the defection of their followers. This had necessitated temporary modification of Bonaparte's plans. Leclerc was further handicapped by the difficulties of the climate. Nature had turned against the Emperor, and malaria was devastating his white armies.

On April 1, 1802, of the seven thousand European troops remaining to Leclerc, over five thousand were in hospitals. The commissary service from France, on which Leclerc depended for the greater part of his supplies, had been very defective for some time and the Captain-General was greatly in need of supplies and without money with which to purchase them. The rainy season, which the blacks hoped would rid them of their enemies, was approaching, and

BLACK DEMOCRACY

Leclerc looked forward with misgiving to this unhealthful period and sent strong pleas to France for additional men, money, and supplies.

The French troops were already suffering from malaria and intestinal troubles, which always appeared with the rainy season, when, in the middle of May, an epidemic of yellow fever broke out at Cap Français. This disease, while more or less prevalent in the summer months, had hitherto been comparatively little feared, few precautions were taken, and under the wretched conditions prevailing in the crowded and unsanitary cantonments, the epidemic spread more rapidly than ever before known in the history of the West Indies. By the end of the first week in June three thousand men had died, and on June 11th Leclerc wrote to Bonaparte that if he wanted to have an army in St.-Domingue he must send it from France because "the ravages of this disease are simply indescribable." Leclerc stated that his losses in officers were out of all proportion to those of the troops, that his ablest helpers were dying, leaving him to bear a burden which was becoming insupportable.

At this time the Captain-General was warned that Toussaint contemplated another uprising. That Leclerc so believed is shown by a letter to Bonaparte dated June 6th, in which he stated that Toussaint was playing false, as he had expected, and that he had ordered his arrest. "I think," Leclerc wrote, "that I can count on Dessalines (whose spirit I have mastered) to hunt him down if he escapes."

The arrest of Toussaint was accomplished by means which, no matter what evidence the French may have had against him, must be regarded as abominable treachery. About a month after Toussaint had returned to his house at Ennery, he received a letter from General Brunet, then commanding the French troops at Gonaives, inviting him to a conference to settle some matters of importance "which it is impossible to explain by letter."

"FIRST OF THE BLACKS"

General Brunet assured Toussaint that he would find a hearty welcome from "a brave man whose strongest desire is your prosperity and your own personal happiness." Toussaint, depending on these assurances of good will and on the promises of Leclerc, proceeded to Gonaives, where he was immediately arrested. A few days later he was deported to France and there imprisoned in the fortress of Joux until his death in April, 1803.[3]

In a letter to Bonaparte dated June 11, 1802, Leclerc said "the apprehension of Toussaint occasioned some disturbance." This was a mild statement of the facts. The arrest of the former black chieftain and the treacherous manner of his capture and deportation were a profound shock to the blacks and completely destroyed their faith in Leclerc's promises. That no general outbreak followed was due partly to precautions taken by Leclerc, who immediately stamped out the few uprisings which were attempted, but more to the complete disorganization of the black leaders, who distrusted each other, and some of whom, for selfish reasons, were not averse to the elimination of Toussaint.

Leclerc's position was critical. His European troops were dying at an appalling rate. The black troops were showing signs of revolt and he realized that his hold on them depended on their retaining confidence in his ability to reward or punish them. In his desperate situation he decided to disarm the blacks and entrusted this dangerous proceeding to his black generals.

On June 6th, Leclerc reported that the south and west, under Dessalines and La Plume, had been disarmed and that the disarmament of the north, where more difficulty was expected, would next be undertaken. He said that his black generals realized he was destroying their influence, but that they detested each other and feared him. He ended his report by stating that it now seemed probable St.-Domingue would be restored to France.[4]

BLACK DEMOCRACY

If the fever had abated, or if fresh troops had arrived, it is possible that these hopes would have been realized; but the fever did not abate and the European troops were ineffective because, as he reported, "they dropped on the road from disease." Leclerc stated that he had but few colonial troops, for, mistrusting their loyalty, he dared not keep them in great numbers. In spite of this desperate situation, Leclerc still had hopes of success when the extraordinary tidings was received that, by the order of Bonaparte, slavery had been restored in Guadeloupe and Martinique.

This news, which was received with the utmost fury, was the beginning of the end of French rule in St.-Domingue. At the very moment when success was in sight, Leclerc was compelled to report that he faced absolute failure. "All the Negroes here," he wrote, "are convinced by the news that we are about to reduce them to servitude. . . . At the very moment of success these political circumstances have almost destroyed my work; you can no longer count on the moral force I used to have here; it is destroyed. I can reduce the Negroes only by force, and for this I must have an army and money."

Although the black troops were rapidly deserting the French and congregating in the mountains, the prominent leaders had so far remained faithful, even to the extent of ruthlessly punishing their former companions who had revolted. Charles Belair, one of Toussaint's favourites, who joined the insurgents, was hunted down by Dessalines and sent with his wife to Cap Français, where they were tried by court martial and publicly shot. At about the same time Dessalines ordered the execution of several hundred blacks who were accused of killing some French soldiers in the Artibonite Valley. These and other wholesale executions added fuel to the flames, and the insurrection continued to spread with great rapidity.

"FIRST OF THE BLACKS"

In August, 1802, Leclerc wrote to Napoleon: "My position grows trying and may well become worse. Here it is: disease had made such frightful ravages among my troops that when I wished to disarm the Negroes an insurrection broke out. . . . Our first attacks scattered the insurgents, but they fled into other cantons. In the present insurrection there is a veritable fanaticism. These men may be killed, but will not surrender; they laugh at death; and it is the same with the women. I begged you, Citizen Consul, to do nothing to make these people fear for their liberty till the moment when I should be prepared. Suddenly there came the law authorizing the trade, and on top of that General Richepause has just decreed the restoration of slavery in Guadeloupe. With this state of things, Citizen Consul, the moral force I had acquired here is destroyed. I can do nothing more by persuasion; I can only use force, and force I have none. At present, Citizen Consul, now that your colonial plans are perfectly well known, if you wish to preserve St.-Domingue send a new army, and especially send money. I declare positively that if you abandon us to ourselves as you have done so far, this colony is lost; and, once lost, you will never get it back again."

The fever of which Leclerc complained continued to rage, and the reinforcements which arrived in the middle of September succumbed even more quickly than had the earlier troops. On September 13th he wrote of this to the Minister of Marine:

"I have had to throw them into the field to repress the general insurrection discussed in my last dispatches. For the first few days these troops act with vigour and gain successes; then the disease smites them and all my reinforcements are annihilated. People assure me of a certain change of season by the 15th Vendémiaire [7th October], but I greatly fear that by that time I shall have no soldiers.

"I can give you no exact idea of my position; each day

it grows worse, and what will most retard the colony's prosperity is the fact that when the disease ceases I shall have no men for aggressive action. If on the 15th Vendémiaire I have four thousand Europeans fit to march, even counting those now on the sea, I shall be glad indeed. All my corps commanders save two are dead and I have no fit persons to replace them. To give you an idea of my losses, know that the 7th of the line came here 1,395 strong; to-day there are 83 half-sick men with the colours and 107 in hospital. The rest are dead. The 11th light infantry landed here 1,900 strong; to-day it has 163 fit for duty and 200 in hospital. The 71st of the line, originally 1,000 strong, has 17 men with the colours and 107 in hospital. And it is the same with the rest of the army. Thus, form your own idea of my position in a country where civil war has raged for ten years and where the rebels are convinced that we intend to reduce them to slavery.

"Citizen Minister, if the French government wishes to preserve St.-Domingue it must, on the very day that it receives this letter, order the departure of ten thousand men. They will arrive in Nivôse [January, 1803], and order will be entirely restored before the next hot season; although, if this disease habitually lasts three months on end at St.-Domingue, we must renounce this colony."

On the 16th of September a still more pessimistic outline of the situation was sent to France by Leclerc:

"Here is the state of my black generals. Maurepas is a dangerous rascal, but I dare not arrest him at this moment, since this would surely entail the defection of all his troops. Christophe has so maltreated the Negroes that he is hated by them and is therefore not to be feared. Dessalines is at present the butcher of the Negroes; it is through him that I execute all my odious measures. I shall keep him as long as I need him. He has already begged me not to leave him at St.-Domingue when I return home. La Plume, Clervaux,

"FIRST OF THE BLACKS"

and Paul l'Ouverture are three imbeciles whom I shall get rid of at will. Charles Belair has been tried and shot. Next month I hope to have eight thousand men—four thousand white troops, two thousand *gendarmes,* two thousand Negro soldiers. But these forces will not suffice to hold the country, and the longer I put off its submission, the harder the submission will be. Yes, Citizen Consul, such is my position. I have not exaggerated. Each day I have to rack my brains to know how I may repair the ills of the day before. Not one consoling thought to efface or diminish the cruel impressions of the present or the future. The preservation of St.-Domingue since the embarkation of Toussaint l'Ouverture is something more extraordinary than my landing and my capture of that general. If I did not know how much you have the success of this expedition at heart, I should believe myself sacrificed. . . . Citizen Consul, I must have ten thousand men at once. I must have them to assure you St.-Domingue. The disease has put us far back, and the longer you delay, the more men you will have to send to remedy the situation."

It is apparent from this letter that Leclerc was very much in error as to the state of his black generals. Dessalines was still protesting his loyalty, but several weeks before this letter was written he had met Pétion, the mulatto general who later became the first president of the Republic of Haiti, at Plaisance and, in spite of mutual distrust, these two leaders, Dessalines, an illiterate ex-slave, and Pétion, a cultured half-white who had been educated in the best French military schools and had served with the armies of France in Europe, came to an understanding that they would ultimately join in the insurrection. At this meeting, while discussing the deportation of Toussaint, Pétion remarked: "But how could General Toussaint count on the sincerity of the whites, he their former slave, when I have not even the friendship of my own father for the single reason that I have African blood in my veins?" This remark apparently resolved any doubts Dessalines may have entertained of Pétion, and they parted agreed to desert the French when the time was ripe.

On the 26th of September, Leclerc wrote to the First Consul:

"My position grows worse from day to day, and the most terrible thing about the situation is that I cannot tell you when or how it will improve. I thought that the ravages of the disease would slacken with Vendémiaire. I was mistaken; it has taken on new virulence. Fructidor [September] has cost me more than four thousand dead, and to-day people tell me that it may last to the end of Brumaire [November]. If this be true and its intensity continue, the colony is lost.

"Each day the insurgent forces increase, while mine diminish by loss of whites and desertions of the blacks. Dessalines, who up to this time has not thought of rebellion, thinks so to-day. A month ago he was destroying captured arms; to-day he no longer destroys them, and he no longer maltreats the Negroes as he did then. He is a scoundrel. I know him, but I dare not arrest him. I should alarm all the Negroes who are still with me. Christophe inspires more confidence. Maurepas is a rascal, but I cannot yet order his arrest.

"Never was general in a more dreadful situation. The troops that arrived a month ago no longer exist. Each day the rebels attack and the firing can be heard in Le Cap. I cannot take the offensive—it crushes my troops—and even should I attack, I could not follow up the victories I might gain. I repeat what I have said before: St.-Domingue is lost to France if by the end of Nivôse [January, 1803] I do not receive ten thousand men in a body. The partial reinforcements you send me might feed the army in ordinary times, but they can never reconquer St.-Domingue."

"FIRST OF THE BLACKS"

This letter was followed on the next day by an even more pessimistic statement:

"You will never subdue St.-Domingue without an army of twelve thousand acclimated troops besides the *gendarmerie;* and you will not have this army until you have sent seventy thousand men."

On the tenth of October, General Clervaux, described by Leclerc as an imbecile whom he would get rid of at will, deserted, taking with him the large body of mulatto troops under his command, and a few days later, backed by a multitude of blacks, he made a desperate attack on Cap Français, which was now defended only by a few hundred effective regulars and about two thousand white national guards and volunteers. Clervaux failed to capture Le Cap, but the defection of this prominent leader and his mulatto troops decided the blacks and mulattoes who were still wavering, and a few days later Christophe joined Clervaux with a host of well-trained black troops.

On October 13th, Pétion, learning that his arrest had been ordered, deserted the French, taking with him the demi-brigade which was guarding the southern outposts of Cap Français. Dessalines and other leaders immediately followed, and the French forces held only Le Cap in the north, St.-Marc and Port-au-Prince in the west, and Jérémie, Aux Cayes, and Tiburon in the south.

The position of Captain-General Leclerc was now desperate. The garrison at Le Cap did not exceed two hundred effective Europeans and fifteen hundred colonial troops, on whose loyalty it was impossible to depend. The hospitals were crowded with dying French soldiers, and Leclerc himself was seriously ill.

Leclerc's last letter, dated October 7, 1802, stated: "Here is my opinion of this country: We must destroy all the mountain Negroes, men and women, sparing only children under twelve years of age. We must destroy half the Negroes of the plains and not allow in the colony a single man who has worn an epaulette. Without these measures the colony will never be at peace, and every year, especially deadly ones like this, you will have a civil war on your hands which will jeopardize the future."

"This letter," says Stoddard, "was Leclerc's last will and testament. He had written it in the flush of a new malarial crisis which prostrated him for some time, and scarcely had he shown signs of recovery when the first symptoms of yellow fever appeared. For eleven days his iron will battled with the disease, but on the morning of the 28th of November the French army learned that its general was dead. Leclerc has been much blamed for the French failure in San Domingo, but when, in the light of all the attendant circumstances, we picture the Captain-General dragging himself from his bed in the flush of fever or the shiver of ague-chill to pen his luminous dispatches, we must agree with Roloff that it is a wonder he did so well."

Leclerc was succeeded by General Rochambeau, who, at the time of Leclerc's death, was commanding the French forces at Port-au-Prince. He did not reach Le Cap until early in December, when he immediately repeated the demands of his predecessor for additional troops.

Except for some important skirmishes and movements to concentrate their forces, little activity was displayed by either French or blacks for some months. But in October, 1803, Dessalines, with an army of over twenty thousand veterans, captured Port-au-Prince and, leaving Pétion to hold that city, hastened with the greater part of his men to strike the final blow at the remnant of Napoleon's army, now concentrated at Cap Français. After several engagements Rochambeau, despairing of further aid from France, sent a flag of truce to Dessalines, and on November 19th the following articles of capitulation were agreed upon:

"FIRST OF THE BLACKS"

To-day, Brumaire twenty-seventh, year twelfth, November nineteenth, eighteen hundred and three, Adjutant-Commander Duveyrier, having been empowered by General-in-Chief Rochambeau, commanding the French army, to treat of the surrender of the city of Le Cap, and Jean Jacques Dessalines, General-in-Chief of the native army, have come to an agreement on the following articles: viz.,

Art. 1st. The City of Le Cap and its dependent fortresses will be surrendered within ten days, beginning the twenty-eighth inst., to General-in-Chief Dessalines.

Art. 2nd. The ammunition stored in the barracks, the arms, and artillery which are in the city and fortresses will be left in their present condition.

Art. 3rd. Men-of-war or other ships which General Rochambeau will deem necessary for the transportation of the troops and inhabitants, as well as for the evacuation, will be permitted to leave on the appointed day.

Art. 4th. The officers and civil officials, the troops now garrisoned in Le Cap, will leave with the honours of war, carrying away their arms and the belongings of their demi-brigade.

Art. 5th. The sick and wounded unable to be transported will be nursed in the hospital until their recovery; they are especially recommended to the humanity of General Dessalines, who will see them off for France on neutral ships.

Art. 6th. General-in-Chief Dessalines, while giving the assurance of his protection to the inhabitants who may stay in the country, claims from General Rochambeau's spirit of justice the release of all natives, of whatever colour, who in no case can be forced to go on board with the French army.

Art. 7th. The troops of both armies will remain in their respective positions until the tenth day set for the evacuation of Le Cap.

Art. 8th. General Rochambeau will send, as a guarantee of the present convention, the Adjutant-Commandant Urbain Devaux, in exchange for whom General-in-Chief Dessalines will send back an officer of the same rank.

BLACK DEMOCRACY

Made in duplicate and in good faith at the General Head-quarters of "Haut du Cap," the day, month, and year aforementioned.

[Signed] Dessalines.
Duveyrier.

A true copy: The General-in-Chief:
Rochambeau.

Rochambeau, completely ignoring these articles of agreement, sent on the same day two officers to the commandant of the British fleet, which had for some time blockaded Le Cap, to negotiate a surrender. He proposed to evacuate Cap Français and that his troops should be conveyed to France *without being considered prisoners of war.*

This offer was naturally refused by the British, who, in ignorance of Rochambeau's capitulation to Dessalines, offered to accept the surrender of the French, send "the troops in health" to Jamaica as prisoners, and arrange, at the expense of the French government, for the transportation of the sick to America or to France.

Hearing no further from Rochambeau and learning of the capitulation, the British commander requested pilots of Dessalines in order that he might enter the harbour and take possession of the French shipping.

To this request Dessalines replied that he himself would take possession of Le Cap on the following day (the ten days provided for in the capitulation then elapsing), and further stated: "It is a matter of regret to me that I cannot send you the pilots that you require. I presume that you will not have occasion for them, as I shall compel the French vessels to quit the road, and you will do with them what you think proper."

A report of the British admiral gives a final view of this concluding scene of the last act of the struggle for independence of the blacks:

"FIRST OF THE BLACKS"

REPORT OF SIR THOMAS DUCKWORTH
Port Royal [Jamaica], *December 18, 1803.*

Having, in my letter No. 3, by this conveyance stated to you, for the information of my Lords Commissioners of the Admiralty, that General Rochambeau has made proposals for capitulating which, though inadmissible, I thought soon must lead to others more reasonable, the event has justified my opinion; but I am sorry to say that officer, whose actions are too extraordinary to account for, had, on the 19th ultimo (previous to his proposal to Captain Loring, through the General of Brigade Boyce and Commander Barre), actually entered into a capitulation with black General Dessalines, to deliver up the Cape to him, with all the ordinance, ammunition, and stores, on the 30th; I conclude, flattering himself that the tremendous weather which our squadron was then, and had been, experiencing for three weeks, would offer an opening for escape, but the perseverance and watchfulness thereof precluded him from even attempting it. On the 30th the colours of the blacks were displayed at the forts, which induced Captain Loring to dispatch Captain Bligh to know General Dessalines' sentiments respecting General Rochambeau and his troops; when, on his entering the harbour, he met Commodore Barre, who pressed him in strong terms to go on board the *Surveillante* and enter into some capitulation which would put them under our protection and prevent the blacks from sinking them with red-hot shot, as they had threatened and were preparing to do, which Captain Bligh complied with, when they hastily brought him a few articles they had drawn up; which he (after objecting to some particular parts, that they agreed should be altered to carry his interpretation to Jamaica) signed and hastened to acquaint General Dessalines that all the ships and vessels in port had surrendered to His Majesty's arms, and with great difficulty he obtained the promise to desist from firing, till a wind offered for carrying them out (it then blowing hard directly into the harbour); this promise he at length obtained, and the first instant the land-breeze enabled them to sail out under French colours, which, upon a shot being fired athwart them, the vessels of war fired their broadsides and hauled down their colours.

This was the final act of the attempt by Bonaparte to regain for France the lost colony of St.-Domingue, an enterprise which reflected no credit on its instigator and less on the chief instruments employed by him.

In all, there had been sent from France, in this undertaking, over forty-three thousand soldiers, not including the French troops on the island at the time of the arrival of Leclerc's expedition. The eight thousand survivors who sailed from Le Cap were captured by the British fleet. On the 29th of November Dessalines occupied Le Cap, and a few days later the French evacuated their last foothold at Mole St. Nicholas.

Between August, 1791, and November, 1803, over twelve years, this unhappy island had been in a state of almost constant warfare. France, England, and Spain had expended untold treasure and thousands of lives in their endeavours to secure what had once been the richest of colonial possessions. The Spanish gained nothing and eventually were dispossessed from their old colony of Spanish Santo Domingo. The British retired after an inglorious campaign lasting over five years and an immense expenditure of money and troops, too great, Bryan Edwards said, for the value of all the West Indian colonies ever to repay. A most prosperous and promising economic development had been almost completely ruined and there remained a country bountifully endowed by Nature but devastated by man, and a people, free, it is true, from slavery, but, as events proved, totally unprepared to face the difficult problems of reconstruction which confronted them.

CHAPTER V

DESSALINES, DICTATOR AND EMPEROR

PROCLAMATION OF DESSALINES, CHRISTOPHE, AND CLERVAUX, CHIEFS OF ST.-DOMINGUE

The Independence of St.-Domingue is proclaimed. Restored to our primitive dignity, we have asserted our rights; we swear never to yield them to any power on earth. The frightful veil of prejudice is torn to pieces. Be it so for ever! Woe be to them who would dare to put together its bloody tatters!

Landholders of St.-Domingue, wandering in foreign countries! by proclaiming our independence, we do not forbid you all, without distinction, to return to your property. Far be from us so unjust a thought! We are not ignorant that there are some among you who have renounced their former errors, abjured the injustice of their exorbitant pretensions, and acknowledged the lawfulness of the cause for which we have been spilling our blood these twelve years. Towards those men who do us justice, we will act as brothers. Let them rely for ever on our esteem and friendship; let them return among us. The God who protects us, the God of free men, bids us stretch out toward them our conquering arms. But as for those who, intoxicated with foolish pride, interested slaves of a guilty pretension, are blinded so much as to believe themselves the essence of human nature and assert that they are destined by Heaven to be our masters and our tyrants, let them never come near the land of St.-Domingue! If they come hither, they will only meet with chains or banishment. Then let them stay where they are. Tormented by their well-deserved misery and the frowns of the just men whom they have too long mocked, let them still continue to live, unpitied and unnoticed by all.

We have sworn not to listen with clemency to any who

would dare to speak to us of slavery. We will be inexorable, perhaps even cruel, towards all troops who, themselves forgetting the object for which they have not ceased fighting since 1780, should come from Europe to bring among us death and servitude. No sacrifice is too costly and all means are lawful to men from whom it is wished to wrest the first of all blessings. Were they to cause streams and torrents of blood to flow; were they, in order to maintain their liberty, to fire seven-eighths of the globe, they are innocent before the tribunal of Providence, which never created men to groan under so harsh and shameful a servitude.

In the various commotions that have taken place, some inhabitants against whom we have no complaints have been victims of the cruelty of a few soldiers or cultivators too much blinded by the remembrance of their past sufferings to be able to distinguish the good and humane landowners from those who were unfeeling and cruel. We lament, together with all who feel, so deplorable an end, and declare to the world, whatever may be said to the contrary by wicked people, that the murders were committed contrary to the wishes of our hearts. It was impossible, especially in the crisis in which the colony was, to prevent or stop those horrors. They who are in the least acquainted with history know that a people, when torn by civil dissensions, though they may be the most civilized on earth, give themselves up to every species of excess; and the authority of the chiefs, not yet firmly based, in a time of revolution cannot punish all that are guilty, without meeting with perpetual difficulties. But to-day the dawn of peace cheers us with glimpses of a less stormy time; now that the calm of victory has succeeded to the tumult of a dreadful war, all affairs in St.-Domingue ought to assume a new face and its government henceforward be one of justice.

Done at Head-quarters, Fort Dauphin,
November 29, 1803.

[Signed] DESSALINES.
CHRISTOPHE.
CLERVAUX.

True copy:
B. AIMÉ, Secretary.

DESSALINES, DICTATOR AND EMPEROR

Thus ran the liberators' proclamation, but oratory does not solve problems of government and the new black rulers were entirely lacking in training to meet the difficult problems which faced them. In 1791 the French part of St.-Domingue had been a prosperous and rapidly developing colony in which a comparatively small body of whites were proprietors, not only of the soil, but of ninety per cent of the human beings who dwelt thereon. Now, only thirteen years later, not one single foot of land was owned by a white man, and the Negroes, who a few years before had been slaves, and many of whom had been born in Africa, were in complete possession of all that remained of the property which, together with their own bodies, had constituted the wealth of their former masters.

The political changes resulting from this revolution were perhaps no more sweeping than those which had accompanied other successful struggles for freedom. But history does not record any parallel to the tremendous social cataclysm that followed the expulsion of the whites from St.-Domingue. The comparatively small number of the "people of colour," less than thirty thousand in all, included a few who had been educated in France. Among the blacks such extraordinary characters as Toussaint l'Ouverture, although slaves, had acquired the rudiments of an education, though few, even of the mulattoes, had any knowledge of, or experience in, self-government.

Not only did this new state lack trained administrators, but few of its citizens had any background on which to base an intelligent conception of the rights and duties of citizenship. The first acts of the revolting slaves had been to wipe from the face of the earth every evidence of their former condition. Bells installed to call them to toil were dismantled, and the bell towers razed to the ground; plants and factories, the scenes of their former labours, were destroyed, and skill in the industries and trades, particularly

BLACK DEMOCRACY

in the operation and maintenance of machinery and the production of finished commodities, being no longer in demand, was forgotten. The natural impulse of the ex-slaves was to demonstrate their freedom by refusing to perform any but the most necessary labour. The despoiled plantations provided the simple necessities of a people who had no conception of the incentive which inspires free men in more civilized countries to orderly and sustained occupation.

The Negroes had found that expulsion of the whites and emancipation from slavery had changed their condition in form, though not materially in substance. During the short rule of the commissioners of the French Republic, an attempt had been made to substitute for slavery a system of compulsory labour little removed from serfdom.

Under the agricultural system enforced by Toussaint, the whip had been abolished as a punishment, but the *cocomacaque*, a no less effective substitute, had been employed. The people were familiar with no form of control other than the absolute despotism of their former masters or the equally despotic rule of their military chiefs.

The brief period of prosperity during the administration of Toussaint, when very material progress had been made in the rehabilitation of agriculture, had resulted in the creation of an autocracy of the more intelligent and ambitious military leaders, but had made little improvement in the condition of the mass of the people; while the wars which followed the coming of Leclerc, during which practically every able-bodied Haitian was under arms, not only had devastated the country but had destroyed all respect for authority other than that based on military rank.

On the first of January, 1804, the chiefs of the armies of St.-Domingue met at Gonaives and swore to "abjure for ever allegiance to France, to die rather than live under her domination, and to fight to the last for the preservation of their independence." The name St.-Domingue was for

DESSALINES, DICTATOR AND EMPEROR

ever abolished and the aboriginal name of Haiti reestablished.[1] This convention of generals framed a declaration of independence, and the following act was read to the assembly of the people: "In the name of the people of Haiti we, generals and chiefs of the Island of Haiti, grateful for the benefits received from the Commander-in-Chief Jean Jacques Dessalines, the protector of the liberty which we are enjoying; in the name of Liberty, Independence, and the people he has made happy, proclaim him Governor-General of Haiti for life. We swear entire obedience to the laws he shall deem fit to make, his authority being the only one we acknowledge. We authorize him to make peace and war and to appoint his successor."

The title Governor-General signified to the blacks supreme authority, and although it was only a few months before that Dessalines had been described by Leclerc as the butcher of the Negroes, he had been their leader in the final struggle for freedom and was now the acknowledged chief among the blacks, and as such was believed by them to be entitled to dictatorial power, the only government of which they had any conception. Christophe, Pétion, Geffrard, and Gabart, four of the most prominent leaders, were placed in command of Departments. The country was put under strict military rule and every citizen made subject to military duty.

The new governor found himself confronted by a stupendous task, for which he was utterly untrained. The whites who had administered the affairs of the country had either been annihilated, driven from the island, or completely deprived of authority. An entirely new body of administrators was to be created, and the men available for such positions, although courageous fighters, had little or no knowledge of civil affairs.

The most pressing task was to make provision against attempts of the French to regain their lost colony, and the extraordinary energy of Dessalines was focussed on this enterprise. Each of the department commanders was ordered to prepare for defence. Christophe undertook the construction of the Citadel Laferrière. Pétion built Fort Jacques and Fort Alexander, while in the south Geffrard constructed many forts and fortifications. The country was an armed camp, with a considerable proportion of the inhabitants engaged in preparations to resist the return of the French.

At the time the French troops evacuated Cap Français, the white residents received an opportunity to leave the colony on the French fleet, but it was certain that they would be captured by the British and lose, as prizes of war, such of their property as they could carry with them; and many elected to remain and trust to the mercy of their former slaves.

In this choice of two evils they were influenced by the memory of Toussaint's friendly attitude toward the former French proprietors and by the forbearance exhibited by Christophe and other Haitian leaders in their treatment of prisoners and hostages. If Dessalines had been animated by this same spirit, it is probable that the whites who remained would have been safe. But to Dessalines a white man, particularly a Frenchman, was an abomination. He had been an insubordinate slave and had suffered terrible punishment for his insubordination. He bore on his body marks of this punishment which he often exhibited. In his heart burned a fanatic hatred of the French and everything that had contributed to maintain the system of slavery.

Dessalines, however, did not hesitate to promise protection to the French. His first act as general-in-chief had been to issue a proclamation addressed to the people of Cap Français to tranquillize their fears, in which he stated that the war which had been waged had no relation to the inhabitants of the colony, and that he had uniformly held

DESSALINES, DICTATOR AND EMPEROR

out protection and security to inhabitants of every complexion, further assuring them that on the present occasion he would adhere to the same lines of conduct, and pointing out that the manner in which the people of Jérémie, Aux Cayes, and Port-au-Prince had been treated "afforded a certain pledge of his good faith and honour." He invited those who did not wish to leave the country to remain, and promised them that they would enjoy security under his government.

It was, however, soon made evident that Dessalines had resolved on the complete destruction of the French in St.-Domingue. Immediately following his appointment to the office of governor-general, he published an inflammatory proclamation reciting the crimes of the French and urging vengeance upon them.

"It is not enough," he said, "to have driven from our country the barbarians who for ages have stained it with blood. . . . It has become necessary to ensure, by a last act of national authority, the permanent empire of liberty. . . . It is necessary to deprive an inhuman government of every hope of enslaving us again. Those generals who have led your struggles against tyranny have not yet done. The French name still darkens our plains; everything reminds us of the cruelties of that barbarous people. Our laws, our customs, our towns, everything bears the impress of France. What do I say? There still remain Frenchmen on our island. . . . When shall we be tired of breathing in the same air with them? What have we in common with that bloody-minded people? Their cruelties compared to our moderation, their colour to ours, the extension of seas which separate us, our avenging climate, all plainly tell us they are not our brethren; that they will never become so, and if they find an asylum among us, they will still be the instigators of troubles and divisions.

"Citizens, men, women, young and old, cast your eyes

on every part of the island; seek there your wives, your husbands, your brothers, your sisters. What did I say? Seek your children—your children at the breast. What is become of them? Instead of these innocent victims, the affrighted eye sees only their assassins—tigers still covered with their blood and whose frightful presence upbraids you with your insensibility and your slowness to avenge them. Why do you delay to appease your *manes?* Do you hope that your ashes can rest in peace by the side of your fathers unless you shall have made tyranny to disappear? Will you descend into their tombs without having avenged them? Their bones will repulse yours. And, ye invaluable men, intrepid generals, who, insensible to private sufferings, have given new life to liberty by lavishing your blood; know that you have done nothing unless you give to the nations a terrible though just example of the vengeance that ought to be exercised by a brave people who have recovered their liberty and are determined to maintain it. Let us intimidate those who would dare to attempt depriving us of it again; let us begin with the French; let them shudder at approaching our shores, if not on account of the cruelties they have committed, at least at the terrible resolution we are about to make: to devote to death whatever native of France dares to soil this shore with his sacrilegious footstep. . . . Accursed be the French name—eternal hatred of France—such are our principles. Swear, then, to live free and independent, and to prefer death to anything that would lead to replacing you under the yoke! Swear to pursue for ever the traitors and enemies of your independence."

Fortunately this proclamation did not reflect the feelings of the majority of the leaders nor of the people, and no general massacre of the whites was attempted. But in February Dessalines issued a second proclamation enjoining proceedings against the actors in the "inhuman massacres coolly perpetrated under the government of Leclerc and

DESSALINES, DICTATOR AND EMPEROR

Rochambeau," in which, he asserted, over sixty thousand Haitians had been drowned, suffocated, hanged, shot, or otherwise put to death. "Nothing," he said, "shall ever avert our vengeance from those murderers who have delighted to bathe themselves in the blood of the innocent children of Haiti." So strongly were the people in general opposed to these measures that Dessalines, after further vain efforts to incite a popular massacre of the whites, determined to accomplish his purpose himself. He visited in turn the towns where the French were congregated and, under his personal supervision, selected troops massacred a very large proportion of the French men, women, and children who still remained on the island.[2]

The last act of this tragedy was a climax of cruelty and perfidy. Dessalines issued a proclamation stating that vengeance was satisfied and inviting all refugees who had escaped death to appear in public and receive tickets of protection. Many hundreds of terrified whites who had contrived to secrete themselves, or who had been hidden by friendly foreigners or blacks, determined, in desperation, to avail themselves of this offer and assembled at the Place d'Armes at Cap Français, where they were surrounded by troops and at once taken to execution. It is said that the little stream which then ran through the town by the present custom house was for many hours literally dyed red with the blood of the victims of this atrocious plot.[3]

In justice to the people and a majority of their leaders, it is recorded that these bloody and treacherous measures were generally disapproved. Dessalines took full responsibility when later he proclaimed: "I have saved my country. The avowal I make in the face of earth and heaven constitutes my pride and glory. Of what consequence to me is the opinion which contemporary and future generations will pronounce upon my conduct? I have performed my duty. I enjoy my own approbation; for me that is sufficient."

BLACK DEMOCRACY

When Dessalines became ruler of Haiti the inhabitants of the Spanish part of the island had withdrawn from their agreement made originally with Toussaint and had put themselves under the protection of France, and a small detachment of French troops now occupied Santo Domingo City. The commander of these troops most impolitically announced that Haitians captured on the border might be held in Spanish Santo Domingo as slaves, and Dessalines, incensed by this proclamation, determined to expel the French from their last hold on the island and to resubject the inhabitants of the Spanish area. This he proceeded to undertake with his usual energy. He assembled an army of thirty thousand men and, with no arrangements for a commissary department, advanced on Santo Domingo, at the time warning the inhabitants, by proclamation, that he was coming with a victorious army to receive their submission.

After some initial success Dessalines laid siege to Santo Domingo City, but, being without artillery, he failed to capture this strongly fortified town and, learning that French reinforcements were coming by sea, he abandoned his project and led his army back to Haiti, laying waste the country as he proceeded.

Shortly after his return from this unsuccessful enterprise, he decided to change his title from Governor-General to Emperor, and on the 8th of October, with great ceremony, Jean Jacques Dessalines, "the avenger and deliverer of his fellow citizens," was crowned Emperor of Haiti.

This imperial dignity was further confirmed by a new constitution which decreed the creation of the empire of Haiti as a free sovereign and independent state. The new constitution abolished slavery for ever, prohibited white men, of whatever nation, from acquiring property of any kind, and adopted the generic name of "blacks" for all subjects to Haiti, of whatever colour. The new "empire" was

DESSALINES, DICTATOR AND EMPEROR

divided into six military divisions, with a general in command of each who was independent of all but the Emperor, on whom the title of Majesty was conferred.

Dessalines had now arrived at the height of his ambition; his power was supreme. The blacks of the peasant class, relegated to the same position they had occupied under the rule of Toussaint, were practically serfs. The law provided imprisonment as the sole punishment for idleness, but this law was openly disregarded and a heavy cane (*coco-macaque*) was substituted for the whip of the slave days. Labourers were forbidden to leave the plantation to which they were attached without written permission. Most of the plantations, now ostensibly owned by the state, were farmed out to military officers or favourites of the Emperor, who paid rentals to him, based not on the extent of fertility of the land, but upon the number of cultivators attached to the property. Many of the estates of the *anciens libres,* free men before the revolution, were still held by their owners, and some of the mulattoes who had been able to present proof of paternity from former white proprietors were placed in possession of the lands of their fathers. These, with the more prominent black military chiefs, constituted an aristocracy for whom the great peasant class laboured on an arbitrarily enforced system under which one-third of the harvest was *supposed* to be paid to them for their toil.

The sugar estates, destroyed during the successive wars and internal convulsions, had become overgrown with thickets, and the elaborate irrigation works, mills, and factories were in ruins. The manufacture of sugar had practically ceased, and coffee from the neglected but still productive plantations in the hills was the principal wealth of the island.[4]

Dessalines had secured his advancement by his untiring and ferocious energy, his courage, and undoubted military genius. In a position of supreme power he could be nothing less than a despot. He had no qualifications for civil rule, and his administration degenerated into a tyranny under which he and his officers systematically exploited the people. "Pick the chicken but don't let it squall" was a maxim of this government, said to have been originated by the Emperor himself.

When Dessalines finally realized that the scandalous conditions had completely antagonized the people, it was too late to stem the revolt which, originating in the south, where he was bitterly hated, spread rapidly throughout the country. Soon the whole south was in arms. General Pétion, who commanded the Department of the West, joined the insurrection before Dessalines suspected him of any thought of defection. Leaving his home town in the plain of the Artibonite, accompanied only by a few officers, Dessalines rode to Port-au-Prince to suppress the revolt. At Pont Rouge, in the outskirts of the capital, he encountered a detachment of troops of the empire who made no move to salute him. Furious because his approach was not received with the usual military honours, he spurred his horse and galloped up to the bridge, loudly demanding the reason for this strange conduct. The reply was a fatal shot fired by a non-commissioned officer. Dessalines fell and the soldiers returned to Port-au-Prince, leaving the body of the Emperor where it fell, and where it remained lying for hours until finally an old peasant woman gave it burial. "Thus," says Léger, "expired the liberator of Haiti, a victim of the sad customs of the time and of the very cause of liberty of which he had been the successful defender."

CHAPTER VI

CHRISTOPHE AND PÉTION

THE death of Dessalines left Henri Christophe the only surviving one of the three black generals who had led their fellows in the wars for independence. This remarkable man, the most powerful leader in Haiti and, with the possible exception of Toussaint and Dessalines, the outstanding figure in Haitian history, was a pureblooded African, born a slave. He was first a waiter in a hotel and later a steward on a French warship. When the Comte d'Estaing, admiral of the French West Indian fleet, disregarded orders from France and went to assist Lafayette, then a general officer in the American Continental Army, he stopped in St.-Domingue for reinforcements. Christophe was one of the eight hundred recruits who helped the Americans win the Battle of Savannah. On his return to St.-Domingue, he resumed his old occupation of waiter in an inn at Cap Français.

From his association with the white men, Christophe learned many things, and he served with such distinction in their armies that he attained the rank of major-general in the army of St.-Domingue. His person was handsome and commanding, and his natural personal dignity impressed both blacks and whites. Although unable to read or write, he had acquired a considerable knowledge of books through employing secretaries to read to him. His rule, though brutal, was amazingly efficient, and by stern discipline he brought prosperity to the northern portion of the island. Arrogant, forceful, and possessed of extraordinary personal

~ The Citadel of King Christophe ~

courage, this man, despite the excesses and cruelties which marked the latter part of his reign, stands out as one of the strongest and greatest of the many rulers of Haiti.

After the death of Dessalines a military council named this man the "Provisional Chief of the Nation," and summoned an *Assemblée Constituante* to adopt a constitution and elect a chief magistrate. This assembly, the first actual legislative body to be created in Haiti, met at Port-au-Prince on December 18, 1806.

Christophe, as first lieutenant to Dessalines and the acknowledged chief of the blacks, was the logical successor of the "Liberator." If it had not been for the influence of the more enlightened and educated mulatto minority, led by Pétion, he would have succeeded Dessalines without recourse to the formality of a national election. That the recently emancipated blacks, who were vastly in the majority, were competent to exercise civil rights, or had any conception of a democratic form of government, cannot for a moment be supposed. There were, even among the mulattoes, only a few who had anything but the most vague conception of democracy.

Christophe knew the blacks whom he had commanded under Toussaint and Dessalines. The only government that he could understand was a despotism such as had already existed, and he realized that it was the only government suited to his people. Through control of the prosperous and thickly settled districts of the north and the Valley of the Artibonite, he believed his supremacy so firmly assured that he did not attend the assembly but merely sent his deputies to Port-au-Prince, fully confident of his control of the situation.

His only rival, Pétion, a highly educated mulatto, had graduated from a French military school and had served creditably as an officer in the armies of France. The natural leader of the mulatto caste in Haiti, he dreamed of an ideal

CHRISTOPHE AND PÉTION

republic controlled by his own people and planned to convert the ex-slaves to democratic institutions by dividing the land among them, and to encourage agriculture by persuasion and example rather than by the despotic methods of Dessalines. He schemed to acquire through diplomacy the power which he was unprepared to seize by force. Fearing to defy Christophe openly, Pétion resorted to a clever political expedient. He was the most influential member present at the organization of the assembly, which he proceeded to handle as the Jacobins had conducted such bodies in France. In spite of protests from Christophe's delegates, he arranged for the election of deputies from districts in the south and west which had never before been accorded representation. These districts were opposed to Christophe, and through the support of their delegates Pétion was chosen chairman of a committee to draft a constitution.

This was the opportunity for which the mulatto leader had been striving; Christophe had drafted and sent by his deputies a constitution embodying his despotic ideas, but this draft Pétion completely ignored. In its place he drew up a constitution which so restricted the powers of the chief executive as to be obviously unacceptable to Christophe.

On December 27th a draft of a constitution establishing a government with the executive, legislative, and military powers practically confined to the senate was submitted and, Pétion's influence prevailing, was approved by the assembly. The senate, as thus constituted, had the sole right to appoint the civil and military functionaries and to determine their duties, had the direction of foreign affairs, was authorized to negotiate all treaties, and was given the initiative in the matter of laws and legislative measures. The privileges of a supreme court were also invested in this body. With powers thus curtailed, the President was little more than a figurehead. Although he was commander-in-chief of the army, he was without power to appoint officials or confer any title or rank. This, so far, was a complete victory for Pétion.

On the following day the assembly chose Christophe chief executive of the new state and ordered that he should be notified of his election. Christophe had been in close touch with the proceedings of the assembly through his deputies, one of whom had informed him that "if he accepted the constitution he would have no more power than a corporal." Indignant at the limited powers thus conferred on him, Christophe determined to ignore both the constitution and his election. He issued a proclamation accusing Pétion and other leaders of having so framed the constitution as to place the real power in their own hands, and, branding them as traitors, he called on his people, the blacks of the north, to "take up arms in defence of their liberties," and, promising them unlimited plunder, advanced on Port-au-Prince.

At the end of December, 1806, Christophe passed through St.-Marc with a large and well-equipped army. Pétion delayed his preparations but finally, forced to action, left Port-au-Prince on January 1st, leading a greatly inferior force, and on the same day, a few miles from the capital, was utterly routed. Barely escaping with his life, the mulatto leader returned to Port-au-Prince, where he rallied his forces and on January 6th succeeded in defeating Christophe's army. Contemporary reports of this battle and of the subsequent proceedings of the two leaders are conflicting. It is difficult to understand why one of the two did not press decisive action. Pétion's generals are said to have severely censured him for not following up his victory. As it was, after some further ineffective operations in the vicinity of Port-au-Prince, Christophe returned to the north, taking with him a large part of the wealth which Dessalines had amassed.

At Cap Haitien, on February 17th, Christophe assembled

CHRISTOPHE AND PÉTION

his military leaders and by them was elected "President of the State of Haiti," and through a constitution ratified by a so-called "Assembly of the Mandatories of the People" he conferred upon himself absolutely dictatorial powers.

Meanwhile delegates from the West and South had assembled at Port-au-Prince and had appointed Pétion to "maintain order" in the Department of the West and General Gerin in the same capacity in the South. Christophe was declared an outlaw and the constitution he had rejected was promulgated on December 27, 1806. On the ninth of March, 1807, Pétion was elected "President of the Republic of Haiti" and on the next day took the following oath of fidelity to the Constitution: "I swear faithfully to fulfil the office of President of Haiti, and to maintain, to the utmost of my power, the Constitution. May the arms confided to the people for the defence of liberty pierce my breast if ever I conceive the audacious and infamous project of violating their rights, or if ever I forget that it is after having punished with death a tyrant whose existence was an insult to the nation, and after having aided to proscribe another whose ambition has lighted up civil war among us, that I now find myself President of Haiti."

T. Madiou, one of Haiti's foremost historians, has thus compared the constitution of the "Republic" of the South and that of the "State" of the North:

In that of the "State" the chief magistrate commanded all forces, naval and military, and also could name a successor, but only among the generals of the army. In the "Republic" of that day, the president at the head was under the control of the senate.

The president of the "State" was chosen for life. The president of the "Republic" was elected for four years.

In the "State" the legislative council was confined to a council of State. In the "Republic" this was confined to a senate chosen by the people.

BLACK DEMOCRACY

In the "State" the president nominated to all offices and honours. In the "Republic" this was done by the people, through the senate.

Thus two separate governments approximately equal in resources and man power were created in the little territory which had formerly been the French colony of St.-Domingue; the "State of Haiti," comprising the districts of the North and the Valley of the Artibonite, and the "Republic of Haiti," which included the West and the South. The profound and far-reaching effect of this division can hardly be exaggerated. To it may be traced the enmity and discord between these two sections of the people, which inaugurated the internal strife that has characterized the history of the Haitians since their emancipation from slavery. It is obvious that the Haitian people were totally unfitted to organize or maintain a democracy, and it is equally certain that, for a time at least, Christophe's autocratic form of government was far better suited to their condition than was the utopian democracy planned by Pétion. But, as events proved, neither Christophe nor Pétion was allowed a fair opportunity to test his theories.

The people of the North generally accepted the dictatorship of Christophe; but the inhabitants of the districts bordering on the Republic were inclined to Pétion's more lenient rule and many of them passed over the border and became citizens of the Republic. Until the death of Christophe and the consolidation of the two areas under one government, the border was in a constant state of unrest. Christophe made several attempts to overthrow Pétion and would probably have succeeded if it had not been that the dread of his tyrannical rule inspired the people of the Republic to desperate resistance.

In 1810 the situation was further complicated by the arrival in Haiti of Rigaud, the former mulatto leader. Although Rigaud was bitterly jealous of the position attained

CHRISTOPHE AND PÉTION

by his previous subordinate and Pétion greatly feared him, the two met with every evidence of friendship and Pétion, through a mistaken idea of policy, appointed Rigaud to the important position of commander-in-chief of the Southwestern Department. Rigaud abused this trust by almost immediately establishing himself there as the head of an independent government.

The conflict between Christophe and Pétion, and this civil war precipitated by Rigaud within the Republic, completely demoralized the South and West and severely handicapped the rehabilitation of the North. Plantations were practically abandoned and the peasants, instead of being employed in farming, were engaged in warfare. Production for export had almost ceased and, while the people in their newly acquired independence were killing one another, famine threatened to complete the annihilation of the race. During this period Santo Domingo presented the singular spectacle of five independent governments—those of Christophe, Pétion, Rigaud, the bandit Gauman, and of old Spain—in an island having an area of only twenty-eight thousand square miles and a population of less than 700,000.

Fortunately for Pétion, Rigaud died about a year after his return to Haiti and on his death the South-western Department was again incorporated in the Republic. This consolidation of the military resources of the South and West discouraged further aggressions by Christophe, who now directed his energy toward the resumption of agricultural production within his territory. He farmed out the neglected plantations to his military chiefs, restored to their former occupations the peasants who had been forced into his armies, and promulgated the most stringent laws compelling them to labour. In the South, Pétion adopted less forceful measures. He instituted a system of distribution of land in small plots, either as a reward for military services or by sale, and made every effort to create a self-sustaining class of cultivators.

Pétion was re-elected to the presidency in 1811 and again in 1815. In June, 1816, a complete revision of the constitution of the Republic was effected, the authority being divided between the executive, legislative, and judiciary powers. A supreme court was established and many of the restrictive provisions of the former constitution eliminated. A clause in this revised constitution providing that the president be elected for life is a blot on Pétion's reputation. This vicious provision, repealed in 1843, re-established in 1846 and again repealed in 1860, re-established in 1868 and finally abolished after the execution of Salnave in 1870, has been the cause of much of the "revolutionary spirit" which has so greatly retarded the progress of the Haitian people.

From the first days of the Republic, great fears were entertained of active aggression from France and vast sums of money were spent on military preparations. That these fears were not groundless was demonstrated soon after the downfall of Bonaparte.

The overwhelming disaster of the Leclerc expedition and the fact that Bonaparte was fully occupied at home had prevented any immediate attempt to recover the French colony. But no sooner did Louis XVIII ascend the throne of France than the ex-colonists renewed their efforts to regain their former possessions. With this end in view, a number of the former colonial proprietors presented a petition to the French Chamber of Deputies, citing the conditions in Haiti and asking for an investigation.[1] A committee appointed for this purpose reported that no authentic information had been obtained by the French government as to the disposition of the two chiefs, Christophe and Pétion, now ruling the divided colony. With an astonishing lack of any conception of the situation, the chairman of this

CHRISTOPHE AND PÉTION

committee, who had formerly served in the colony and should have been better advised, stated that he fully believed both Christophe and Pétion would eagerly acknowledge the sovereignty of the King of France, "but that, as this hope, however, might possibly be disappointed, His Majesty should be advised to send a sufficient number of land and sea forces to occupy the colony."

The committee urged the immediate dispatch of an expedition to put the ex-colonists in possession of their former estates, and to establish laws for the regulation of the colony "with a view to the blacks who were already there and *those who should hereafter be introduced.*"

It is almost incredible that anyone of intelligence could have supposed that either Christophe or Pétion would for a moment entertain a proposal to submit again to French rule. And the absurdity of such expectations was quickly demonstrated by the reply of each leader to interrogations from France. Christophe at once stated that the King of Haiti would treat with France only as one independent power with another; and Pétion announced that on the first appearance of a hostile force he would set fire to all the buildings in the cities and destroy everything that could not be removed to the mountains. Nothing but the admirably firm and vigorous attitude of Christophe and Pétion prevented more active measures by France. Only their preparation for defence saved Haiti from the horrors of another invasion.

Aside from their apprehensions of trouble with France, Haiti had during these years little to do with the rest of the world, and may be said to have taken no part in making history other than her own.

Haiti did, however, give a hearty welcome to Simon Bolivar and many Venezuelan families driven into exile by the Spaniards in 1816. Pétion extended to them all the assistance in his power and secretly equipped Bolivar with rifles, powder, cartridges, and all kinds of provisions. Pétion was moved to this dangerous and generous action by his sincere desire to assist in freeing the slaves of South America, and Bolivar promised to abolish slavery in all provinces he might liberate. After freeing Venezuela, Bolivar sent Pétion his beautiful gold sword, in gratitude to "the author of our liberties." [2]

Pétion strove earnestly for the betterment of his people, but his administration was from the beginning seriously handicapped. The mulattoes, of whom he was the leader, were greatly in the minority, and feeling it necessary to propitiate the blacks, he was driven to temporizing measures. He fully realized the need for increased agricultural production, on which the commerce of the country must depend and which was the only source of revenue for the people and for the state. But he was in no position to enforce labour, nor did he dare punish idleness or crime. It was soon demonstrated that his ideas were utopian and unfitted to the time and to the people, who were neither by inclination nor by training ready for self-government. Only sixteen years before the establishment of the Republic, a vast majority of its citizens had lived in abject slavery. And the interval between the first revolt of the slaves and the first election of Pétion to the presidency had been marked by a series of conflicts, involving unspeakable crimes against civilization, during which opportunities for the inculcation of civic virtues or for lessons in self-government were conspicuous by their absence.

The costly military establishment necessary to combat insurrections and to repel the possible attempt of the French to regain their lost colony, diverted from commercial and agricultural development both money and man power, which, if employed under the system of small land holdings devised by Pétion, might have largely increased the prosperity of the country. While extremely popular with, and

CHRISTOPHE AND PÉTION

beloved by, the common people, Pétion was, owing to the very qualities which endeared him to them, unfitted to control a nation so turbulent and undisciplined.

In the North the despotic rule of Christophe had created and maintained a degree of prosperity and order, and the treasury of his kingdom was amply provided. But in the South the people were ungovernable and indolent. Production was hardly sufficient to maintain the population, and the financial resources of the country failed to support the current expenses of the government. The contrasting conditions proved to Pétion that he had failed in the chief object of his ambition, and he took the matter so much to heart that the realization gradually undermined his health, till, in March, 1818, he became seriously ill. The announcement of a possibly fatal termination to this illness was received with consternation by the people of the Republic and by foreign merchants established there. Fears of an attack by Christophe and of another revolution in the South were general. The senate met and conferred on the dying president the right to appoint his successor. Pétion then designated General Jean Pierre Boyer, who had been for years his faithful lieutenant. Shortly afterward Pétion died, declaring to his friends that he was weary of life. The appointment of Boyer met with general approval and the new president was peacefully installed in office.

Christophe had ruled the North as president of the State of Haiti until March, 1811, when he caused to be enacted the *Loi Constitutionnelle du Conseil d'Etat qui établit la royauté à Haïti.* The chiefs of the army and notables of the North assembled on June 2nd at Cap Haitien, where an immense pavilion had been erected, furnished with a throne, galleries for the audience, chapels, oratories, and all arrangements necessary for an august ceremony. Here the Archbishop of Haiti, recently appointed by Christophe, consecrated him king under the title of Henri I.

BLACK DEMOCRACY

This illiterate ex-slave, now nominally the brother of Europe's kings, had used despotic power to raise the North of Haiti from a war-desolated waste to a prosperous though tiny kingdom. He now turned his efforts to rivalling the kings of the whites, and in doing so gave free rein to his arbitrary will. He fully recognized his own limitations, but he unquestionably entrusted to men of ability the tasks he could not himself perform, as is evidenced by the Code Henri, comprising the laws affecting civil rights, commerce, civil and criminal procedure, and military service. It is true that, when opposed to the despotic will of the sovereign, these laws were ignored, and that they may have been partly inspired by the Code Napoléon. Yet his was not merely an imitation of the formalities of other kingdoms, but the sincere though often blundering attempt of a black man to raise his people, by giving them the government best suited to their needs. Many of his plans were unquestionably good. He invited men of science from Europe. He established schools. He built fortifications to protect the country from foreign invasion. He disciplined an efficient army, protected foreigners, and encouraged commerce.

Towards the end of his reign his discipline degenerated into savage cruelty. Driven to desperation by continued desertions to the South and the fear of invasion, he doubtless felt justified in any measures which would save his people. Legends have arisen concerning him, but they are the mighty legends of a national hero, and if it is true that he recognized no law save that of his own savage passions, those passions were inspired by his determination to benefit his wretched, wearied people.

This extraordinary man left two monuments to his terrific energy, the Royal Palace of San Souci at Milot, and the Citadel of La Ferrière. It is said that Christophe, in building San Souci, selected as his model the palace of Pauline Leclerc, the ruins of which are still visible at Cap

~ Ruins of Sans-Souci from the Air ~

CHRISTOPHE AND PÉTION

Haitien, but instructed the builders of San Souci to build a palace equal in size and grandeur to any in Europe. The result, though in some respects an architectural monstrosity, was an astonishing achievement. It is now abandoned and in ruins, yet in Christophe's day it must have been truly impressive. "The rooms were spacious and lofty, the floors and side panels of polished mahogany, or beautifully inlaid with mosaic; the apartments are said to have been sumptuously furnished and the gardens and the baths were all in keeping with the general splendour. The coach-house and stables were magnificent; a number of the royal carriages still remain; the panels of each, gilded and emblazoned by the royal arms, show at how great a cost they must have been constructed; one of the coaches was built in London and cost £700 sterling." [3]

The Citadel is even more imposing. This stupendous structure stands on the summit of Bonnet-à-l'Evêque, twenty-six hundred feet above sea-level. It was intended as a stronghold in the event of an invasion, and no site could have been better chosen. Occupying the crest of the mountain, it commands every height which in those days could have threatened it.

The walls of this extraordinary building are in some places 140 feet high, the average number of floors is four, and the main gun corridor, which was designed to protect the eastern and most vulnerable approach, is 30 feet in width and 270 feet in length. In the Citadel were installed hundreds of pieces of artillery, some of them bronze cannon over eleven feet in length and of six-inch calibre. Many of these guns are of English make, relics of the ill-fated British invasion of Haiti; some are French and a few Spanish, some of them bearing the names of the ships for which they were cast.

The Citadel has been declared one of the wonders of the Western Hemisphere and is said to have cost the lives

~ The Citadel of King Christophe ~

of twenty thousand peasants in the building, but probably no structure in the world has involved so much useless labour and expense. It was never occupied, the dreaded French invasion did not materialize, and its builder gained nothing from the money and lives sacrificed in its building except personal satisfaction for his abnormal egotism.

The peaceful acceptance of Boyer by the people of the Republic and the prompt military measures taken by the new president to protect the boundary were a great disappointment to Christophe. He had hoped that dissensions within the Republic would afford him an easy opportunity to add the South and West to his kingdom. Nevertheless, he threatened another invasion of the Republic, and for many months, during which hostilities between the two states were expected, his severity reached such an intolerable pitch that his people fled to the Republic in increasing numbers and those who remained were subservient only through dread of his ferocity. The country was seething with revolt, and some of his most powerful leaders were already conspiring against him, when, in August, 1820, while attending service at the church of Limonade, Christophe suffered a paralytic stroke. For three days he lay paralysed in the priest's house while the peasants killed every fowl in the neighbourhood lest the King's quiet be disturbed. Removed from Limonade to the royal palace of San Souci, he was informed by his Scotch physician that he was permanently paralysed from the waist down. News of the serious illness of the King spread rapidly throughout the North. In St.-Marc the royal troops killed their commander and sent his head to Boyer with a message that they were through with Christophe and his kingdom and desired to swear allegiance to the Republic. This precipitated a revolt at Cap Henri (Cap Haitien), and on the eighth of October the regulars and a mob from the city advanced on the royal palace at Milot. Christophe, with his indomitable courage, made one

CHRISTOPHE AND PÉTION

last endeavour to overcome his malady. He attempted to mount his horse in order personally to take command of the still loyal household troops, but fell on his face in the mud and was carried back to his palace, where, learning that the household guards had joined the insurgents, he retired to his private apartments and shot himself.

CHAPTER VII

THE HAITIAN REPUBLIC FROM 1818 TO 1908

JEAN PIERRE BOYER, unanimously elected president of the Republic of Haiti for life, commenced his career of twenty-five years as chief of state on March 20, 1818.

Boyer was a free mulatto. He had been sent to France at an early age and there received a military education. When sixteen years old, he entered the French army and served with some distinction in several campaigns in Europe. Returning to Haiti with Rigaud, he served under him until the defeat of the mulattoes by Toussaint in 1800, at which time he, with Rigaud, Pétion, and others, took refuge in Paris. Two years later Boyer went back to Haiti as a captain in the Leclerc expedition and held responsible positions with the armies of France until after the deportation of Toussaint, when he joined in the insurrection and assisted in the expulsion of the French. On the election of Pétion he became major-general in the army of the Republic and military commander of Port-au-Prince. As actual chief of the military forces of the Republic he showed decided administrative ability, and it was largely due to him that Christophe's attempts to overthrow the Republic were unsuccessful.

Boyer had been elected without opposition and had nothing to fear from rival generals plotting to depose him. He was the accepted chief of the mulattoes, then in control of the Republic, and he possessed the confidence of the merchants. But he had inherited from the lax administration of his predecessor a most difficult situation. The commerce of

HAITIAN REPUBLIC FROM 1818 TO 1908

the Republic was demoralized and the condition of the treasury deplorable. For years bandits had infested the district of Grande Anse, keeping the whole South in a state of alarm, while Christophe still threatened the border. Boyer's first task, which he promptly assumed, was to disperse the bandits gathered under a chief named Gouman, who, acting in conjunction with Christophe, had even extended their depredations to the environs of Port-au-Prince.

In this enterprise the new president was completely successful, and on the death of Christophe, in 1820, the area of the former colony of St.-Domingue was united under his rule. One year later the Spanish part voluntarily joined the Republic, and the whole island of Santo Domingo (Haiti) was, until Boyer's death in 1843, united in a Haitian Republic.

Boyer succeeded in improving commercial and financial conditions, but in this he was greatly handicapped. At the time of his election to the presidency, the Republic of Haiti had been in existence for fourteen years; yet not one foreign nation, not even Colombia, which owed its very existence to Pétion, had recognized the Haitian Republic. England, France, and Spain were all slave-owning states, and the United States, the great Republic of the Western World, not only maintained slavery, but, for political reasons, consistently refused to recognize the Republic of Haiti.[1] Recognition by France was essential to the commercial development of the Republic, and this Boyer endeavoured to obtain.

Twice during Pétion's rule and in 1821, three years after Pétion's death, negotiations between France and Haiti for the acknowledgment of the independence of the Republic had been undertaken. In August, 1823, at a conference held in Brussels, Haiti had requested the full recognition of her independence, offering in return that for four years French goods in French bottoms should be exempted from duties

BLACK DEMOCRACY

and after that should pay one-half the duties imposed on other nations. This was agreed to by France only on condition that Haiti should also pay a heavy indemnity, which Haitian representatives refused.

In November, 1823, negotiations were reopened, and in May, 1824, Boyer sent a commission to France empowered to offer an indemnity in money or produce and certain mutual concessions in customs duties. These offers were accepted, but on the most extraordinary condition that this should apply only to the French part of the island, the representative of the French government stating that "the King of France could not stipulate for the King of Spain." This amounted to a refusal to recognize the Republic of Haiti as then constituted, and as it was further stipulated that the King of France would reserve to himself the *Souveraineté Extérieure,* these proposals were naturally refused.

In July, 1825, Baron Mackau arrived at Port-au-Prince with a squadron of fourteen French ships of war and presented an ordinance of Charles X in which the independence of Haiti was recognized on condition that ports of Haiti should be open to all nations, but that the French flag should pay only half duties, both import and export, and that one hundred and fifteen million francs should be paid in five equal instalments in order to compensate the former colonists who might claim indemnity.[2] Boyer, intimidated by this show of overwhelming force, accepted these terms, thereby saddling his country with a vast burden of debt for which there existed no apparent means of liquidation. On July 11, 1825, the senate approved the ordinance.

The senate, which reluctantly took this action, was dominated by the mulattoes, who, although greatly in the minority, had maintained political control for over twenty years, but the blacks were ever conscious that they had won their independence by years of warfare, and the thought that they were to be deprived of some of their hard-won liberties and must again accept any sort of French domination infuriated them.

The general indignation among the blacks, who constituted more than nine-tenths of his people, at the terms of this humiliating compact grew so pronounced that Boyer, realizing his only hope lay in the possibility of some modification, sent a commission to France instructed to negotiate a new and less distasteful treaty. But these negotiations met with complete failure.

The chief revenue of the Republic was then, as now, derived from heavy export and import taxes. This revenue, the only source from which to meet the indemnity payments, had been greatly limited by the terms of the ordinance which imposed a reduction in all duties on commerce with France. And the treasury, already drained by heavy expenditures for the military establishment, was unable to meet these payments. To complicate the situation further, the inhabitants of the Spanish part of the island refused to contribute to an indemnity which they asserted concerned the French part of the island alone. The disclosure that an additional payment of thirty million francs had been agreed upon to reimburse France for fortifications and public buildings, added to the people's indignation.

A loan of thirty million francs, floated in France, netted the Haitian government only twenty-four million francs, and the measures taken to raise in Haiti the additional six million francs required to make up the first payment brought home to the people a realization of the burden which had been laid upon them. Rebellion was averted only by prompt military measures.

The laxity of Pétion's administration and the failure of his successor to enforce labour on the plantations had demoralized the "cultivators." Agricultural production had greatly diminished, and consequently the revenues of the

Republic were inadequate even for the administrative needs of the government. To correct this condition, laws were passed compelling a certain amount of labour from each "cultivator." These laws were enforced by military discipline, and even on the plantations of the President labourers worked under the supervision of armed guards.

Failure to meet the indemnity payments and the interest on loans resulted in a rupture of relations with France, and it was not until February, 1838, when a new and less onerous treaty was signed, that relations were resumed.

In May, 1842, an earthquake wrecked Cap Haitien, Port-de-Paix, Mole St. Nicholas, and Fort Liberté. Boyer's enemies, claiming that he had neglected proper measures for the relief of the sufferers from this catastrophe, became more active. In January, 1843, Major Charles Herard took up arms against the President, and the country rose in revolt. In March, 1843, Boyer sent his resignation to the senate and sailed for Jamaica on a British sloop of war. He died in Paris in 1850.[3] His retirement ended thirty-six years of mulatto domination, a perpetuation of the dictatorship established by Pétion, which, with all its faults, at least was comparatively free from discord and civil war.

Boyer was succeeded by Charles Herard, who entered the capital on March 21st amid an extraordinary demonstration of popular approval.

In April a provisional government revised the constitution. Presidency for life was abolished and the powers of the chief executive greatly curtailed. No measure of the President was to become effective until countersigned by the Minister of State entrusted with its execution. The new constitution provided for the popular election of judges, trial by jury was established, and the right to originate legislation conferred on the senate and chamber of deputies. The army was declared "a law-abiding body," while strict measures were enacted guaranteeing personal freedom and respect for property. These commendable innovations were, however, nullified by the incapacity and insincerity of the President, who, in spite of his pre-election promises, openly supported the military party.

The Spanish part of the island had separated from Haiti on Boyer's death to found a separate republic, and Herard, with a stupid lack of appreciation of his unpopularity at home, personally led an army in a futile campaign to restore Santo Domingo to the Republic. Shortly after his departure on this exploit a revolution was started in the North, and on May 3, 1844, General Philippe Guerrier was acclaimed president of Haiti. A month later Herard abdicated and sailed for Jamaica.

Guerrier, a veteran of the Revolution, who was eighty years old at the time of his election, filled the office, for which he was obviously unfitted, for only eleven months. He died on April 15, 1845, and was succeeded by General Louis Pierrot, another aged veteran, who retired after less than eleven months. On the retirement of Pierrot, General Jean Baptiste Riche was proclaimed president of the Republic.

Riche appears to have made a conscientious effort to improve the deplorable conditions inherited from his predecessors. He chose able ministers, took active measures to suppress banditry, and attempted to reorganize commerce by encouraging foreign merchants; but, unfortunately for Haiti, Riche died less than a year after his election.

Some sixteen years before, when news was brought to Boyer that an insurrection had started against him in the South, he prophesied a period of disorder and is said to have remarked that "any man in Haiti may become president of the Republic, even that stupid Negro over there," pointing to Soulouque, then an officer in his guards. Soulouque is supposed to have answered: "Please, Mr. President, don't make a fool of me." Soulouque had in no way distinguished himself in the interval, but after a prolonged attempt to elect either of the two rival candidates of their own party, the ministers of Riche, who had held political control for some time, selected this inconspicuous black for the highest office in the land. Four days after the death of Riche, General Faustin Soulouque, very greatly to his own surprise, was elected president of Haiti.

Soulouque, an illiterate, superstitious, and totally inconspicuous "general," with no particular record for public service and practically no political following, was obviously chosen as a man who would be completely subservient to his sponsors. But as a tool he proved a bitter disappointment. Ignorant as he undoubtedly was, he had a will of his own and an inordinate vanity which, coupled with an unscrupulous disregard for orderly procedure, maintained him in office for almost twelve years. Shortly after his election he replaced the ministers of Riche by nonentities and advanced to the highest rank some of the most ignorant blacks in the army. He caused a general massacre of mulattoes in the spring of 1848, during which many of the prominent mulatto leaders were executed, those who escaped being compelled to go into exile.

Following this successful campaign against his "detractors," Soulouque turned his attention to affairs of state. His first move was an ill-advised and disastrous attempt to recover the Spanish part of the island. As every attempt was made to conduct this campaign with secrecy, little became known to the public except reports of victories until some weeks later, when the President entered Port-au-Prince amid the roars of cannon and the plaudits of the people, who learned during the day that the expedition had been a complete and miserable fiasco.

Soulouque, realizing that this campaign, instead of adding to his glory, had greatly intensified the disaffection of the people, and in order to give them something else to think about besides their very real wrongs, decided to create an empire. In the cathedral at Port-au-Prince, on August 26, 1849, he declared himself Emperor, under the title of Faustin I, and the second Empire of Haiti was inaugurated. The ceremonies on this occasion were comparatively simple. It was not until April, 1852, all preparations having been made and the elaborate regalia secured from abroad, that the final coronation took place. The Emperor did not hesitate then, at lavish expenditure of the public funds, to add to the impressiveness of the occasion. It is said that the imperial crown, one of the few relics of Haiti still in possession of the government, cost $100,000, and that $150,000 was spent for the rest of the paraphernalia. The ceremony took place in the Champ de Mars at Port-au-Prince, where an immense tabernacle capable of seating seven thousand people had been constructed. An eyewitness reported the scene in the following words:

"As early as three o'clock A.M. the roll of drums was heard, calling the troops together and reminding the inhabitants of the capital of the great event which was to distinguish that day. Soon after daylight, 'le Champ de Mars' was filled with all of the brilliant and gay, both civil and military.

"At an early hour, the roar of artillery, the shouts of vivas, the din of arms, with the confusion of bugles, trumpets, and various bands at different points, announced the approach of the imperial state carriage, which, for splendour, was worthy of the occasion and was drawn by eight noble American greys.

"On arriving at a side tent, some three or four hundred feet from the main one, the imperial family alighted, and from thence, after a rather long pause, all being well adjusted, his Majesty, duly robed and sceptred, marched with a brilliant procession of newly created nobles in open air until they reached the entrance of the great tent, and then,

~ The Coronation Ceremony, April 18, 1852 ~

⇀ Faustin the First, Emperor of Haiti ↽

continuing under its spacious canopy, they ultimately arrived in front of the great altar, now loaded with blazing tapers and gorgeous decorations of every kind; here seats were provided for all parties, according to their rank and honour.

"The costumes, on this occasion, of most of those who held offices of any kind were designedly antique, rather imitating the court and time of Louis XIV. In fact, the splendour and riches displayed on the occasion, although it seemed to throw one back to another age by the antique, not to say gorgeous, appearance of much that was seen, gave at the same time an elevated idea of the wealth and taste of the Haitian people. Nor would any European infantry have presented a neater or more imposing appearance than was seen in the Haitian soldiery on this occasion, while the attire of the simple citizens was that of gentility and worthy of the day.

"Numerous priests were in attendance, but there was neither sermon nor oration on the occasion; the chanting, however, and general music were good, although wanting in good brass instruments. The Emperor crowned himself, and then the Empress.

"At the end of this pompous ceremony, the roar of cannon broke forth again, which, with the sound of arms and the confused music of widely scattered bands, all mingling together at the same time, overwhelmed everything; yet all passed off well and the shades of night were welcome."

In establishing his empire, Faustin did not overlook the desire of his generals to share in the trappings of royalty. He created a nobility and elevated to rank four princes and fifty-nine dukes, as well as innumerable counts, barons, and chevaliers. The Legion of Honour and Imperial Order of St. Faustin were established and insignia provided, as well as most elaborate rules and regulations for royal receptions and court procedure. The constitution of the empire was a strange combination of aristocratic and republican institutions. But Soulouque, or Faustin I, as he now called himself, adopted the motto, "I am the State and my will is law," and the constitution for all practical purposes was a dead letter, protests being quickly silenced by imprisonment, or more often by sudden death.

"Let us rejoice," said Faustin; "we await the future when a time shall come when people will say, what a beautiful epoch was that of Soulouque." This optimistic prediction, however, was never realized; far from rejoicing, the people became more and more discontented with the autocratic rule of the Emperor and his utter disregard for the rights of individuals.

In 1855 Faustin again invaded the territory of the Dominican Republic. This campaign, which was miserably organized and directed, met with disastrous failure and added greatly to the general discontent. After the Dominican campaign Great Britain and France interfered and secured an armistice between the belligerents. In this these two powers had the support of the United States. Daniel Webster, then Secretary of State of the United States, wrote to the American representative in Port-au-Prince: "The material interests of these three countries [Great Britain, France, and the United States] are largely involved in the restoration and preservation of peace between the contending parties in Santo Domingo. France is a creditor of the government of Soulouque to a large amount. She cannot hope for a discharge of her debt when the resources of his country, instead of being developed by pacific pursuits and a part, at least, applied to the purpose, are checked in their growth and wasted in a war which countermines the state. . . . If the Emperor Soulouque shall insist upon maintaining a belligerent attitude . . . you will unite with your colleagues in remonstrating against this course on his part. If remonstrations shall prove to be unavailing you will signify to the

Emperor that you shall give immediate notice to your government, that the President [of the United States], with the concurrence of Congress, may adopt such measures, in co-operation with the governments of England and France, as may cause the three powers to be respected."

This attitude of the three great powers, following the disgraceful failure of his military campaign, completely eliminated the Dominican question, and Faustin faced a disgruntled and thoroughly dissatisfied people without any hope of arousing enthusiasm by military conquests.

Of the Dominican campaign Léger says: "The responsibility of the failure of this undertaking was cast on the Emperor. Confidence in him was shaken, the empire might yet have been saved by taking wise measures in regard to the interest and welfare of the people. But the government, in order to maintain its authority, resorted instead to intimidation and violence, which methods had once proven to be successful. No regard was paid to public liberty. Bad financial measures, added to faulty management of the nation's revenues, soon aggravated the situation. Such was the state of affairs when General Fabre Geffrard considered that the time had come for the overthrow of the man who had, in reality, assumed dictatorial power."

Geffrard had gained great popularity in the army during the ill-fated invasion of Santo Domingo, his courage and ability having saved several regiments from complete destruction. Warned by Geffrard's popularity and the increasing disaffection of his people, Faustin kept a close watch on the General and finally ordered his arrest. But Geffrard escaped and at Gonaives, on December 22, 1858, inaugurated an insurrection against the Emperor. This movement was received with the greatest enthusiasm, and a few days later, supported by the people of the North, Geffrard advanced on Port-au-Prince at the head of six thousand men.

Faustin made a feeble attempt to stem the rebellion, but

~ The Empress Adelina ~

finding that his troops were deserting, he returned to Port-au-Prince and, on January 15, 1859, took refuge in the French legation. A few days later he ended a dictatorship of over eleven years' duration by sailing on a British ship for Jamaica.

Geffrard, "appointed" on the twenty-third of December, 1858, took the oath of office as president of the re-established republic on January 20, 1859. He was a *griffe*, the son of a black father by a mulatto mother, and he endeavoured to employ this circumstance to ingratiate himself with both parties, but apparently fully succeeded with neither.

From the beginning of his administration Geffrard was handicapped by conspiracies against him. Nevertheless he succeeded in introducing many reforms. The army was reorganized, a system of primary and high schools started, as well as a school of medicine and one of music, while a concordat, which is still in effect, was ratified by the Holy See. In November, 1864, a treaty of amity, commerce, and navigation was signed between Haiti and the United States.

Co-operating with certain prominent abolitionists of New England, Geffrard made elaborate plans to bring to Haiti "industrious men of African descent." Some few such emigrants actually arrived, but the plan failed, owing partly to lack of proper preparation to receive and care for these people, but more because of the absence of any public interest either in Haiti or in the United States.

In July, 1864, Geffrard suppressed a revolt headed by Sylvain Salnave, who later succeeded him as president, but in May, 1865, Salnave captured Cap Haitien. During the following August, Geffrard took personal command of the army and left for the North, but failed to dislodge Salnave from his hold on Cap Haitien. On the nineteenth of November a British merchant ship loaded with arms, ammunition, and supplies for the government forces, attempting to enter

BLACK DEMOCRACY

Acul Bay, a port near Cap Haitien then used as a base by Geffrard's troops, was chased and would have been captured by an insurgent steamer had it not been for the interference of a British gun-boat. Salnave, highly incensed at what he claimed was unwarranted interference, forcibly removed from the British consulate some of his opponents who had taken refuge there. This violation of the British consulate resulted in the bombardment of the fortifications of the Cape by the British, the sinking of the Haitian steamer, and the destruction of a British gun-boat.

Shortly after this the British *chargé d'affaires* reached the Cape on a man-of-war and, failing to obtain satisfaction from Salnave, fired on the city. During the ensuing excitement the government army which had been besieging the Cape succeeded in storming the town, and Salnave and his generals took refuge on an American warship.

This disgraceful affair, due entirely to the "impetuosity" of Salnave, was, for some reason difficult to analyse, laid at the door of Geffrard, and conspiracies against him multiplied. In September, 1866, the arsenal at Port-au-Prince was blown up with the loss of many lives and great destruction of property; and in February, 1867, the *Tirailleurs*, Geffrard's favourite regiment, mutinied. On the thirteenth of March, Geffrard resigned and sailed for Jamaica.

Léger, in the final paragraph of his review of Geffrard's administration, says: "In restoring the Republic, Geffrard made a great mistake in accepting the presidency for life. Had a time been fixed for the duration of his power, his opponents would have been more patient and his administration would have marked the beginning of a new epoch for Haiti. Ideas of reform and progress were uppermost in the minds of the people. A strong reaction had followed the downfall of monarchy. After a long period of restraint enforced by Soulouque, the Haitians, once aroused, were not easily repressed; they wished to secure then and there

HAITIAN REPUBLIC FROM 1818 TO 1908

the reign of liberty. This ideal of political liberty and freedom of thought was to be the cause later of much friction and disagreement with the Executive Power, always slow in yielding to public opinion."

In April, 1867, Major Sylvain Salnave arrived at Port-au-Prince and became a member of the provisional government composed of himself and two others, one of them being Nissage-Saget, later president of the Republic. A few weeks later Salnave assumed the title of "Protector of the Republic" and the powers of a dictator. The national assembly met at Port-au-Prince and, on the fourteenth of May, adopted a new constitution which abolished the presidency for life and fixed the term of office at four years. On the same day Salnave was elected president.

The new president resisted all attempts to put into effect the parliamentary form of government guaranteed by the constitution, and relations between the executive and legislature were soon strained to the breaking-point. An insurrection headed by General Leon Montas was followed by the forcible dissolution of the national assembly, which the President claimed was in sympathy with the rebels. Salnave suspended the constitution and, re-establishing the presidency for life, assumed a complete dictatorship. But, under the leadership of Nissage-Saget, Boisrond-Canal, and others, the insurrection became general and Salnave found himself besieged at Port-au-Prince.

At St.-Marc, in September, 1868, Nissage-Saget was proclaimed provisional president, and later in the month Domingue, insurgent leader of the South, was "acknowledged" president of the "Meridional State," with headquarters at Aux Cayes.

In August, 1869, Salnave, realizing that his position was critical and hoping that he might yet be able to allay the general discontent by relinquishing the absolute power he had usurped, appointed a council of state, but a few months later caused this body to elect him president for life. In December an army of twelve hundred men under General Brice and Boisrond-Canal landed at the capital. During the fight which followed, a shot fired from a government man-of-war that had been captured by the rebels struck the palace and exploded the powder magazine. After this catastrophe Salnave escaped to Santo Domingo, but was arrested and returned to Port-au-Prince, where he was tried by court martial, tied to a pole in the ruins of his palace, and shot. Since then no president has ventured to revive the "presidency for life."

After the execution of Salnave a provisional government was organized, and two months later the national assembly met in Port-au-Prince and elected Nissage-Saget to the presidency.

Attempts of the legislative body to put into effect the parliamentary system of government guaranteed by the constitution were again resisted by the president chosen by them. Samuel Hazard, who had during this period visited Haiti as correspondent of the *New York Herald* in connexion with President Grant's project to annex Santo Domingo, wrote:

"On the 29th of May, 1870, the present incumbent, Nissage-Saget, was named (it cannot be said elected) President for four years.

"What is this experiment of 'self-government,' so described by some over-zealous or badly informed people? Do they not know that at present there exists in Haiti another of those military despotisms for which the island is famous; that passes are required by the country people to come to town; that the only police are soldiers; and that not a year goes by unaccompanied by revolution and bloodshed?

"Do they not know that there are no general means of education or communication, except for roads ordinarily fit only for animals, most of which even were originally made in the time of the French; that bridges going to decay are not repaired; that there is no general system of agriculture and absolutely no manufacture of any kind and that neither foreigner nor native dare express their honest views, if they are not in accord with the Government? Do they know that this Government is bankrupt, its coin depreciated to four hundred dollars of paper to one of silver; while France threatens it for a settlement of its claims and Prussia has been forced within three months past to forcibly seize Haitian war-vessels in settlement of her claims, only too glad, doubtless, to strengthen her hold upon an island whose principal trade she monopolizes, whose merchants are principally composed of her citizens?

"Do they know that the men of the island exist upon the industry of the women, who are really the only labourers; and that, furthermore, at least two-thirds of the population do not speak any language recognized by the civilized world; that there is not a town on the island not remaining in ruins more or less caused by their revolutions?

"Again, do they not know that, with acres and acres of splendid sugar-cane, there is hardly a steam mill, that, with a soil especially adapted by nature for coffee raising, there cannot be said to be a dozen coffee estates in the island, and that even the coffee, which, left thus in its wild state, grows in such abundance that it cannot all be harvested, is in the marts of commerce valued as an inferior article, not from any demerit of its own, but from the fact that the people are too lazy to clean and prepare it properly for market?

"I could here quote many paragraphs from Haitian writers themselves showing how conscious they are of their own shortcomings, but space does not permit me; yet I cannot refrain from quoting a few passages from the works of their most celebrated historian (Ardouin), who says: 'In general the people of Haiti are incapable of industry;

a thousand means besides those of agriculture are offered to them to arrive at a state of great prosperity, but they do not avail themselves of them. In the towns where there is a surplus of inhabitants, there is no lack of labour, but few of the workmen acquit themselves well in their tasks. A great part remain idle, they like better to vegetate than live honestly by labour. The youth of the country give themselves up to foolishness and frivolity and to that idleness which is the mother of all vice. The crime most frequently committed is theft and the greatest number of the criminals are the young.' "

That these unfortunate facts were generally recognized is confirmed by the following extract from an editorial in the *Gazette du Peuple*, Port-au-Prince, April 6, 1871: "For sixty-eight years . . . what have we done? Nothing or almost nothing. All our constitutions are defective, all our laws are incomplete, our custom houses are badly administered, our navy is detestable, our finances are rotten to the core; our police is badly organized, our army is in a pitiable state; the legislative power is not understood and never will be; the primary elections are neglected and our people feel not their importance; nearly all our public edifices are in ruins; the public instruction is almost entirely abandoned."

In January, 1870, the American minister at Port-au-Prince notified the Haitian government that his country was in negotiation with the president of the Dominican Republic for the annexation of the latter country to the United States and requested Haiti to refrain, or desist, from any interference in Dominican affairs. The Haitian government replied, promising to observe this request, but the American government, evidently doubting the good faith of these assurances, made further representations, thereby arousing great indignation among the Haitians. The failure of the United States Senate to ratify President

Grant's treaty for the annexation of Santo Domingo ended this episode and probably avoided a definite break in the relations between the two countries.[4]

Saget's administration closed unaccompanied by the usual revolution. But fate determined to deny to the Haitians an orderly change of government. The House of Representatives and Senate, acting as a national assembly, being unable to choose a successor to Saget, a *dissidence* was created and the Council of Secretaries of State assumed the executive functions of the government. In May, 1874, Saget appointed Michel Domingue, who was his choice as candidate for the presidency, commander-in-chief of the army and retired to private life.

General Michel Domingue, the commander of the Southeastern Department, immediately left Aux Cayes for Port-au-Prince with a strong body of troops. The Council of Secretaries of State, who held the executive power, had taken measures to facilitate his election, and his opponents realized the impossibility of holding out against him. Profiting by the lack of a quorum, which prevented the legislative body from executive sessions, the Council declared the two houses of Congress divested of their functions, and issued orders for the election of a Constituent Assembly.

The "election" was held on June 11, 1874, and General Domingue, the successful candidate, was elected for a term of eight years, of which he served less than two.

Not only was Domingue utterly incompetent, but he seems to have realized his limitations. He appointed his nephew, Septimus Rameau, to the office of vice-president of the Council of Secretaries of State and turned over the government to him. Rameau, one of the most unscrupulous scoundrels in the history of the Haitian people, proceeded to loot the government. A loan was floated in Paris for twenty-six million francs, only a very little of which sum reached the Haitian treasury, and it is said that a considerable part of the proceeds of the loan found its way into the pockets of Septimus Rameau.

This scandalous financial transaction greatly increased the dissatisfaction already existing in Haiti, and in anticipation of a popular uprising, Rameau ordered the arrest of General Brice, Montplaisir Pierre, and Boisrond-Canal, three of the most influential men in the Republic.

"On May 1st, taking advantage of an assembly to celebrate the *Fête de l'Agriculture,* Rameau ordered an attack to be made on the three rivals he most feared. General Brice was sitting writing in his office when the soldiers sent to murder him appeared; his bravery, however, was so well known that they dreaded to approach him but, firing at a distance, gave him time to seize his arms and defend himself. But having only revolvers, he thought it prudent to endeavour to take refuge in the English legation. He was wounded fatally in doing so. . . . Montplaisir Pierre was attacked in his own house, but being better armed, he made a long defence; he killed seventeen soldiers, wounded thirty-two, most mortally, and could only be subdued by the employment of artillery. . . . The third destined to death by the government was Boisrond-Canal. While defending himself, Brice had thought of his friend and had sent his clerk to warn him of his danger. On the approach of the soldiers he and his friends readily put them to flight, but then were forced to disperse, Canal taking refuge with the American Minister, who after five months of tedious correspondence was enabled to embark him in safety." *

The killing of these two prominent citizens produced an effect precisely opposite to that intended by Rameau, and it soon became evident that his days of dictatorship were numbered. On April 15, 1876, a report that the government was sending the public funds out of the country resulted in

---

* Sir Spencer St. John. See Bibliography.

HAITIAN REPUBLIC FROM 1818 TO 1908

the murder of Rameau and the flight of the President, who, after taking refuge in the French legation, sailed for Jamaica.

Boisrond-Canal, who succeeded Domingue, was elected on July 17, 1876, for a term of four years, of which he served three. During his administration, France, Spain, Great Britain, and the United States all made claims against the Haitian government. The Domingue debt to France was adjusted by the acknowledgment of an indebtedness of twenty-one million francs, other claims being withdrawn or settled. Boyer-Bazelais, leader of the so-called Liberal party, which had bitterly contested the election of Canal, continued actively to oppose him. In July, 1879, a serious disturbance took place in the Chamber of Deputies, which adjourned in a riot in which many prominent men, including two brothers of Boyer-Bazelais, were killed. Léger says of this situation: "The insane ambition of what was called the Liberty party thus ruined the most honest government Haiti had seen since the days of Boyer. These disturbances in the capital were followed by others in the provinces; and Boisrond-Canal, disquieted with the treatment he had received from those who should have supported him, resigned and left the country with his chief ministers, July 17, 1879. Great sympathy was shown him by the people, who cheered him as he left the wharf." *

After the departure of Boisrond-Canal, the constitution was again modified and the presidential term of office changed from four to seven years.

Lysius Salomon, elected to the presidency on December 3, 1879, was the leader of the National party. He was a man of education and much political and diplomatic experience. He had been Minister of Finance in Soulouque's first cabinet, and when the latter created the Empire of Haiti, Salomon was named Duke of Saint-Louis de Sud. Later he

* *Haiti: Her History and Her Detractors.* See Bibliography.

was Minister to France, and had lived over twenty years in Europe.

The rivalry between the Liberal and National parties, quieted for a time by the absence of Boyer-Bazelais, who had taken refuge in Jamaica, was revived in March, 1883, when Bazelais landed at Mirogoane and started another insurrection, which was finally suppressed.

But claims for damage suffered by foreigners during the fighting, and the expenses of maintaining the army, resulted in serious drains on the public funds. In spite of these added burdens, Salomon succeeded in inaugurating a number of genuinely constructive projects. Haiti was admitted to the Universal Postal Union, and communications with the outside world were further improved by the laying of a submarine cable. The constitution of 1879 expressly prohibited the immediate re-election of a president. This, however, did not deter Salomon's ambition and he had the constitution modified. On the thirtieth of June, 1886, Salomon was re-elected president for a new term of seven years. This proceeding was held by his opponents to be an attempt at re-establishing the presidency for life, and the usual insurrection followed. The President at once declared he was willing to resign his office, and left for France.

Salomon left Haiti on the tenth of August, and on the twenty-fourth General Télémaque entered Port-au-Prince with ten thousand men. A provisional government, instituted on that day by the revolutionary committee, included Télémaque, Hippolyte, Boisrond-Canal, and Légitime. Télémaque held the portfolio of War and Navy, Boisrond-Canal was president of the provisional government, while Légitime's power was limited to his personal influence and his great popularity with the people. On the seventeenth of September the delegates to the national assembly, which was to choose a president, were elected.

Rivalry between the Northern troops of Télémaque and

HAITIAN REPUBLIC FROM 1818 TO 1908

the soldiers of Port-au-Prince resulted in a riot during which Télémaque was killed. The origin of this conflict is as obscure as the results were deplorable. Hippolyte, in the North, organized a provisional government. The West and South chose Légitime "Chief of the Executive Government," and on the sixteenth of December elected him president of the Republic. This election was protested by the North, but Légitime was recognized by the foreign powers, the United States alone withholding recognition. It is claimed by Haitian writers that the refusal of the United States to recognize Légitime and its partiality to the claims of Hippolyte caused the downfall of the Légitime Government.

After a brief rule of eight months Légitime, "being unable to maintain his authority," resigned and left the island.

Légitime, the only surviving ex-president, lives at Port-au-Prince and is highly respected by both Haitians and foreigners.

On September 24, 1889, the Constituent Assembly met at Gonaives and, after amending the constitution, elected Florvil Hippolyte to the presidency for a term of seven years.

It was claimed by representatives of the United States government that promises had been made by Hippolyte and his minister Firmin that, in return for aid rendered the revolutionary cause, the Mole St. Nicholas would be leased to the United States for use as a naval base. This demand was met by a decided refusal, Hippolyte and Firmin denying the existence of such an agreement, and after prolonged parleys the project was abandoned.[5]

During the administration of Hippolyte the telephone was introduced in Haiti, telegraph lines were constructed, a number of public buildings, which still bear the name of the President, were built, and an attempt was made to provide proper docking facilities at some of the principal ports.

BLACK DEMOCRACY

In 1896 a loan was floated in Paris for fifty million francs which netted eighty per cent of its face value. On March 24, 1896, Hippolyte, who had for some time been in poor health, died from a stroke of apoplexy.

General T. Simon Sam, the Secretary of War, elected to the presidency seven days after the death of Hippolyte, took the oath of office on April 1, 1896. His administration of over six years, while not marked by any notable achievement, was comparatively peaceful. In 1897 a controversy with the German government over the arrest of German citizens, which for a time threatened to become serious, was settled through the intervention of representatives of foreign powers.

Towards the end of the administration of Simon Sam, a discussion of the duration of his term of office was the principal subject engaging the attention of the newspapers and politicians. Sam was elected on March 31, 1896. The constitution provided for a term of seven years, but specified that "his [the president's] power must always close on the fifteenth of May, even if the seventh year of his term be not completed."

A decree of the national assembly had prescribed that he should retain office until the fifteenth of May, 1903, but, influenced by a very decided opposition to this decision, Sam did not even wait until the end of his term, *i.e.*, May 15, 1902, but "to prevent misunderstanding" sent his resignation to the national assembly on the twelfth of May, and on the thirteenth left Port-au-Prince. The task of maintaining order was, as usual, entrusted to a provisional government.

Three candidates for the presidency immediately entered the field. Two of them contented themselves with campaigns in newspapers and pamphlets, but A. Firmin, formerly Minister of Foreign Affairs in Hippolyte's cabinet, proceeded to the North and, after having been defeated in a campaign to secure his election as Deputy for Cap Haitien, went to Gonaives, where he had been elected to that office.

On the second of September, Admiral Killick of the Haitian navy, who was supporting Firmin, boarded a German steamer in the harbour of Gonaives and forcibly removed arms and ammunition consigned by the provisional government to Nord Alexis, then at Cap Haitien. This was held by the German government to be a piratical act, and a few days later a German gun-boat arrived in the harbour of Gonaives and demanded the surrender of the Haitian warship. Killick asked for a few moments' delay and, sending his crew ashore, blew up the ship and himself with it. Thus deprived of his most effective support, Firmin gave up the contest and departed for Inargua.

In the meantime, "tiring of a seemingly endless struggle," the population of Port-au-Prince put aside the three candidates who were striving for the presidency and, on the night of December 17, 1902, declared in favour of General Nord Alexis. Needless to say, the General was a few days later elected president.

The new president, although over eighty years old at the time of his election, courageously devoted himself to his office and gave personal attention to many public works that were inaugurated during his administration. An investigation of frauds which had been perpetrated in the consolidation of the floating debt disclosed that over a million and a quarter dollars had been stolen from the government and, in spite of the prominence of the guilty parties, the President referred the matter to the courts.

After a prolonged inquiry the grand jury indicted the French director of the national bank, two Germans, and several very prominent Haitians. Tremendous pressure was brought to bear to prevent their trial, but the President refused to interfere and T. Simon Sam, ex-President of the Republic, Vilbrun Guillaume, Minister of War, Tancrede

Auguste, Minister of the Interior, and Cincinnatus Leconte, Minister of Public Works, were convicted. The evidence that these sentences did not "take" is that only one of the above-named men was even arrested and the still more extraordinary fact that the last three were later elected in turn to the presidency of the Republic.

Toward the end of Alexis' term of office he decided not to be a candidate for re-election, but prepared to turn over the presidency to General Turenne Jean-Gilles. This precipitated a rebellion headed by Antoine Simon, the delegate for the Department of the South, who was himself a candidate.

Simon proceeded toward Port-au-Prince with an ill-equipped army of only about three hundred men which might easily have been defeated if it had not been for the treachery of the commander of the government troops, who apparently deliberately allowed Simon to advance on the capital.

Nord Alexis, deserted by his friends, was forced to abdicate and take refuge on a French warship, which transported him to Jamaica.

PART TWO

FOREWORD

A FEW months before the conclusion of the era of comparative peace and prosperity which terminated with the administration of Nord Alexis, J. N. Léger, an eminent Haitian publicist, issued the following optimistic prophecy: "Peace, the advantage of which is daily gaining ground in the appreciation of Haitians, in procuring security will facilitate the exploitation of the many natural resources of the country with the help of foreign capital." Yet, a year after Mr. Léger's book was published, President Nord Alexis, in spite of his conspicuous services to the Republic, was forced to abdicate.

Within the following period of six and a half years, seven presidents were elected and deposed. Of these seven, one was blown up in the national palace; one died, it is said, by poison; and of the other five, all of whom were deposed by revolutions, one was butchered in a massacre of political prisoners, and another was torn to pieces by a mob.

The collapse of the Haitian state was imminent, not only politically, but in the approaching bankruptcy of the governmental finances, which had been avoided for years only by successively more desperate shifts of expediency.

That foreign interests should play an important part in the drama of "ephemeral governments" which preceded the American intervention was inevitable. The great majority of the outstanding government bonds were held in France, and German nationals were the largest owners of property and controlled by far the greater part of the lucrative business enterprises in Haiti.

American interests, although of lesser actual intrinsic

value, were not inactive. The Bank of Haiti and the National Railroad, in which Americans were largely interested, admittedly pursued a policy designed to secure American interference as the only escape for the hopelessly chaotic conditions. The weight of the influence of these interests in the policy of the Department of State has, however, been greatly exaggerated.

In July, 1915, Haiti presented an opening for intervention which had in one form or another been for some time contemplated by the United States. The situation called for some active measures on the part of the United States, and it is difficult to see how armed intervention could well have been avoided. But that this intervention was inspired by a handful of American investors to further the plans of a great American bank is a myth created by propagandists.

The story of the collapse of the Haitian state and the history of the period since the American intervention in 1915 have been told from all sorts of angles. Bitterly prejudiced and often utterly irresponsible criticism has vied with equally irresponsible fulsome praise. But never have the facts been presented clearly in an unprejudiced view. Substantially half of this volume has therefore been devoted to an attempt to tell as clearly and concisely as possible the story of these fateful years in Haiti's history. It also professes to describe accurately the events which led to the present situation in Haiti.

CHAPTER I

THE REVOLUTIONARY PERIOD, 1908–1915

ANTOINE SIMON, on his arrival at the capital, assumed the title of "Chief of the Executive Power," and on the seventeenth of December, 1908, he was elected to the presidency by the national assembly for a term of seven years.

His administration, which lasted two years and seven months, inaugurated the period which is known in Haiti as the Period of Ephemeral Governments (*Epoque des Gouvernements Ephémères*).

The story of this period is a recital of insurrections, revolutions, and assassinations punctuated by a most extraordinary series of bond issues and hectic financial operations, which finally forced the Republic of Haiti into political, moral, and financial bankruptcy.

During this period of less than seven years, the principal occupation of the chief executive and his ministers was raising money to "maintain the government" or taking measures designed to prevent someone else from assuming this privilege.

Reorganization of the National Bank

The gross mismanagement of the Banque Nationale, which was typified by the consolidation scandal mentioned in the previous chapter, resulted in cancelling the charter of this institution, and the organization, in 1910, of the Banque Nationale de la République d'Haïti. The foreign nations holding claims against the Haitian Republic or Hai-

Above: Statue of Dessalines
Below: Old and New Cathedrals in Port-au-Prince

tian government-bonds all actively promoted the plans for this new organization.

German interests, exceedingly powerful in Haiti both commercially and politically, demanded a large participation in the reorganized bank and opposed American participation. The attitude of the French government, however, was emphatically against the inclusion of German capital without American participation, and the final arrangement, completed in 1910, gave only about 2,500 of the total of 40,000 shares of the Banque Nationale de la République d'Haïti to the Disconto Gesellschaft, a semi-governmental German institution. About 6,000 shares were, however, held in New York by three banking houses of close German affiliations. The remainder of the stock, excepting 2,000 shares taken by the National City Bank of New York and a few shares in Haiti, was held in France.

The two prime factors aimed at were monetary reform and a recognized share for the bank in a joint administration of the customs. France, Germany, and England were all concerned through money due for claims of their nationals and interest in the future repayment of outstanding loans. As a matter of fact, within the next few years each of these countries took steps to compel the settlement of claims by force.

In August, 1910, the Simon administration entered into a contract with a syndicate of French, German, and American bankers for a loan of 65,000,000 francs, bearing interest at five per cent.

The proceeds of this loan were to be used, first, for the payment of the government's debt to the old bank; secondly, for the execution of a program of monetary reform, for which 10,000,000 francs were reserved; and, thirdly, for the retirement of the internal debts.

This loan was subscribed for by the syndicate at a price which netted the government 72.3 per cent of its face value.

REVOLUTIONARY PERIOD, 1908-1915

The service of this loan was secured by a tax of one dollar gold on each hundred pounds of coffee exported, and by a special gold surtax of fifteen per cent on import duties.

These taxes were to be received by the Banque Nationale de la République d'Haïti, and the government obligated itself to set aside other revenues in case these taxes did not produce sufficient revenue to meet the obligation.

The terms of this loan were at first not acceptable to the United States government. It is understood that the rate of issue was considered too low and that the provisions for the retirement of the internal debt did not adequately protect American interests. In this connexion it was stated, at the time, that the low price realized for these bonds was largely due to the fact that the syndicate had been compelled to pay a commission of 5,000,000 francs to the officials of the Haitian government who signed the convention. The objections of the United States government were withdrawn after satisfactory assurances had been given that legitimate foreign claims would be properly protected.

A Caco Rising Puts Leconte in Power

In February, 1911, an uprising in the North was mercilessly suppressed by Simon, who personally commanded the government troops. But early in May the North was again in revolt, this time directed by Cincinnatus Leconte, who from exile had planned and financed a well-organized caco * movement. He crossed the Dominican border and assembled a force so well equipped and organized that he had little difficulty in forcing Simon, who had again per-

---

* The origin of this word has long been disputed. It appears for the first time in 1867, when the revolting peasants of Vallières called themselves cacos. The word has never, except erroneously, been synonymous with "bandit." The cacos were peasants from the hills who sold their services to presidential aspirants and made up the chief personnel of the revolutionary armies, especially in the "ephemeral" period. See note 1.

sonally taken the field, to return to the capital. Leconte then proceeded with his cacos to carry out the program which later became the conventional method of securing the office of chief executive of the Republic.

After taking Cap Haitien he marched over the mountain trails to Plaisance, then to Ennery, both small mountain towns, then to the important port of Gonaives, which surrendered to him. From Gonaives he marched to St.-Marc, the next open port, which is connected by railroad with the capital, only sixty-four miles distant. The capture of St.-Marc usually meant the fall of the administration in power, and this campaign was no exception to the rule. On August second, Simon abdicated and sailed for Jamaica, and on the fourteenth of August, 1911, Leconte was elected by the national assembly for a term of seven years, of which he served less than one.

Leconte had been Minister of Public Works in the administration of Tiresias Simon Sam and was one of the prominent Haitians convicted in the consolidation scandal. He, however, immediately instituted reforms in the military establishment and the schools, and became very popular with the people.

Early in the morning of the eighth of August, 1912, an explosion took place in the national palace, under which, during this revolutionary period, it had been customary to store the munitions. This explosion, which may or may not have been accidental, resulted in the death of the President, his grandson, and many soldiers of the palace guard.

During the short period in which Leconte held office he built the Casernes Dessalines, now the United States Marine barracks, and started a program for the construction of public schools.

An internal bond issue of $674,000, bearing interest at six per cent, was placed locally by Leconte at about eighty-one per cent. This loan was the first of a series of internal

REVOLUTIONARY PERIOD, 1908-1915

bond issues, of which there were four within the next three years, all placed to meet the "extraordinary expenses" of the various presidents either in securing their election or in "maintaining them in office." The law authorizing this first issue provided that the proceeds should be used for the payment of debts incurred by Leconte in his revolution against Simon.

No time was lost in choosing the successor to Leconte, and on the day of his death Tancrede Auguste was elected for a term of seven years, of which he served nine months.

Auguste had been Minister of the Interior under Simon Sam. He was very energetic and a man of culture. Although implicated in the consolidation scandal, he had been pardoned by Nord Alexis. Auguste was chosen to succeed Leconte largely through the influence of General Beaufossé Laroche, the governor of Port-au-Prince, who controlled the army. His administration was considered a continuation of the policies of Leconte, whose cabinet he retained practically intact. The short period of Auguste's incumbency ended May 2, 1913, when he died in the palace at Port-au-Prince, it is understood, of poisoning.

Haiti's First Civilian President

During the final ceremonies, and while the body of the ex-president was lying in state in the cathedral, shots were heard from the vicinity of the custom house, immediately followed by scattered firing from all parts of the city. Even the soldiers of the regular army, drawn up in front of the cathedral, fired promiscuously, and pistols were actually discharged in the cathedral itself. In great confusion the body of the ex-president was rushed to the cemetery, followed by an unruly mob. It was evident that the time-honoured preliminaries of a new "election" were under way.

BLACK DEMOCRACY

Beaufossé Laroche and General Defly were both candidates for the presidency. General Poitevien, Commander of the Army, and Ducasse, Commander of the Police, united to oppose both these candidates. General Defly surrounded the chamber of the national assembly with the intention of forcing his own election, but was compelled to withdraw by the superior force of Poitevien and took refuge in one of the consulates.

On the fourth of May, Senator Michel Oreste, "under the protection of Poitevien," was chosen by the national assembly for a term of seven years. This was the first election of a civilian to the presidency in the history of Haiti.

Oreste had long been popular with the people, and had been several times elected to the Chamber of Deputies and to the Senate, in spite of opposition on the part of the government in power. He was a trained lawyer and an accomplished speaker.

Depending on public support for a program of reform of the military establishment, President Oreste's first official acts were to introduce measures to reduce military expenditures. The military chiefs, however, were too strong for him. An insurrection almost immediately gathered headway in the North, and finding that he could not count on his friends or on public opinion, he abdicated, sailing for Jamaica after less than nine months of his seven-year term.

In the short period of Oreste's incumbency, he succeeded in setting aside a considerable sum of money obtained by a special tax on tobacco, for the purpose of building primary schools. This sum was spent in the first weeks of the succeeding administration "for military purposes."

The insurrection in the North against Oreste had been started by Davilmar Theodore, and on Oreste's abdication Theodore proceeded with his caco army in a campaign practically identical with that which had placed Leconte in office. But Theodore made a mistake in choosing his col-

REVOLUTIONARY PERIOD, 1908–1915

laborators. Under President Oreste, Charles Zamor had been delegate of the Department of the North and his brother, Oreste Zamor, had been Commandant of the *arrondissement* of Gonaives. Both of them had resigned in consequence of Oreste's military reform policies. They were, however, very influential in the North and also extremely ambitious, and when Theodore, leading the army of the North, reached Gonaives, a caco army controlled by the Zamors mingled with his troops. In the general excitement, during which the town was burned, Theodore and his cohorts were chased into the hills.

The Zamor brothers then proceeded towards Port-au-Prince. On January 27, 1914, Michel Oreste abdicated and left for Jamaica, and on February 8, 1914, under pressure of the caco army, the national assembly proceeded to elect the elder Zamor to the presidency for a term of seven years, which lasted, however, eight months and twenty days.

Approaching Bankruptcy under Zamor

During Zamor's short-lived but turbulent administration, he was principally engaged in a defensive campaign against Theodore, who had not relinquished his ambition to become president, and in efforts to raise money to "maintain the government." One of his most pressing needs, if he were to retain office, was to satisfy the demands of his caco chiefs for payment for their services.

A second internal bond issue of a face value of $609,000 had been issued under Michel Oreste's administration to meet current expenses. These bonds were offered at 94, but as it was provided that subscriptions would be received in *gourdes* [2] at the rate of 3.50 *gourdes* to one dollar gold, and as the actual value of exchange was then 4.17 *gourdes* to one dollar, the bonds really netted only 78.8.

There was still little or no money in the treasury, a

foreign loan was out of the question, and Zamor resorted to the plan initiated by Leconte and floated an internal bond issue of a face value of $712,000, authorized by law for the purpose of defraying his election expenses and providing funds for current expenses of the government. A large part of the proceeds of the loan, which netted only about 60 per cent, was used for immediate distribution among the caco chiefs.

In June, 1914, while Zamor was in the North endeavouring to quell the Theodore insurrection, a third loan was authorized to meet the "extraordinary expenses of the government." This issue, of $525,000 face value, netted about 56 per cent and was almost immediately followed by another for a slightly smaller amount on practically the same terms.

These internal bonds were subscribed almost entirely in Haiti, largely by German merchants or agents for German banking institutions, and were generally secured by setting aside specific customs duties. They had no fixed date of maturity but were, until 1915, amortized very rapidly, as the yield of customs duties segregated for this purpose in excess of the amount required for payment of interest was used for the amortization of the principal.

Some of these "revolutionary" loans, openly characterized in Haiti as cold-blooded graft, were issued at an absurdly small proportion of their face value. Although there were, from time to time, some genuine investments by local capitalists, most of these loans were subscribed by firms or individuals who received extraordinary profits by assisting the aspirants to the presidency or the government pro-tem to meet their pressing needs. In return for this assistance they received concessions, which virtually handed over to them important customs duties and other valuable privileges.

These privileges were highly profitable to the subscribers, for the chance of backing the winning president was naturally a highly speculative one, and the reward had to be correspondingly high. They were, of course, equally ruinous to the honest creditors of the Haitian government whose claims were secured by these same customs duties. Up to the outbreak of the war, German nationals and German firms were prominent, if not predominant, in these subversive but, under the circumstances, highly natural transactions.

In August, 1914, a law was promulgated by the Zamor Government suspending the retirement of paper money and authorizing the use "for current expenses" of the interest on the 10,000,000 francs which had been set aside for the retirement of government bills and also the use of funds from certain duties which had been pledged for this same purpose. This "law," in so far as the use of these pledged funds was concerned, the bank held to be contrary both to the sense and to the spirit of the contract under which it operated. On the advice of eminent Haitian counsel, the Bank refused to pay out pledged funds except as specifically provided in the convention.

In the fall Zamor, who had again taken the field against Theodore, was decisively defeated. Retreating to Gonaives, he sailed on a Dutch steamer for Port-au-Prince.

First Steps toward American Intervention

In the meantime the United States government had been closely watching events. United States warships had visited Port-au-Prince in January, 1914, and on the twenty-eighth of that month an American ship had, in company with forces from British, French, and German warships, landed marines to protect foreign interests. An American warship had remained continuously in the harbour of Port-au-Prince from January 25 to February 23, 1914, and other ships made repeated visits during the spring and summer of this year.

In October, 1914, the Zamor Government was approached by the American minister in connexion with negotiations for a treaty between the two governments, and a rumour to this effect was used by Zamor's opponents to weaken his already precarious position. Zamor arrived at Port-au-Prince on October 29th, and on that day resigned his office without leaving the Dutch ship on which he had come from Gonaives.

The way now being open, Davilmar Theodore entered Port-au-Prince at the head of his caco army, and on the seventh of November, 1914, he was elected to the presidency for a term of seven years. He served three months and fifteen days.

The United States withheld recognition of the Theodore Government and proposed a commission for the purpose of drawing up a convention on the lines of the Dominican-American Treaty of 1906, which had already effected a complete reform in the finances of that country.[3]

The Secretary of State for Foreign Affairs, on December third, reported to the Haitian Senate that the American minister had made proposals to the Haitian government relative to a convention for the control of the customs; this announcement was greeted with hoots of disapproval. On the tenth of December the American minister presented to the Haitian government a project for a convention. The Haitian government replied that it could not accept such an agreement, and on the nineteenth the American minister stated that the United States would not insist on the project, saying that in expressing its willingness to do in Haiti what had been successfully done in the Dominican Republic, the United States "was actuated entirely by a disinterested desire to give assistance."

Under the terms of the Loan Contract of 1910, the

REVOLUTIONARY PERIOD, 1908-1915

Banque Nationale de la République d'Haïti was designated as the sole treasury of the government and, as such, received all customs collections and other government revenues, and was empowered to hold such moneys intact until the end of each fiscal year.

While there was nothing in this contract specifically providing for the advancement of money for current government needs, the bank, under a budgetary convention, had extended certain accommodations to the government, in spite of the fact that these advances endangered the punctual payment of pledged funds. In July, 1914, the American minister in Haiti had notified the Department of State that the bank was planning to refuse to renew the budgetary convention on its expiration at the end of the fiscal year (September 31st), and stated that the suspension of the convention most likely would bring the government to a condition where it could not operate. "It is just this condition," said the minister, "that the bank desires, for it is the belief of the bank that the government, when confronted by such a crisis, would be forced to ask the assistance of the United States in adjusting its financial tangle, and that the American supervision of the customs would result." *
On October first, the bank refused to renew this convention.

Theodore was in a most critical situation. The usual revolutionary program was in full swing in the North. The President had no money with which to satisfy the leaders, and the soldiers of the Republic, practically never paid, had no heart to oppose the caco bands of the North.[4]

Customs receipts, on which the government depended for revenue, were largely pledged to guarantee domestic or foreign loans, and being unable to raise funds by further bond issues, Theodore resorted to the expedient of issuing 12,000,000 *gourdes* [2] in treasury notes. These notes, issued in small denominations, were for a time accepted in payment

* *Foreign Relations of the United States,* 1914.

of surtaxes on imports, but the bank protested their legality and they were gradually outlawed.*

Salvaging $500,000 of Haiti's Pledged Funds

Although Davilmar Theodore had been in office only a few weeks, the position of his Government was generally recognized as precarious, and when, in December, he threatened to seize by force certain government funds held by the bank pledged to the redemption of paper money, the bank requested the United States Department of State to remove these funds and hold them for safe-keeping.

On December 17, 1914, the U.S.S. *Machias,* acting under instructions from the Navy Department, landed marines at Port-au-Prince and removed $500,000 of the reserve funds. This money, which was in gold coin, was taken to New York and deposited in the National City Bank, where it remained until 1919, when, a monetary reform agreement between the government and the bank having been executed, the money was returned with two per cent (per annum) interest.

There seems no doubt but that the bank, which was supported by the ablest Haitian lawyers, acted in defence of its rights to prevent the misappropriation of national funds for which it was rightfully a trustee, and which would have been promptly dissipated for that euphemism so familiar in Haiti, "military expenses."

Shortly after his election, Davilmar Theodore had acceded to the demand of General Vilbrun Guillaume Sam that he should be appointed a "delegate" of the Departments of the North and North-west. About the middle of January, General Sam convoked a meeting of civil and military authorities at Cap Haitien and informed them that

* In 1925 these so-called Davilmar notes were redeemed by a judgment of the international claims commission at far less than their face value.

REVOLUTIONARY PERIOD, 1908-1915

the city was threatened by a revolutionary army which it was impossible for him to resist. He also reminded his hearers that he was himself a candidate for the presidency. A few days later General Metallus entered Cap Haitien with one thousand cacos and proclaimed Vilbrun Guillaume Sam *chef du pouvoir exécutif*. The people of the Departments of the North and North-west generally accepting Sam as their candidate for the presidency, a new revolution was inaugurated.

In January, 1915, the American consul at Cap Haitien requested the presence of an American vessel. This consul, a very intelligent American Negro married to a Haitian lady of a prominent family, was perhaps the best qualified man in Haiti to judge as to the necessity for such assistance. The revolutionary movement started by Vilbrun Guillaume Sam was pursuing the usual course, the North was seething with "revolutionary spirit," and the Cape, crowded with revolutionary troops, was threatened with an attack from a Haitian warship reported to be proceeding to that port. The American consul had vainly endeavoured to send messages to Admiral Caperton, then at sea, and had protested to General Sam against orders that had been issued to withhold the use of the cable from him.

Admiral William B. Caperton, U.S.N., who arrived on the U.S.S. *Washington* on January 23rd, was informed by the American consul of the usual methods pursued by the revolutionary armies. He was told that Sam, who had placed himself at the head of the revolution, planned to proceed from Cap Haitien to Gonaives, thence to St.-Marc, and finally to Port-au-Prince, capturing each of these towns as he proceeded. At the suggestion of the American consul, Admiral Caperton met General Sam "unofficially" and exacted a promise that there should be no looting or burning of towns on the proposed march to the capital.

As Sam's army, following the usual procedure, moved

out of Cap Haitien towards the South, Admiral Caperton, with the U.S.S. *Washington,* sailed for Port-au-Prince, assigning other ships to Gonaives and St.-Marc, and instructing their commanders to remind Sam of his promise not to burn or loot the cities and towns.[5] In view of the financial condition of the Haitian government, and the revolutionary movement in the North, Admiral Caperton decided to keep in close touch with the American minister at Port-au-Prince and stand by for any emergency. As a precaution he mounted a field radio set at the American legation.

Admiral Caperton "Personally Conducts" a Revolution

Gonaives was taken by Sam's forces during the first week in February, and on the eighth the commanding officer of the U.S.S. *Des Moines* reported that St.-Marc was in the hands of the revolutionists. It was generally believed that Theodore would leave Haiti on a Dutch steamer momentarily expected at Port-au-Prince, which he did, sailing on the twenty-second of February, and on the twenty-third Sam's army entered the capital.[6]

So solicitous was Admiral Caperton that the comparatively peaceful program of revolution as prescribed by him be carried out by Sam's army that during the campaign American naval forces had virtually extended to the revolutionists a personally conducted tour to Gonaives, St.-Marc, and Port-au-Prince. As each large town was reached on the 180-mile journey, General Sam was increasingly amazed to find American officers awaiting him, who repeated the Admiral's warning. The towns along the way were consequently spared any serious disorder, but it is said that this new idea in revolutions mystified the caco army as much as it did the government forces.

On March 4, 1915, the national assembly elected Vilbrun Guillaume Sam President of Haiti, and on the following

REVOLUTIONARY PERIOD, 1908–1915

day ex-Governor Fort of New Jersey and Mr. C. C. Smith, commissioners to Haiti from the United States, arrived at Port-au-Prince. Sam was inaugurated on the ninth of March, and on the following day the American commissioners held an official conference with the President and later with the Minister for Foreign Affairs regarding the proposed convention between the two governments.

American Commissioners Fail to Negotiate a Treaty

On the twelfth, Governor Fort cabled the Department of State that the commission had full possession of the facts and that a "longer stay or further efforts would not accomplish more." * As a matter of fact, the Minister for Foreign Affairs held that this commission was without proper credentials to negotiate a treaty and, naturally being most unwilling to negotiate, he used this as a reason for refusing further conferences. Governor Fort and Mr. Smith left Haiti on March 15th.

About two months later, Paul Fuller, Jr., arrived at Port-au-Prince accredited as the Special Agent and Minister Plenipotentiary of the United States to the government of Haiti. On May 21st he was received by the President, to whom he explained the object of his mission, and on the following day he presented to the Minister for Foreign Affairs a project of a treaty. Ten days later the minister sent Mr. Fuller a counter project, and after some further negotiations Mr. Fuller left for the United States and these negotiations were not resumed.

Less than two months after Sam's election, Dr. Rosalvo Bobo, Minister of the Interior in the cabinet of Theodore, inaugurated another revolution in the North, and by the middle of June he had occupied Cap Haitien with a caco army. On June 19, 1915, the government troops entered the town, Bobo retired with his army, and the French cruiser

* *Foreign Relations of the United States,* 1915.

BLACK DEMOCRACY

Descartes landed fifty marines at Cap Haitien to protect the French consulate and the bank, which was then controlled by French interests. This landing resulted in the immediate dispatch of Admiral Caperton, then at Vera Cruz, with orders to proceed to Cap Haitien, thank the French commander, and take necessary steps to "protect property and preserve order."

Admiral Caperton arrived at Cap Haitien on the U.S.S. *Washington* on July 1, 1915, having detailed the U.S.S. *Eagle* to proceed to Port-au-Prince for news of conditions there. The commander of the *Descartes* explained that, acting on instructions from the French minister to Haiti, he had landed a detail from his ship to protect the French consulate and the bank and that his landing had been protested by the Haitian government and the German minister at Port-au-Prince. He placed himself at the disposal of the American admiral and inquired if Admiral Caperton's instructions interfered with his remaining at Cap Haitien, stating that in any event the French cruiser would have to leave shortly for coal.

After conferences with the American and French consuls and with the commanding officer of the government forces then holding Cap Haitien, Admiral Caperton decided that he would not allow any fighting within the city walls, and drew up an order stating that he was present to protect lives and property of foreigners, which would, he believed, be threatened should there be any fighting at Cap Haitien, and that he must therefore *"insist that no fighting whatever take place in the town of Cap Haitien and that the contending factions fight their battles well clear of the town."* He added that *"he had no intention of questioning the sovereignty of the Haitian nation, or of maintaining any but a neutral attitude towards the contending factions."* * But

* *Hearings before Select Committee on Haiti and Santo Domingo, U.S. Senate, 1921, p. 307.*

REVOLUTIONARY PERIOD, 1908-1915

he also stated that if it should become necessary he was prepared to land United States forces at Cap Haitien. This order, which was issued, the Admiral has testified, in conformity with his instructions from Washington to protect lives and property of foreigners, was served on the commandant of the government troops, and a copy sent to Dr. Bobo, then on the outskirts of the city.

On July 3rd, Admiral Caperton, who had not previously landed troops, sent a small detail ashore to set up and man a field radio set in the railroad yard. This was done with the previous knowledge of the commander of the government troops, who made no objection. From this date until the twenty-seventh, the Admiral lay off the Cape watching the movements of the revolutionary forces. On the morning of the twenty-seventh, reports were received of a serious situation at Port-au-Prince, and in reply to a cable to the American *chargé d'affaires* at the capital, Admiral Caperton was informed that the palace had been attacked, that the President was in refuge at the French legation, that many political prisoners had been assassinated, and that the presence of a warship at the capital was urgently necessary. On receipt of this dispatch, the Admiral withdrew his landing forces and proceeded at full speed for Port-au-Prince, leaving an American gunboat at the Cape. On the following day the gunboat, at the request of the French consul, landed twenty men to protect foreign interests.

Up to this time active intervention in the affairs of Haiti had been confined to occasional landing of troops to protect foreign lives and property, attempts to persuade the Haitian government to enter into an arrangement somewhat similar to the American-Dominican convention, and Admiral Caperton's warnings that the lives and property of foreigners should not be endangered by fighting in the streets of the cities or by the looting and burning of towns.

BLACK DEMOCRACY

But events were going forward at Port-au-Prince destined to change the history of Haiti, and to bring at last to a culmination the steps already taken toward American interference in the Republic's affairs.

CHAPTER II

THE AMERICAN INTERVENTION

IN Port-au-Prince most of the month of July had passed in comparative quiet. The situation was, however, recognized by everyone as extremely precarious, and the progress of Bobo's revolution in the North was watched with intense interest.

President Sam, convinced of the existence of plots against him in the capital, initiated a clean sweep of suspects and incarcerated in the national prison many of the most prominent men of Haiti. The legations, however, with the exception of that of the United States, which since 1908 had refused to harbour political refugees, were crowded with men who, anticipating arrest, had sought asylum under foreign flags. From these places of safety conspiracies against Sam were conducted with little risk to the plotters, and towards the end of the month it was common knowledge in Port-au-Prince that plots against Sam were maturing. The stage was set for the usual revolutionary program, and if Sam had played his part in a conventional manner he would have sailed for Jamaica or some other West Indian island, and Bobo, with his caco army, would have entered the capital and "elected" himself president of the Republic.

Revolutions had seldom involved actual fighting in the capital, but when a revolution did start in the city, or when citizens of the capital participated, it was customary to divide the forces into bands, one to attack the palace, one the bureau of the *arrondissement,* one the bureau of La Place, one the bureau of the Port, and in the event that political prisoners of prominence were confined, a strong detachment was sent to the national prison to liberate them.

The Situation on the Night of July 26th

On this occasion there were, however, unusual conditions: first, the presence in Haitian waters of United States warships and the arbitrary orders issued by Admiral Caperton that fighting in the cities would not be tolerated, and, second, the presence in the capital of a large force of cacos under the command of General Metallus, the same leader who had proclaimed Sam president in the Cape. Another unusual feature was the character of the President, who was known for his unscrupulous and relentless cruelty and personal courage.

To sum up the situation as it existed on the night of July 26th at Cap Haitien: Bobo, with his cacos, was threatening the town, then held by government troops, and Admiral Caperton, with the U.S.S. *Washington,* was in that harbour, watching events. At Port-au-Prince, President Sam, fearing an uprising in the city, had encamped his caco troops in a yard adjoining the palace, but since it was known that these cacos had been tampered with, and that their loyalty to Sam was questionable, their action in the event of an uprising was problematical. By this time the political prisoners confined in the national prison numbered about two hundred, and the foreign legations were crowded with refugees, including some of the most influential men in Haiti.

It was known that conspiracies against Sam were coming to a head, and the President, anticipating an attack, spent the night of July 26th on the porch of the palace, surrounded by his aides and body-guard. Towards morning, as the guard was changed at the palace gate, a small band led by Charles de Delva rushed the guard and opened fire on the palace. Accounts of what followed are confusing and

THE AMERICAN INTERVENTION

conflicting. It is known that for a short period some of Sam's personal body-guard made a valiant effort to defend him, but his caco army, after a little indiscriminate shooting, abandoned the President to his fate. Shortly after daybreak Sam, realizing that he had been deserted by his friends, took refuge in the French legation, which adjoins the building then used as the national palace.* Being unable to open an iron door in the wall, he was compelled to scale the barrier and, wounded in the leg, fell within the legation grounds and was assisted to the building by General Charles Zamor.

At the request of President Sam, the French minister sent a messenger to Charles Oscar Etienne, the commander of the *arrondissement*. This hastily written note, which was a few hours later taken from the dead body of General Etienne, is reproduced herewith:

July 27, 1915.

My dear Oscar:
   Having been assured by Minister Bonami that the Arrondissement, the Place, and the Port were in the hands of the revolutionists, which information he affirmed he had received from an authoritative source, and as up to later than half past eight not one of the authorities had come to my assistance, I decided to make my way to the French legation, where I now am. I greatly regret having been misinformed. As regards yourself, take such measures as your conscience shall dictate. Too much to say.
                                    Vilbrun Guillaume.

The Atrocity in the Prison

During the interval between the first attack on the palace and the dispatch of this note, there had taken place one of the most horrid and inexcusable crimes ever recorded against governmental agents in the history of Haiti, and

---
* Now the United States Marine Brigade Head-quarters.

—Note Found on the Body of General Charles Oscar Etienne, July 28, 1927—

BLACK DEMOCRACY

although it is impossible to doubt that Sam was aware of this atrocity, his note made no mention of it and expressed no regret or disapproval, but only complained that his Minister of Finance, Bonami, who, by the way, was at that very moment concealed in the grounds of the French legation, had misinformed him in stating that the chief military posts of the city were in the hands of the revolutionists.

Massacre in the National Prison

A few minutes after 4 A.M., Charles Oscar Etienne, the chief military officer of the Haitian government and a close friend of the President, hurried to the national prison, where ensued the bloody massacre of some 167 prisoners who were held only as political suspects without being even charged with any crime. Among the victims were members of the most prominent families of Haiti, including ex-President Oreste Zamor, Charles Germain, ex-commandant of the *arrondissement,* and others of equal social and political standing. The following is believed to be the first accurate account of the circumstances of the atrocity to be published.

Stephen Alexis, one of the political prisoners who escaped death in the massacre, has testified before the claims commission that on the morning of the twenty-eighth of July he was awakened by the prisoner who shared his cell and told that there was firing in town. He heard shots being fired with increasing intensity, and at twenty minutes past four the sound of voices in the *conciergerie* and the order, "To arms, sound the bugle, prepare for action; fifteen men, forward march." As the firing squad reached the first cell, Alexis heard Chocotte, the adjutant of the prison, say, "Fire close to the ground; a bullet in the head for each man," and when the second cell was reached a loud voice cried, "Every one of the political prisoners must die. The *arrondissement's* orders are that not one be left standing," and later he heard the gaoler remark, "They don't know the kind of man that General Vilbrun [President Sam] is; they are all going to bite the dust." Finally, when the carnage had ended, Alexis heard a voice in the *conciergerie* saying, "The *Arrondissement* congratulates you upon the good work you have done."

The work had, indeed, been thoroughly performed. Except for the very few who escaped by a miracle, the political prisoners were all slaughtered like cattle, their bodies slashed and horribly mutilated, limbs hacked off, the skulls of some of the corpses smashed in, and the bodies of others disembowelled. Another of the political prisoners who escaped testified that it appeared to him that Oscar strove to delay the execution, but was dissuaded from doing so either by Chocotte, Thrasybule Zamor, or Paul Herard, all three prison officials in responsible positions, one of whom said to Oscar, "No, the President has given orders to start killing at the first shot fired."

The report of the claims commission says: "The barbarous act perpetrated in the prison in Port-au-Prince is all the more inexplicable in that it had no act of war for excuse. There had been no revolt in the interior of the prison. The prisoners were locked into their cells. The prison had not been attacked. The bureau of the *arrondissement*, which adjoined the prison, had not had to repulse any offensive on the part of the revolutionists. It was with appalling cold-bloodedness that Haitian officers, in whom military authority had been vested, to whom the care and security of the prisoners had been entrusted, perpetrated, with the assistance of their subordinates, the wholesale slaughter of July 27."

News of this butchery and of Sam's escape to the French legation was received by the people with the utmost rage and horror. General Polynice, a man with a long record for distinguished service, rushed to the Dominican legation, where General Oscar Etienne had taken refuge, and, dragging him to the street, shot him three times through the body, one shot for each of the three young sons of Polynice who had been butchered in the prison. Within a few hours after Oscar met his well-deserved fate, and while the body still lay on the pavement, his home in Port-au-Prince was not only looted but actually ripped to pieces, so completely demolished that nothing was left except the foundations.

The prison, which had been forced open by the mob, was surrounded by a mass of sorrowing and enraged citizens. Hardly a prominent family in the capital but numbered among the victims one or more of its members. The bodies not too badly mutilated for identification were removed from the prison and, on the following day, conveyed to the cemetery and there buried. During the day of the massacre a huge mob surrounded the French legation and threats were made that Sam would be forcibly removed. In the afternoon a squad of soldiers led by Charles Zamor entered the legation grounds with the purpose of securing Sam, but were dissuaded by the young daughter of the French minister, who reminded General Zamor that for the past four or five months, while he was in refuge in the legation which he was then attempting to violate, she had herself attended to his comfort. Zamor, greatly moved by her pleading, led his men from the house and promised that the legation would not again be entered by soldiers, which promise he faithfully carried out.

The Murder of President Sam

On the morning of the twenty-eighth, as the people were returning from the funeral of the victims, the smoke of an American warship was seen in the outer harbour. The lead-

THE AMERICAN INTERVENTION

ers, realizing that the landing of foreign troops would prevent any chance of vengeance on Sam, led the people at once to the French legation. The mob remained without the gates, but a small body of well-known citizens, after courteously explaining to the French minister that the people were no longer to be baulked of their revenge, entered the house and, finding Sam under a bed in a spare room on an upper floor, pulled him down the stairs, dragged him along the driveway, and threw him over an iron gate to the mob. It is not known who did the actual killing, but it is said that the first mortal wound was inflicted by a woman. The body was then cut in pieces and paraded through the streets.

The U.S.S. *Washington* arrived in the harbour at 10:30 A.M. and was immediately boarded by the American *chargé d'affaires*. Admiral Caperton, while listening to the report of conditions ashore, had in his hands his glasses. "I was about a mile off," said the Admiral in his testimony at the Senate inquiry, "and I saw much confusion, people in the streets, and apparently there was a procession, as if they were dragging something through the city, and I afterwards found out, from officers whom I sent ashore, that this was the body of President Guillaume Sam, which had been mutilated, the arms cut off, the head cut off, and stuck on poles, and the torso drawn with ropes through the city."

Officers sent ashore to investigate returned to the U.S.S. *Washington,* accompanied by the French minister and the British *chargé d'affaires,* who united with the American *chargé* in assuring Admiral Caperton that there was no government or authority in Port-au-Prince. The President had been murdered, the French and Dominican legations violated, and a wild mob was in possession of the city. They united in strongly urging the immediate landing of American troops. In his testimony at the Senate inquiry, Admiral Caperton stated: "I think it but fair and just that I make some mention of the intense feeling and desire with which the French minister especially and the British *chargé d'affaires* insisted upon my landing immediately. The French minister has a family consisting of a wife and two daughters, and he said, 'They are there at the legation with no one to protect them. Now you see what is going on in the city.' And he begged that I land as quickly as possible, as did also the British *chargé d'affaires.*"

Admiral Caperton had already decided to order a landing when, at 3 P.M., he received from the Secretary of the Navy the following message:

> State Department desires that American forces be landed at Port-au-Prince and that American and foreign interests be protected; that representatives of England and France be informed of this intention—informed that their interests will be protected and that they are requested not to land. . . . *

At 5 P.M. on July 28, 1915, a provisional regiment consisting of two companies of marines and three of bluejackets was landed at Bizoton, about three miles from the centre of the town.

The Inception of the American Occupation

From Bizoton the American troops marched to the city, where guards were placed at the legations and the main body bivouacked for the night. While this was not by any means the first time the United States had intervened in the affairs of Haiti, this moment marks the inception of the intervention by the armed forces of the United States.†

On July 29th, Admiral Caperton cabled the Navy De-

---

* *Hearings before Select Committee on Haiti and Santo Domingo, U.S. Senate,* 1921, p. 307.

† In order not to break the chronological thread of this story of Haiti, the author has placed in the Appendix a brief but comprehensive review of the many interventions of the United States in Haiti. See note 1.

THE AMERICAN INTERVENTION

partment that a landing force had been established, and that as there was no existing government it was necessary for him to assume military authority. He further stated that a regiment of marines would be absolutely necessary.

After consultation with a committee of public safety which had been organized by prominent Haitians, the Admiral, assuming complete authority, proceeded to disarm the citizens and soldiers. The committee of safety, which was practically unanimous in favouring the candidacy of Dr. Bobo, proposed the dissolution of the national assembly and even issued a proclamation to this effect. Admiral Caperton, however, holding that this committee was self-constituted and without authority, refused to countenance its action. The Admiral has stated that his procedure in landing troops was in accordance with orders which he had received to protect lives and preserve property, and the following dispatch sent by him to the Secretary of the Navy, on August 2nd, appears to be the first forecast of the policy later pursued in Haiti:

> Large number Haitian revolutions, largely due existing professional soldiers called cacos, organized in bands under lawless, irresponsible chiefs, who fight on side offering greatest inducement and but nominally recognize the government. Cacos are feared by all Haitians and practically control politics. About 1,500 cacos now in Port-au-Prince, ostensibly disarmed, but retain organization and believed to have arms and ammunition hidden. They have demanded election Bobo, President, and Congress, terrorized by mere demand, is on point of complying, but restrained by my request. Present condition no other man can be elected account fear of cacos. Believe can control Congress. Can prevent any cacos outbreak in Port-au-Prince after arrival regiment of marines U.S.S. *Connecticut*. Stable government not possible in Haiti until cacos are disbanded and power broken.
>
> Such action now imperative at Port-au-Prince if United States desires to negotiate treaty for financial control

of Haiti. To accomplish this must have regiment of marines in addition to that on *Connecticut*. Majority populace well-disposed and submissive, and will welcome disbanding cacos and stopping revolutions. Should agreement with Haiti be desired, recommend Capt. Beach, U.S.N., be appointed single commissioner for United States, with full instructions and authority. He has conducted my negotiations on shore, and I believe has confidence generally of Haitians. As future relations between United States and Haiti depend largely on course of action taken at this time, earnestly request to be fully informed of policy of United States.

CAPERTON.*

Contemporary Reasons for Interventions

In reply to a question by one of the members of the Senate committee which investigated the American occupation in Haiti and Santo Domingo as to what was meant by the clause, "such action now imperative if United States desires to negotiate treaty for financial control of Haiti," the Admiral stated that he did not know why he mentioned "financial control" but that he had in mind that "if we wished to form a treaty with Haiti for all purposes, and a treaty like the one we finally did succeed in getting ratified, the expression 'financial control' would be one part of the treaty." In reference to the last part of this dispatch, in which he said, "As future relations between the United States and Haiti depend largely on course of action at this time," the Admiral was asked if he had been informed of any policy of the Navy Department prior to that date, and made the somewhat extraordinary reply, "No definite policy," but further stated that on August 7th, which was about ten days after the landing of troops, he received from Washington the following message:

Senate Hearings, p. 313.

THE AMERICAN INTERVENTION

Conciliate Haitians to fullest extent consistent with maintaining order and full control of situation, and issue following proclamation: "Am directed to assure the Haitian people United States of America has no object in view except to insure, establish, and help to maintain Haitian independence and the re-establishing of a stable and firm government by the Haitian people. Every assistance will be given to the Haitian people in their attempt to secure these ends. It is the intention to retain United States forces in Haiti only so long as will be necessary for this purpose." Acknowledge.

BENSON, acting.*

Additional light on the policy of the United States towards Haiti at the time of the intervention was cast in a letter from Robert Lansing to the Senate committee investigating the occupation of Haiti and Santo Domingo in 1922, in which the ex-Secretary of State said that the two dominating ideas of the policy of the State Department at the time of the intervention were:

> To terminate the appalling conditions of anarchy, savagery, and oppression which had been prevalent in Haiti for decades, and to undertake the establishment of domestic peace in the Republic in order that the population who had been downtrodden by dictators and the innocent victims of repeated revolutions should enjoy prosperity and an economic and industrial development to which every people of an American nation are entitled.
> A desire to forestall any attempt by a foreign power to obtain a foothold on the territory of an American nation, which, if the seizure of customs control by such a power had occurred, or if a grant of a coaling station or naval base had been obtained, would most certainly have been a menace to the peace of the Western Hemisphere and in flagrant defiance of the Monroe Doctrine.†

---

* *Senate Hearings*, p. 313.
† *Ibid.*

BLACK DEMOCRACY

German Aspirations

Mr. Lansing further stated that he had information that Germany not only contemplated but had taken preliminary steps towards securing exclusive customs control of Haiti and a naval base at Mole St. Nicholas.

This had been denied by Germany in 1914, but at that time Germany stated that "the German government has joined with other European governments in representing to Washington that the interests of European countries in Haiti are so large that no scheme of reorganization or control can be regarded as acceptable unless it is undertaken under international auspices." This challenge to the then well-known endeavour of the United States to secure a convention with Haiti could not be ignored, and undoubtedly influenced the attitude of the American State Department towards Haiti. Nor can too much emphasis be laid on the fact that at the time the American government actually had to decide on intervention in Haiti, it was by no means assured that Germany might not later, after a victory over the Allies, make good its plainly expressed pretensions.

During the five years which preceded the American intervention, the foreign relations of the Haitian government had become seriously involved because of pressure from the governments of Great Britain, France, Germany, Italy, and the United States to obtain settlement of claims of their nationals, and armed forces of foreign powers had been landed at Haitian ports. It is possible that the attitude of the Department of State was influenced by the situation created by the World War, but it is certain that there had for some time been reason to fear foreign interference in Haiti and the possible seizure of an important strategical position on the island by a foreign power.[2] Mr. Root has said the Monroe Doctrine rests upon "the right of every sovereign state to protect itself by preventing a condition of

THE AMERICAN INTERVENTION

affairs in which it will be too late to protect itself," and John Bassett Moore has written that the American intervention in Cuba was "analogous to what is known in private law as the abatement of a nuisance." It is evident that the United States government considered that the psychological moment for the abatement of this particular nuisance had arrived.

Preparing for the Presidential Election

On the 31st of July the Chamber of Deputies had proposed a presidential election, but had deferred action at the "request" of Admiral Caperton. In the North, revolutionary activities had continued unabated, Cap Haitien was threatened, and the French minister had requested that steps be taken to guard the French legation. On August 1st, Admiral Caperton, pursuing his policy of control of the situation, sent a commission to the Cape for the purpose of disbanding the opposing armies. This commission, which included ex-President Légitime, Archbishop Conan, General Polynice, Charles Zamor, and André Chevallier, returned to Port-au-Prince on the fifth of August with Dr. Bobo and twenty-six "generals." On the same day Admiral Caperton sent the following message to the Secretary of the Navy:

> To-day Haitian congress published notice it would elect president Sunday, but was postponed at my request because time is inopportune. Am informed congress would elect Menos, Haitian minister at Washington, if here. In absence Menos am informed president of senate, Dartiguenave, will be elected. From many other sources hear Dartiguenave is man of personal honour and patriotism. Has never been connected with any revolution, is of good ability, and anxious for Haiti's regeneration, realizes Haiti must agree to any terms laid down by the United States, professes to believe any terms demanded will be for Haiti's benefit, says he will use all his influence with

Haitian congress to have such terms agreed upon by Haiti. If elected must be sustained by American protection. Same condition applies to whoever else is elected. Bobo only other prominent candidate. Bobo said to be man of intellectuality, honour, and patriotism. Friends maintain would work solely for Haiti's good. Bobo could be elected only through fear of cacos, and if elected revolution against him would undoubtedly start unless prevented by United States.

Great relief expressed by all classes except cacos at presence of American troops. Americans afford hope of relief from government by terror. Universally believed that if Americans depart, government will lapse into complete anarchy. My opinion is that United States must expect to remain in Haiti until native government is self-sustaining and people educated to respect laws and abide by them. Should president be elected now there would be complete machinery for all government functions. With American protection and influenced by United States, progress towards good government could be soon commenced. Haitian people anxious to have president elected, because at present no central government in Haiti except as directed by me. Also people uneasy, fearing United States may not permit continuance of Haitian independence.*

That a policy had by this time been determined upon is shown by the following message from the Secretary of the Navy, received by Admiral Caperton on August 10th:

Allow election of president to take place whenever Haitians wish. The United States prefers election of Dartiguenave. Has no other motive than that establishment of firm and lasting government by Haitian people and to assist them now and at all times in future to maintain their political independence and territorial integrity. United States will insist that the Haitian government will grant no territorial concessions to foreign governments. The government of the United States will

* *Senate Hearings*, p. 312.

THE AMERICAN INTERVENTION

take up the question of the cession of Mole St. Nicholas later along with the other questions to be submitted to the reorganized government with regard to its relation to the United States.*

The Quizzing of the Presidential Candidate

At the same time the Secretary of State advised the American minister in Haiti that in view of the fact that Admiral Caperton had been instructed by the Navy Department that he might allow an election for the president "whenever the Haitians wished," it was desired that the Minister confer with the Admiral to the end that, in some way to be determined between them, "the following things be made perfectly clear":

> First: Let Congress understand that the government of the United States intends to uphold it but that it cannot recognize action which does not establish in charge of Haitian affairs those whose abilities and dispositions give assurances of putting an end to factional disorder.
> Second: In order that no misunderstanding can possibly occur after election it should be made perfectly clear to candidates, as soon as possible, and in advance of their election, that the United States expects to be entrusted with the practical control of the customs and such financial control over the affairs of the Republic of Haiti as the United States may deem necessary for efficient administration. The government of the United States considers it its duty to support a constitutional government. It means to assist in the establishment of such a government and to support it as long as necessity may require. It has no design upon the political or territorial integrity of Haiti. On the contrary, what has been done, as well as what will be done, is conceived in an effort to aid the people in establishing a stable government and maintaining domestic peace throughout the Republic.†

* *Senate Hearings*, p. 315.
† *Ibid.*

BLACK DEMOCRACY

Among other prominent Haitians who were approached in connexion with becoming candidates for the presidency were Mr. J. N. Léger, Mr. Salon Menos, and ex-President Légitime. Mr. Léger Admiral Caperton later described as one of the most distinguished of living Haitians, "a gentleman educated in Paris, a famous traveller, author, and diplomat, former minister at Paris and Washington," and as a man who would have been "undoubtedly satisfactory to the United States." But, approached by Admiral Caperton's chief of staff, Mr. Léger replied: "Tell the Admiral I will do everything in my power for Haiti, but I must watch and see what the United States will demand of Haiti and be in a position to defend Haiti's interests in case the demands should be unreasonable. At this time I could not possibly accept the presidency. I am for Haiti, not for the United States."

Mr. Menos, then the Haitian minister at Washington, peremptorily refused to accept the presidency, as did also ex-President Légitime, a venerable Haitian who had the confidence of all classes.

The night of the tenth of August and the day of the eleventh passed quietly at Port-au-Prince, but there was considerable uneasiness; some small demonstrations took place, owing to the approaching election, and a number of cacos were arrested.

A few days previously Admiral Caperton had arranged a meeting between Dr. Bobo and Senator Dartiguenave, then the two most prominent presidential candidates, for the purpose of ascertaining their views and their feelings towards the United States.

At this meeting, held at the American legation, were present Senator Dartiguenave, Dr. Bobo, and two United States Navy staff officers. Dartiguenave and Bobo were addressed as follows: "Gentlemen, it seems likely that one of you will be elected president of Haiti. Haiti is in great

THE AMERICAN INTERVENTION

trouble; she has suffered much. The United States has come to Haiti as a good friend, interested only in Haiti's welfare, in her happiness, in her prosperity. The United States has determined that revolution and disorder and anarchy must cease in Haiti; that unselfish and devoted patriotism must characterize hereafter the acts of the Haitian government. Senator Dartiguenave and Dr. Bobo, realizing this momentous crisis in Haitian history, with the eyes of Haiti and of the United States upon you, do you promise that if elected president of Haiti you will, in your official acts, be guided solely by earnest devotion to Haiti's honour and welfare?"

Admiral Caperton has reported that Dartiguenave replied, "I will so promise," "I have no other ambition than to be of service to my country"; and that Bobo exclaimed, rather theatrically, "I promise. I would be happy to lay down my life for my beloved country." The Admiral's report continues: "Senator Dartiguenave, in case Dr. Bobo should be elected, will you promise that you will exert every influence in your power to assist him for Haiti's good; that you will join him heartily and helpfully and loyally?" "If Dr. Bobo is elected president I will give him the most loyal, earnest support in every effort he may make for Haiti's welfare," replied Dartiguenave, with simple dignity.

"Dr. Bobo, if Senator Dartiguenave is elected president, will you help him loyally and earnestly in his efforts to benefit Haiti?" "No, I will not!" shouted Bobo. "If Senator Dartiguenave is elected president I will not help him. I will go away and leave Haiti to her fate. I alone am fit to be president of Haiti; I alone understand Haiti's aspirations; no one is fit to be president but me; there is no patriotism in Haiti to be compared with mine; the Haitians love no one as they love me." * This seems to have been Bobo's swan song.

* *Senate Hearings*, p. 316.

BLACK DEMOCRACY

Admiral Caperton, in his testimony, said, "I might mention another meeting that I had, trying to ascertain the feelings and purposes, and what these gentlemen would do if they were elected president, because I did not know. I felt, as the talk grew about Senator Dartiguenave, that I desired to know something about him. This, I might add, was previous to the other meeting. I sent two of my staff officers to converse with Senator Dartiguenave. My particular purpose was to gain a personal knowledge of Senator Dartiguenave and of his views and attitude towards Haiti and the United States. My idea was that the man most suitable for the Haitian presidency was one in whom the Haitians had confidence, one whose animating purpose would be Haiti's welfare, to which purpose he would give unselfish devotion; and also one who combined such qualifications with confidence in the United States, who was friendly disposed towards the United States, who wanted her help, and who would listen sympathetically to the intentions of the United States. There was never any bargaining of any kind whatever with Dartiguenave, as far as I know. No pressure of any kind was brought to bear upon any Haitian elector in Dartiguenave's interest. The Haitians themselves without any outside influence or pressure or bargaining made him, later, their president." *

While it is generally conceded that no actual pressure was brought to bear on the individual electors (the vote stood 94 for Dartiguenave out of a total of 116), it is certain that the caco element, supported by many influential men of Port-au-Prince, was united for Bobo, and obvious that Dartiguenave could not have been elected if the presence of the armed forces of the United States had not prevented the caco army from repeating the time-honoured program. Moreover, Admiral Caperton had been informed "by law-abiding Haitians" that Dr. Bobo and his adherents,

* *Senate Hearings*, p. 317.

THE AMERICAN INTERVENTION

realizing that if an election were held at that moment Bobo would be defeated, had determined to prevent an election by starting a riot.

On receiving this information, Admiral Caperton notified the committee of safety, which was understood to have inspired and planned this by no means novel proceeding, that their conspiracy to plunge Port-au-Prince into riot and bloodshed was known and would be prevented, and he informed them that they were no longer to exercise any authority whatever in the capital.

The committee, according to the Admiral, made no pretence of denial or innocence but seemed to be fearful that they might be unable to stop the riot. One of the members contented himself with remarking in a jocular way, "Admiral, you have won."

After taking the oath of office, President Dartiguenave announced that he had been elected because he belonged to no political faction, and was free from all political obligations; that it was the understanding of all Haiti that he, as president, would have the support and help of the United States; but that he had made no promises, and was under no obligation except as expressed in his oath of office.

Dr. Bobo had resigned his self-assumed office as "chief of the executive power" on his arrival at Port-au-Prince, but his supporters were still in the field, and the next step taken by the Admiral was to disband them and to disarm the government troops. This was accomplished with little difficulty, and a short time later Bobo, thoroughly disgusted with events, left Haiti.

CHAPTER III

THE HAITIAN-AMERICAN TREATY

THE intervention having been peacefully accomplished and a president representing the best political classes in Haiti placed securely in office, it was thereupon necessary to lay the foundations which were to govern the relations between Haiti and the United States during the emergency situation then existing in fact, if not recognized in political theory. That is, it was necessary to frame the terms of Haiti's temporary tutelage. The draft of a treaty designed to accomplish that purpose, which had already been drawn up in Washington, was the basis for the negotiations that now ensued.

Three days after the election of President Dartiguenave, the American *chargé d'affaires* was instructed by the Department of State to call the attention of the President-elect to the fact that for more than a year the Haitian government had been familiar with the terms of a treaty proposed by the United States government, and to advise him that "the department believes that as a guaranty of sincerity and interest of the Haitians in orderly and peaceful development of their country . . . the Haitian congress will be pleased to pass forthwith a resolution authorizing the President-elect to conclude, without modification, the treaty submitted by you." *

The *chargé* was also instructed *that when such a resolution was passed by Congress* he should extend to the President-elect the formal recognition of this government. In

* *Senate Hearings*, p. 327.

~ President Dartiguenave, His Cabinet, and Officers of the *Gendarmerie* ~

THE HAITIAN-AMERICAN TREATY

other words, the American diplomatic representative at Port-au-Prince was instructed to intimate to the President-elect of Haiti that the recognition withheld from his predecessor would be accorded to him only when an agreement as to this treaty had been reached.

On the seventeenth of August, 1915, a draft of the proposed treaty was delivered to the President together with a memorandum relative to the desire of the Department of State that the Haitian legislature should pass a resolution directing the President to conclude the treaty.

In spite of repeated assurances that the treaty would soon be accepted without modification, negotiations proceeded most unsatisfactorily.

The American *chargé* reported that the President continued his favourable attitude, but that unfavourable sentiment had developed in the legislature against the proposed customs control and against the American occupation in general. This "sentiment" was very greatly intensified by Admiral Caperton's action in restoring to the National Bank of Haiti the treasury service of the Haitian government which had been illegally transferred by President Sam to private banking houses,[1] and was further aggravated when, within the next few weeks, orders were received from Washington to take over the Haitian custom houses.

Admiral Caperton has stated that he believed that the funds collected in some of the custom houses were being improperly used, and that some of the money held by the private banking houses for the account of the government was in jeopardy of being turned over to "whosoever may exercise sufficient control or persuasion in the name of the government or revolution to obtain it."

The custom houses are all located at the open ports of Haiti, the principal commercial centres, and in many of these towns the election of Dartiguenave had been unfavourably received. Some of them even maintained a "committee of public safety" or a "revolutionary committee" which refused to recognize the government.

When Admiral Caperton received instructions that it was desired that he should assume charge of the custom houses, he sent a long message to Washington in which he outlined the situation and pointed out that the United States *"has now actually accomplished a military intervention in the affairs of another nation."* The Admiral further explained that "hostility exists now in Haiti and has existed for a number of years against such action" and that serious hostile contacts had been avoided only by prompt military action. He further pointed out the need for additional forces, and explained that to occupy the seven open ports, which action the taking over of the custom houses would necessitate, meant practically the military occupation of the seacoast of Haiti.*

On August 19th the State Department had directed that all funds collected from the customs be used, first, for the organization and maintenance of an efficient constabulary; secondly, for conducting such temporary public works as would afford immediate relief through employment for the starving populace and discharged soldiers, and, finally, for the support of the Dartiguenave government. In these instructions the Admiral was directed to confer with the American *chargé d'affaires* for the purpose of having the President [of Haiti] solicit the above action, but, whether the President so requested or not, he was directed to carry out the State Department's desires.† On August 21st the custom house at Cap Haitien was formally taken over, and on September 2nd the control of the customs service of Haiti was completed by taking over the custom house at Port-au-Prince.

Although several positive declarations had been received

* Some 1,100 kilometres.
† *Senate Hearings*, p. 335.

THE HAITIAN-AMERICAN TREATY

that the President and his cabinet were in accord with the American legation as to all the principles involved, and that only slight matters of detail would be further discussed, the American *chargé,* on August 27th, was astonished to receive a written reply from the Haitian government to his last previous message, in which reply practically every stipulation of the treaty as drafted was either omitted or so changed as to defeat its purpose.

This procedure was quite typical of the Haitian attitude towards diplomatic negotiations, a time-honoured method of bargaining which naturally confused the less experienced Americans and added tremendously to the difficulties under which they were struggling.

As a matter of fact, the President and his cabinet were fully conscious of a very strong and almost universal disinclination among the Haitian *élite* to consummate any treaty with the United States. These officials were in a position where the acceptance of a treaty was obligatory, but were endeavouring to evade the issue and trying in the meantime to extract as many teeth from the instrument as possible.

They agreed to sign the treaty, but only in a modified form; they were willing, for instance, to give customs "control," but not to allow the United States actual administration of customs collections. They were willing to accept the provision that the United States should by armed force secure the "pacification" of Haiti, but wished to provide that the forces of the United States should be withdrawn at the request of the Haitian government.

In answer to emphatic protests, the Admiral and the American *chargé* were informed that the treaty could be agreed to only in this modified form, and on September 1st the Admiral informed the Secretary of the Navy that in view of the uneasy situation, the possibility of disturbance, and the apparent attitude of some of the members of the cabinet towards the government, an outbreak at Port-au-Prince was possible and that a declaration of martial law might be necessary.[2]

Three days later Admiral Caperton issued a proclamation declaring that the existing government of Haiti was confronted with conditions which it was unable to control, and that therefore, under his authority as commanding officer of the forces of the United States of America in Haitian waters, he proclaimed that martial law existed in the city of Port-au-Prince and the immediate territory now occupied by the forces under his command. This apparently had the desired effect, as on the seventh, after a conference between the President, his cabinet, and the American *chargé,* the cabinet, with the exception of the ministers of Foreign Affairs and of Public Works, agreed to accept the treaty without modification.

Immediately after the above-mentioned conference, the President requested and received the resignation of the two ministers who had refused to accept the treaty, and on the sixteenth of September the treaty was signed by Mr. Louis Borno, the new Minister for Foreign Affairs, and by Robert Beale Davis, Jr., American *chargé d'affaires.*

Under the constitution the treaty, to be binding, had to be ratified by the Senate and the Chamber of Deputies, and it was quite apparent that opposition would develop in both bodies.

On October 3rd, President Dartiguenave pointed out to the American *chargé* that as the custom houses, practically the only source of revenue, were in the hands of the Americans, his government was without funds, and that without money to pay overdue salaries and meet current expenses the government could not continue and he would be forced to resign. The President, later in the day, was informed by Admiral Caperton that funds would be immediately available *upon the ratification of the treaty.*

THE HAITIAN-AMERICAN TREATY

In reporting the result of this interview, Admiral Caperton stated that the President seemed utterly discouraged and pointed out once more how the delay in ratifying the treaty was not due to any lack of effort by himself or his cabinet, but that the withholding of funds only gave another weapon to the opposition, and that if the United States government persisted in withholding funds ratification would become so difficult that he and his cabinet would resign rather than attempt to force the treaty through the Senate. The Admiral apparently believed, and so reported, that the President was really trying to secure the ratification of the treaty but that opposition in the Senate was strong, owing, the Admiral said, to the fact that many senators were "unscrupulous politicians or fanatics" who wished either to embarrass the United States government by blocking the ratification of the treaty, or to overthrow the Haitian administration. He further stated that he was informed that pressure was being brought to bear by outside interests which would be glad to see the Dartiguenave Government forced to resign.

Funds collected in the custom houses had been expended for the first of the purposes outlined in the instructions of August 19th; but not one cent had been turned over to the Haitian government for expenses, and Admiral Caperton recommended that, in view of the extreme urgency of the case, he be authorized to turn over needed sums to the Haitian government. To this request the Secretary of the Navy replied authorizing the Admiral to furnish the Haitian government weekly amounts necessary to meet current expenses, and to use for the purpose funds collected from Haitian customs. He was further informed that "the question of payment of back salaries would be settled by the department immediately after ratification of treaty." *

* *Senate Hearings*, p. 383.

BLACK DEMOCRACY

On October 6th, the Chamber of Deputies ratified the treaty; but opposition in the Senate continued, and on the sixteenth it was currently reported that the government intended to force favourable action in the Senate, regardless of the conclusions of the committee on revision, which was employing dilatory tactics to block the ratification of the treaty.

In spite of pressure from the executive branch of the government and the efforts of the American officials, the Senate continued to delay action, and on the tenth of November, in reply to a message outlining the situation, the Secretary of the Navy instructed Admiral Caperton to arrange with the President that he call a cabinet meeting and allow the Admiral to make a statement in which, among other things, he should inform the cabinet that he was confident that if the treaty failed of ratification the United States government "has the intention to retain control in Haiti until the desired end is accomplished, and that it will forthwith proceed to the complete pacification of Haiti so as to insure tranquillity necessary to such development of the country and its industry as to afford relief to the starving populace now unemployed." * The Admiral was further instructed to say that meanwhile the Dartiguenave Government would be supported in its efforts to secure stable conditions, whereas those offering opposition could expect only such treatment as their conduct merited.

This dispatch, which was signed by Secretary of the Navy Daniels, concluded, "It is expected that you will be able to make this sufficiently clear to remove all opposition and secure immediate ratification." † That this expectation was warranted is shown by the action of the Senate, which met

* During all these proceedings the United States Marines had been operating in the North against caco bands, and the northern part of Haiti was in a state of unrest, business was practically suspended, and the people generally were suffering from extreme poverty.
† *Senate Hearings*, p. 394.

THE HAITIAN-AMERICAN TREATY

on November 11th and, after a protracted debate, ratified the treaty by a vote of 26 to 7.

The treaty was announced by the President in a proclamation dated November 15, 1915, in which he stated that "this event, the most important in our national history, is the foundation of Haitian independence, of the solemn consecration of the new era of progress for the nation. . . . Without entering into a discussion of facts anterior to the coming of the Americans, remember that in a moment of our supreme despair the powerful and generous nation of North America saw our unhappiness, taking pity upon us, and came in the name of humanity and universal fraternity to offer us the hand of friendship and succour."

The preamble of the treaty reads in part as follows:

> The United States and the Republic of Haiti, desiring to confirm and strengthen the amity existing between them by the most cordial co-operation in measures for their common advantage;
> And the Republic of Haiti, desiring to remedy the present condition of its revenues and finances, to maintain the tranquillity of the Republic, to carry out plans for the economic development and prosperity of the Republic and its people;
> And the United States, being in full sympathy with all these aims and objects and desiring to contribute in all proper ways to their accomplishment; etc.

Among the more important provisions of the treaty are:

Article I. The Government of the United States will by its good offices aid the Haitian government in the proper and efficient development of its agricultural, mineral, and commercial resources, and the establishment of the finances of Haiti on a firm and solid basis.

Article II of the treaty provides for the nomination by the President of the United States and appointment by the President of the Republic of Haiti of a general receiver to supervise customs, and of a financial adviser. Article X provides for the establishment of the *gendarmerie d'Haïti*, to be organized and officered by Americans nominated by the President of the United States and appointed by the President of Haiti. Article XIV provides that, should the necessity occur, the United States "will lend an efficient aid for the preservation of Haitian independence and the maintenance of a government adequate for the protection of life, property, and individual liberty," and, furthermore, that the United States and the Republic of Haiti "shall have authority to take such steps as may be necessary to insure the complete attainment of any of the objects comprehended in this treaty."

Article XVI provides that this treaty "shall remain in full force and virtue for the term of ten years . . . and further for another term of ten years if, for specific reasons presented by either of the high contracting parties, the purpose of this treaty has not been fully accomplished." *

On November 29, 1915, a *modus vivendi* was signed, stipulating that, pending the sanction of the United States Senate, the treaty would provisionally go into full effect and remain in full force until the United States Senate had acted upon it.

The Senate ratified the treaty on February 28th, and the exchange of ratifications took place on May 3, 1916.

Breaking the Insurrection in the North

Shortly after the landing at Port-au-Prince, on July 28th, marines were sent to the North to disarm the revolutionists, and during all the treaty negotiations operations against the cacos had been carried on with success, but with a considerable number of caco casualties, and Admiral Caperton had been repeatedly urged from Washington to limit mili-

* For full text of treaty, see Exhibit B.

THE HAITIAN-AMERICAN TREATY

tary operations, in so far as possible, to the preservation of order and the protection of innocent people.

A few days after the ratification of the treaty by the Senate, the Admiral reported that operations against the cacos had resulted in dispersing all but a few roving bands and that the country people were returning to their crops. The backbone of the insurrectory movement had been broken, and, except for scattered bands of ill-armed brigands, the area patrolled by the marines, which included practically all of the North, was now peaceful.

It was perfectly obvious, however, that this situation was due solely to the presence of a small but highly efficient body of United States marines who had in a few months established patrols throughout the so-called caco country and, by forced marches and untiring vigilance, had rounded up the leaders of the caco movement and disarmed most of their followers.

Although there had been some protest against this early campaign, emanating largely from people who were entirely opposed to the American intervention, the general feeling in Haiti was highly favourable, and the Haitian people as a whole were profoundly relieved by the assurance that there would be no immediate renewal of the "revolutionary" activity which had kept the country in a state of unrest since the beginning of the revolutionary period in 1908. It was generally realized, moreover, that the Dartiguenave Government was totally powerless to function without military aid, and that if the American forces were withdrawn the usual revolution would immediately materialize.

The Dartiguenave Government had little or no authority outside of the capital, and in the North large numbers of cacos still retained their arms. For many months business had practically ceased. Throughout the country a serious state of poverty existed. While a large proportion of the able-bodied men had been under arms, their crops and cattle had been destroyed and their farms abandoned. This was fully realized by the Haitian people and by the president of Haiti and his advisers, but the seizure of the custom houses, the declaration of martial law, and the modes of procedure followed in securing the ratification of the treaty were bitterly resented by the majority of Haitians who had sufficient intelligence to know what was going on.

The governing class realized that foreign intervention could no longer be delayed, and that under the circumstances American intervention of some sort was inevitable. They were, as a matter of fact, glad enough to have military protection against the repetition of cacoism, but they were alarmed at the assumption of power by the Americans and resented and feared the pretensions of the white men so derogatory to their standing in their own country. In spite of a certain measure of appreciation of services rendered by the Americans in pacifying the country and a relief from fear of an immediate renewal of anarchy, they surveyed the future with doubt and misgiving.

The position of President Dartiguenave was extremely difficult. He realized the necessity of conciliating the United States government, was conscious of definite pledges as to certain programs, but was naturally jealous for the prestige of his own government and also desired to stand well with the Haitian people. Many of the steps taken by him or with his approval were sharply criticized by both Americans and Haitians, the Americans claiming that he was deliberately refraining from carrying out promises he had made, and the Haitians accusing him of constantly sacrificing their sovereignty and repeatedly assenting to "encroachments" of power by the American treaty officials.*

* See *Foreign Relations of the United States*, 1915; *Reports of the Secretary of the Navy, U.S.A.*, etc.; *Exposé général de la situation de la*

THE HAITIAN-AMERICAN TREATY

At the moment of the intervention the leading Haitians of the upper class, already disgusted with the situation, were ready to accept almost any procedure which would assure peace and order. They welcomed the intervention but expected impossible achievements, and as time passed and it became evident that the Government, "advised" by the American officials, was gradually elaborating the scope of the intervention as expressed in the treaty—"encroaching," as the Haitians expressed it—there naturally developed a party which capitalized and exaggerated the real errors and invented others and, having little else to do, spent much of its time endeavouring to block the program of the President and his American "advisers."

This gradual loss of sympathy between the American occupation and the Haitian people will be more readily understood when the first obstacles the American occupation officials had to contend with are considered in the next chapter. But it should be frankly admitted at this point that contributing not a little to this attitude of obstruction was the very decided racial antagonism which has always been more pronounced between Americans and Haitians than between the Haitians and other white peoples; and this feeling was naturally emphasized by the fact that Americans, most of whom were in the military service of the United States, held practically all the executive and administrative positions.

There were a certain number of Haitians of considerable influence who might have been of the greatest service if their co-operation had been secured, but who held aloof from any participation and confined themselves to more or less restrained criticism of both the Haitian Government and the American intervention. This critical attitude was greatly intensified when, less than a year after the ratifica-

---
République d'Haïti, 1917; *Report to the President of Haiti by Louis Borno, Secretary of Foreign Affairs*, 1917; etc.

tion of the treaty, the duration of this instrument was extended for ten additional years.

The "additional act" extending the duration of the treaty to May 3, 1936, was signed at Port-au-Prince on March 28, 1917, by the American minister and the Haitian Minister for Foreign Affairs. (See Exhibit C.)

Article XVI of the treaty reads: "The present treaty shall remain in full force and virtue for the term of ten years, to be counted from the day of exchange of ratifications (May 3, 1916), and for a further term of ten years if, for specific reasons presented by either of the high contracting parties, *the purpose of this treaty has not been fully accomplished.*"

Haitian and American critics of the intervention hold that this extension of the treaty was unjustified and invalid, first, because it was improper to invoke Article XVI until after a sufficient time had elapsed to determine whether or not the purposes of the treaty were, or were likely to be, accomplished, and, secondly, because while the "additional act" was signed by the Haitian Minister for Foreign Affairs and the American minister to Haiti, it had not been ratified by either the United States Senate or the National Assembly of Haiti.

In reference to this agreement it is stated in *Relations with Haiti*, a pamphlet issued by the Office of the American High Commissioner (1926):

> On March 1, 1917, the Haitian Government requested the good offices of the United States in securing for Haiti a loan of $30,000,000 for the purpose of refunding and consolidating the existing public debt and to provide for public works and improvements necessary to the development of the country's resources. In order that the projected loan might be arranged upon terms most advantageous to Haiti, that Government notified the United States of its desire to exercise the option conferred by Article XVI of the treaty, thus extending the treaty until

THE HAITIAN-AMERICAN TREATY

May 3, 1936. The considerations which prompted this action are obvious. Haitian bonds in any large amount could not be placed advantageously unless the prospective purchasers could have the assurance that such bonds would be properly secured as to payment of interest and amortization. This security was fully provided as long as the participation of the United States in the administration of Haitian affairs within the scope of the treaty should continue. That participation would, however, cease in 1926 unless it should be extended by agreement between the two governments. A loan of the amount proposed for a period of less than ten years was out of the question. On the other hand, provision for the possible prolongation of the treaty was contained in that instrument itself.

It is further stated in this pamphlet that it was not necessary to submit the agreement to the United States Senate "inasmuch as that body had already given its approval to the treaty of which the provision for extension by supplementary agreement was an integral part."

Whether or not this loan and the agreement for the extension of the treaty were inspired by the American treaty officials, it was obvious that the first step towards the rehabilitation of the Haitian finances, to which the United States was pledged, must be the floatation of a loan. This was recognized by the Haitians, but they strenuously objected to the precipitancy in extending the duration of the treaty, and these objections were emphasized as time passed and the contemplated loan, which was not in fact effected until June, 1923, failed to materialize.

CHAPTER IV

THE OCCUPATION

THE TREATY OFFICIALS INSTALLED IN OFFICE
PROTOCOL OF 1909 (LOAN AGREEMENT)
DISSOLUTION OF THE HAITIAN LEGISLATURE
NEW CONSTITUTION ADOPTED

DURING the interim between the ratification of the Haitian-American treaty by the Haitian legislature (September 11, 1915) and its ratification by the United States (February, 1916), the administration of the customs service, public safety, public works, and public health, and to a large extent the disbursement of public funds, were directed by officers of the United States Navy or Marine Corps. After the ratification of the treaty, the American officials provided for therein were gradually installed in office. The first to assume his duties was the chief of the *gendarmerie.*

In Article X of the treaty, the Haitian government obligated itself to create without delay an efficient constabulary composed of native Haitians, to be organized and officered by Americans appointed by the President of Haiti upon the nomination of the President of the United States. The Haitian army consisted, on paper at least, of thirty-eight regiments of the line, four regiments of artillery, four regiments of the President's guard, and a *gendarmerie* of forty-three companies. The high-ranking officers included over three hundred generals and about fifty colonels. This army was completely disbanded shortly after the intervention, and an officer of the United States Marine Corps was

~ A Crack Troop of the Old Army ~

THE OCCUPATION

detailed to organize a constabulary in accordance with a *"gendarmerie* agreement," a protocol of the treaty, which had been tentatively agreed upon and which was finally ratified in August, 1916.

On the first of February, 1916, the positions of commandants of communes and chiefs of sections were abolished and the military and police duties of the commandants of *arrondissements* were assigned to the *gendarmerie,* which on that date assumed the responsibility for the policing of the Republic of Haiti. In July, 1916, the municipal and rural police were abolished and their duties taken over by the *gendarmerie.*

Pending the organization of the *Bureau Technique* (Department of Public Works), the *gendarmerie* also assumed control of necessary public works and sanitation and the building and repair of roads and of telephone lines. As a matter of fact, *gendarmerie* district or sub-district commanders, officers or enlisted men of the United States Marine Corps, were veritable potentates in their districts, exercising both civil and military functions. With the exception of a few cases which have received widespread publicity, their work, undertaken under the most trying conditions, was most efficiently performed.

The first financial adviser assumed his duties on July 9, 1916, and almost immediately found that the ideas of the Ministry of Finance as to the prerogatives and duties of the financial adviser, and as to giving aid to his proposals, were often directly opposed to those of the American intervention.

The first general receiver took over the customs service from the naval administration on August 29, 1916. He was greatly handicapped by having to administer an antiquated tariff dating from 1872, revised somewhat in 1905, but not, in fact, replaced by a modern tariff until July, 1926.

The powers granted to the receiver-general of customs

were in general specific and comprehensive, but the wording of the articles defining the rather unique duties and authority of the financial adviser was vague and indefinite.

It was provided, for example, that the President of Haiti should appoint, upon the nomination of the President of the United States, a financial adviser "who shall be an officer attached to the Ministry of Finance, to give effect to whose proposals and labours the minister will lend efficient aid." The financial adviser might "devise," "aid," "enquire into," "enlighten," and "recommend," but he had no specific authority to enforce and there was nothing in the treaty to compel the minister to *lend efficient aid*. Article III of the treaty specifically provided that the Republic of Haiti "will extend to the Receivership and to the Financial Adviser all needful aid and full protection in the execution of the powers conferred and duties imposed herein." But the *extent of such powers* was not clearly stated, nor was adequate authority provided for the officials on whom such heavy responsibility rests. The United States assumed definite obligations toward the Haitian people, but failed to incorporate in the treaty specific authority for the responsible agents nominated by the President of the United States.

At the very beginning there developed considerable friction between the financial adviser and the Minister of Finance, both as to the powers of the financial adviser and as to his policies. The duties of the financial adviser and receiver-general of customs, which have since been united under one head, were to a considerable extent interdependent. In the beginning these two officials, both Americans, co-operated closely, and the definite control of customs revenues granted to the general receiver was used, wherever feasible, to secure the acceptance of the policies of the financial adviser.

There was a considerable delay in organizing the *Direc-*

THE OCCUPATION

tion Générale des Travaux Publics, the bureau of the Department of Public Works, of which an American treaty official is the chief.

The first treaty engineer, a commander in the United States Navy, civil engineer corps, arrived in Haiti in January, 1917, but it was many months before he was provided with funds and assigned assistants and employees. In the meanwhile the military occupation and the *gendarmerie* administered such public works as were undertaken.

The system in Haiti had been, and to a great extent still is, that local public works, excepting only certain municipal improvements, are financed by the public treasury and administered by the national department of public works. But there was no organization to carry on the few public works that were attempted, no accounting system or trained force of engineers, nor any adequate provision under the existing law for the maintenance of public utilities.

It was not until the summer of 1920, in fact, when an adequate "public works law" was enacted, that the engineer in chief was properly equipped to administer his department effectively.

The great irrigation systems, built in French colonial times, were in ruins, and municipal waterworks, even in the capital, were either abandoned or in a most unsanitary and inefficient condition; public highways were practically nonexistent. The telegraph system was deplorably inadequate, and sanitation, from a modern standpoint, was unknown.

Prior to the American intervention, matters of public health and sanitation were under the direction of a central body, having local subsidiary bodies all known as the *Jury Médical.* This organization, for practical purposes, existed in name only. Sanitary conditions, particularly in the cities and towns, were inconceivably bad, and conditions in the few hospitals which existed were indescribable.

The first sanitary engineer, a commander in the medical

corps, United States Navy, took office in October, 1917, and in February, 1919, a law creating the public health service was enacted. A staff of commissioned and warrant officers of the medical corps, United States Navy, was assigned to this service and supplemented by Haitian physicians and pharmacists. While handicapped by a deplorable lack of funds, this service functioned admirably from the beginning, and at once gained the respect and admiration of even the most rabid critics of the intervention.

In considering the achievements and failures of the American treaty officials, which at this time were food for much highly acrimonious discussion, it must be borne in mind that they were labouring under the most distinctly unfavourable conditions. The co-operation of the Haitian people, which they had every right to expect, and the aid of the Haitian government officials, pledged to them under the treaty, were not forthcoming, and they were further handicapped by the lack of any continuous and constructive policy in Washington.

The result of this lack of constructive co-operation was particularly apparent in the financial department of the government. Arrangements for the loan contemplated in the treaty and specified in the additional act of 1917 were undoubtedly impeded by conditions resulting from the World War. But this first step in the rehabilitation of the finances of the Republic was further delayed by a decided feeling of antagonism for the then acting financial adviser and an unfortunate lack of faith in his judgment, and it was not until the fall of 1919 that active negotiations for securing this loan were again undertaken. The principal object of this loan was to stabilize the finances of Haiti by refunding and consolidating the Haitian national debt, which included both external and internal obligations.

The external loans had all been floated in France and were still largely held by French bondholders. Owing to

THE OCCUPATION

the depreciation of French francs, it was evident that a very considerable saving could be effected by floating a dollar loan in the United States and paying off the French loan in francs. The funding of this debt involved the determination of the total obligations of the government and of the validity of a great mass of claims against the state which had been accumulating for years, and in an agreement signed on October 3, 1919, specifying the conditions under which the Republic of Haiti should issue bonds to the extent of not more than $40,000,000, the organization of a claims commission was provided for. This agreement, which was signed by the American minister to Haiti and the Haitian Minister for Foreign Affairs, also provided for the continuance, during the life of the loan after the expiration of the treaty of 1915, of supervision over the collection and allocation of hypothecated (customs) revenues by an officer, or officers, appointed by the President of Haiti on the nomination of the President of the United States.

The report, *Relations with Haiti,* above referred to, in this connexion states:

> The authority of the executive branch of the United States Government to conclude such an agreement was derived from Article XIV of the Treaty of 1915, which empowers the high contracting parties to take such steps as may be necessary to insure the complete attainment of any of the objects comprehended in the treaty. To insure the financial rehabilitation of Haiti, one of the most important objects comprehended in this treaty, the continuance of United States customs supervision appeared necessary. The execution of a protocol with the United States for the settlement of foreign claims against Haiti had been specifically agreed to by Article XII of the treaty.*

This statement, printed in 1926, was obviously inspired

* See treaty, Exhitib B.

by the many criticisms of the protocol from both Haitian and American sources, especially as to the continued supervision over customs revenues. No one, however, has denied that Haiti greatly needed a considerable sum of money, nor is there any question that no such sum as contemplated could have been secured on any acceptable terms unless this provision was incorporated in the agreement. Protests against the protocol were natural enough from Haitians who wished to see the end of the American intervention in the affairs of Haiti at the earliest possible date, but they would have borne much greater weight if there had been any possible cause for the implication that "American interests" in any way profited by this loan to the detriment of the Haitian people.

One of the most difficult and unpleasant aspects of the whole situation has been the constant implication that the American treaty officials were personally profiting by their official acts. It is quite understandable that Haitians cannot appreciate that men who are in a position to handle large sums of money can resist the temptation to profit thereby. But it is absolutely inexcusable that Americans who have had every opportunity to learn the truth of the situation should have either openly or by innuendo suggested that the American policy in Haiti, or the conduct of any one of the responsible American officials, was in any manner influenced by any other than a sincere, if perhaps sometimes misguided, effort to carry out the expressed objects of the Haitian-American treaty for the benefit of the Haitian people as a whole.

As a matter of fact, it is held by many Americans that the policy of the treaty officials towards American investments in Haiti has been so influenced by a determination to protect the Haitian people from "exploitation" as to have seriously retarded the legitimate economic development of the resources of the Republic.

THE OCCUPATION

One may question the wisdom of the policies of the American intervention in Haiti, but it is most unfair and even disingenuous and unintelligent to question the motives which have inspired this policy, or the integrity of the responsible officials.

Shortly after the ratification of the treaty, the question of revision of the constitution arose. Certain of the provisions of the treaty were not consistent with the constitution then in force, and certain others, notably the time-honoured prohibition against alien ownership of land, were held by practically all the Americans and many intelligent Haitians to be decidedly detrimental to the economic development of the Republic.

Some weeks prior to the convocation of the national assembly, which was to meet early in April, 1916, it became evident that any plans of the President and the American officials for a revision of the constitution would be strenuously opposed by a majority of the members of the legislature. It was currently reported that the opposition was planning to refuse to endorse any proposed revision of the constitution, and to impeach the President on the ground that by his official acts he had already violated the existing constitution.[1]

In discussing this situation with the American officials, the President stated that he expected to control the legislature and that he did not believe that the "enemies of the government" would be present in sufficient force to cause such a vote to pass. President Dartiguenave admitted that he had made many enemies by his reform measures, in curtailing expenses, eliminating graft, and suppressing the war department and the navy, all of which measures he felt, however, were for the good of Haiti, and all done with the advice and co-operation of the American officials.

He further believed that there was but one thing to do, and that was to revise the constitution and make it fit the present needs of the country. The following changes, he announced, were imperative: "There are 39 senators and 102 deputies—double the number needed. Their salaries alone amount to one-seventeenth of the entire revenue of the country.

"The number must be reduced to less than half the present number. Article VI of the present constitution provides that no foreigner may acquire or hold property. This prevents foreign capital from entering. Article VI must be suppressed. The revised constitution must suppress the war department and army and substitute a *gendarmerie*.*

"The magistracy and civil service must be reformed, and there are other needed reforms. My government will urge the chambers to take the necessary steps to revise this constitution on these lines. Should Congress be hostile and refuse, there will be but one thing to do. I do not ask the American government to advise me to do this, nor to express any opinion on this matter, but I request the assurance of Admiral Caperton that my government will receive complete military protection. I shall declare both chambers dissolved. I will call for a constituent assembly, which will be formed of about fifty representatives, patriotic Haitians, who will revise the constitution according to present needs." †

The desired assurance of protection was authorized by the United States Navy Department, and, the anticipated opposition having materialized immediately after the convocation of the legislature, the President proceeded to carry out his program and dissolved the Senate. In the same decree he convened the Chamber of Deputies exclusively as a constituent assembly, so that it might, "in co-

---

* Article X of the treaty provides that the Haitian government shall create without delay an efficient constabulary.

† As reported by Capt. E. L. Beach, U.S.N., to Admiral Caperton. See *Hearings before Select Committee, U.S. Senate*, p. 415.

THE OCCUPATION

operation with the executive power, revise the constitution and perform such legislative work as might be called for by the President." At the same time another decree was promulgated creating a council of state composed of twenty-one members whose functions should be, first, to give advice on all projects which the government deems fit to submit to it; secondly, to prepare and formulate laws and decrees on matters in which the government desires its action; thirdly, to give advice on all questions which may be submitted to it by the President and his cabinet.

These measures were eminently successful in forestalling impeachment, but notwithstanding the fact that the Senate had been dissolved on April 5th, the senators on the following day repaired to the official chamber and, finding the doors locked, decided to meet on April 7th at a private dwelling. On the eighth of April the members of the permanent committee of the dissolved Senate met at a private house and decided to protest against the decree of dissolution. Members of the Chamber also decided to take the same action. The proceedings of the following days were hectic.

On April 11th the President, learning that about sixty members of the Chamber of Deputies, which had been convened by him to revise the constitution, had met and done nothing but declare no quorum, published a statement in the official organ of the government in which he said that if the deputies persisted in the refusal to perform the duties which he had assigned to them he would call a general election for a new constituent assembly. In this crisis a committee of "notables," prominent citizens headed by ex-President Légitime, offered to endeavour to bring about an understanding between the President and the legislative bodies. Admiral Caperton, believing that this was not impossible, strongly urged that every effort should be made to come to an amicable settlement. These conferences, however, failed to result in any change in the situation, and on May 2, 1916, Admiral Caperton made public the following notice:

> Rear-Admiral Caperton stated that after having tried for the last three weeks in the most friendly way, with the aid of certain neutral Haitian patriots, to reach an understanding in the conflict of the Haitian government, it is impossible to find a basis of understanding that could be accepted by the two parties to the controversy.
>
> Consequently, in view of the impossibility of reconciling the Government and the opposition, in spite of the conciliatory offers made by the Government to the opposition, he has advised the officers of the Chamber and the Senate which had been dissolved by the decree of April 5, 1916, that his full duty of maintaining peace and order in Haiti rendered it necessary for him to uphold the decree of the constituted and recognized Government of Haiti.

The evidence shows that there is no ground for the oft-repeated accusation that the dissolution of the Senate was inspired by the Americans. Major-General Littleton W. T. Waller, U.S.M.C., then commanding the marine forces in Haiti, has testified that he personally was "bitterly opposed" to the dissolution and that he was told by the President that the dissolution was ordered "on account of the tremendous opposition that he was meeting from members of the legislature." * General Waller further stated that the general feeling at the time and his own impression were that the President had dissolved the legislature because he feared impeachment.

On June 23, 1916, President Dartiguenave decreed the convocation of the Chamber of Deputies to meet as a constituent assembly on the fourteenth of August, but this decree was ignored by the deputies, who continued to defy the President until their authority expired on January 10, 1917.

In September, 1916, the President published a decree

* *Senate Hearings*, p. 623.

THE OCCUPATION

modifying the electoral law, reducing the number of deputies and senators and fixing January 15th and 16th as the dates for new elections of a national assembly.

Shortly after the new assembly convened in April, 1917, the American minister notified the Secretary of State for Foreign Affairs that the United States government had several suggestions to make in connexion with the proposed constitution. The attitude of the new assembly was extremely hostile both to the American intervention and to the proposed constitutional changes, particularly to granting to aliens the right to own property in Haiti, the ratification of the acts of the military occupation, and of the decisions of the military courts, all of which had been suggested by the United States government. This hostility was greatly intensified when the Haitian government, through the council of state, presented to the national assembly a draft of a project for revision of the constitution, and at the same time sent to the assembly the correspondence which had been exchanged between the executive branch of the government and the American legation in connexion with this project.

Colonel Eli K. Cole, U.S.M.C., who had succeeded Colonel Waller as brigade commander, has stated * that the Haitian government, in transmitting the correspondence, "deliberately spilled the beans." They took the whole correspondence, said Colonel Cole, and sent it without comment, practically, to the national assembly. In other words, they said, "Here is not our own recommendation, but here is what practically amounts to dictation from the United States. Now see what you can do with it." The Colonel further stated * that there was no doubt in his mind that this was done with absolute malice aforethought.

As a matter of fact, that disclosure of this correspondence, which was obviously not intended for publication, very

* *Senate Hearings*, p. 696.

greatly strengthened the hands of the opposition, and it was immediately apparent that the assembly would not agree to the proposed revision but was, on the other hand, about to adopt a draft of a constitution which was *absolutely at variance with every expressed wish of the United States government*.*

The situation became extremely critical. The President again feared impeachment, and several times intimated that it would probably be necessary again to dissolve the assembly. To this the American officials were loath to agree, but they did not want the President impeached nor could they countenance the enactment of a constitution embodying principles diametrically opposed to the wishes of the American Department of State and to the understanding which had been arrived at between the two governments. The President was informed that the United States government felt that Haiti should have every chance to show her capacity for self-government and every opportunity to show that her people were capable of relieving the state of affairs "and capable or incapable of performing its duties in such a way as to aid in establishing a proper government in the country, and until the national assembly showed that it was not going to approve of the project and the agreements between the executive branch of the Haitian government and the United States, it would not be wise to have recourse to drastic action." † The President was also advised to endeavour to get his supporters to come out openly in favour of the projects which he himself was supporting.

It now became perfectly evident that certain prominent Haitians were playing a double game and, while ostensibly in favour of the Government's policies, were in reality opposing them. This was confirmed when, a short time later, the committee on revision of the constitution reported

* *Senate Hearings*, p. 696.
† Testimony of Colonel Cole, *ibid.*, p. 697.

THE OCCUPATION

favourably a draft which maintained the provision against alien ownership and failed to include the more important clauses which had been agreed upon between the government of Haiti and the representatives of the United States government.

It was pointed out to the President of Haiti that this proposed constitution would make it impossible to bring about the results contemplated in the treaty and consequently the United States government could not accept it.

On June 16th President Dartiguenave proposed to the American officials that the constitution should be submitted to the people in a popular election. The President appeared convinced that the dissolution of the national assembly was inevitable, and he frankly stated to Colonel Cole that the country was not in a condition to elect a proper national assembly, that elections were and had always been engineered by a few politicians, and that the vast majority of the voters had no idea of what they were voting for, but were simply brought in and made to vote by the candidates or their friends. He said that in his opinion the only government by Haitians which would be satisfactory would be one of a president with a council of cabinet ministers and a further council of state with legislative powers, that such a government should prepare a constitution in accord with the ideas of the United States, promulgate the same, and carry on the government until the people were able to realize by actual experience the benefits resulting from the changes in the constitution. He also reminded the American officials that just such a government had existed in Haiti in 1846. (See Exhibit I.)

In discussing this proposal, the President stated that the reason why the American occupation was so hated by the politicians was that they were prevented from getting their livelihood from the public funds, and added that in former days all the principal politicians expected to get enough money out of public funds to live well and take their families on annual trips to Paris.*

At this time Colonel Cole reported to Washington that he had been informed by the President that, "to avoid possible hostile demonstrations," his own brother (then a member of the cabinet) *had voted against* the provision allowing foreigners to own property in Haiti. This was apparently done with the knowledge and approval of the President.

After a number of conferences with the American officials, the President finally sent for certain of the prominent members of the legislature, and is reported to have informed them it was absolutely essential that a constitution which conformed to the recommendations made by the government of the United States should be passed. Whether or not the President actually did so inform these legislators is not clear, but a few hours later the assembly went into secret session for about half an hour and then in open session hurriedly resumed the reading of its own draft of a constitution where it had left off on the previous day. It was quite evident that the intention of the assembly was to rush its constitution to a vote before dissolution could be effected. This being reported to Colonel Cole, he sent to the palace for the presidential decree of dissolution.

The officer entrusted with this duty was instructed to inform President Dartiguenave that in case he did not sign the decree Colonel Cole would suppress the legislature himself and would recommend the establishment of a military government. The President then signed the decree.

This situation in the Chamber had in the meanwhile become dramatically intense. The reading of the assembly's draft of the constitution rapidly neared completion, and the legislators were congratulating themselves on the success of their stratagem, when the chief of the *gendarmerie*

---
* *Senate Hearings*, pp. 699, 700.

THE OCCUPATION

of Haiti, a major in the United States Marine Corps, entered the hall and presented to the presiding officer the decree of dissolution. This official refused to accept the decree or announce it on the ground that it was not delivered by a cabinet officer, but the chief of the *gendarmerie* proceeded to promulgate the decree himself and after reading it aloud directed that the Chamber be cleared.

The national assembly having been dissolved, it was determined to submit the constitution in the form which had finally been approved by Washington to the vote of the people in a special plebiscite. The new constitution was in general in conformity with the one then in force, but included a number of provisions of fundamental importance, one of which, granting property rights to aliens, is in decided variance with the principles maintained in all of the many previous constitutions of the Republic.

There was little opportunity for public discussion, and the great majority of the electorate were entirely incompetent to analyse the proposed changes.

As very few of the voters could read or write or had ever participated in an election, they were not required to mark the ballot, but two ballots of different colours, one signifying approval and the other disapproval, were entrusted to the *gendarmerie* officials in charge of polling places, and these ballots were presumably issued as requested by the voters. Although orders were issued to all American *gendarmerie* officers to get out as large a vote as possible, less than 100,000 votes were cast.* Of these only 769 were in the negative.

It must be admitted that this proceeding has been sharply questioned both as to its constitutional sanction and as to its common sense as a part of necessary strategy in Haiti. Competent Haitian authorities have defended it on the first count, however, as in accord with previous precedents;

* The population of Haiti is estimated at about 2,500,000.

changes in the basic law have on several occasions been sanctioned by a popular vote. It has also, as some Haitians say, been customary to submit constitutional revisions to the national assembly. But on at least three occasions constitutions including important revisions have been promulgated by a council of state.

As to the broader ground of policy, it is only fair to admit that the project of submitting seriously to a people who never in their history have taken part either in drafting or in ratifying a constitution the draft involving the delicate problems arising from American intervention was in essence farcical. This is not to impeach the transparent honesty of the occupation officials who did it. To them it was the only way to accomplish what they believed was to Haiti's best interest.

What the vote showed, of course, was merely that no substantial body of Haitians was willing or able to register its opposition to the constitution submitted to it. In actual practice, the election was probably as honest a one as Haiti ever had. Elaborate precautions against repeating were enforced even to the rather humiliating detail of marking with indelible ink the thumbs of those who had voted. But the widespread impression that the vote must be "for" was so well understood in Haiti that it was even doubted whether all of the 769 negative votes were genuine.

The principal features of the Constitution of 1918 are:

Provisions for the ownership of land by foreigners and protection of foreigners in Haiti, a four- instead of seven-year presidential term, and the substitution of a *gendarmerie* for the old military establishment.

A special article which ratified the acts of the United States government during the military occupation in Haiti provided that no Haitian shall be subject to prosecution for any act performed in execution of the orders of the occupation, and that the acts of military courts of the occupation

THE OCCUPATION

should not be subject to review by Haitian tribunals; and ratified the acts of the Haitian government up to the time of the promulgation of the constitution.

Certain transitory provisions, which have since been strenuously attacked, creating a council of state to "exercise the legislative power until a duly elected legislative body shall have been constituted," provide for the election of a new legislature only on the call of the President. In other words, the time for the re-establishment of a legislature as provided in the permanent provisions of the constitution was left to the discretion of the President, and pending this time a small appointive body selected by him should function as the legislative body. (See Exhibit D.)

The opposition lost no time in protesting that the new constitution was, in fact, unconstitutional, in that the procedure by which it was enacted was not in conformity with Haitian constitutional traditions.[2] Aside from this comprehensive indictment, the principal objections voiced at the time of the promulgation of the constitution were against the provision legalizing alien ownership of real property and against the special article ratifying the acts of the United States government since the intervention. The latter objection seems futile and illogical, as some such provision was ultimately inevitable. But the opposition to doing away with the time-honoured prohibition of ownership of land by foreigners not only involved a decidedly live political question, but also was inspired by a very real feeling that the removal of this prohibition might result in the ultimate transfer of the best agricultural land in Haiti to foreign ownership.

The imperial constitution of Dessalines (1805) prohibited white men, of whatever nation, from acquiring property of any kind in Haiti. The first constitution of the Republic (Pétion, 1806) contained the same provision in a somewhat modified form.

BLACK DEMOCRACY

Christophe inserted a similar provision in the constitution of the "State of Haiti" (1807), and included it in his Royal Constitution (1811).

The constitution of the Republic, revised in 1816 and again in 1843 and in 1846, retained this traditional policy, as did the Imperial Constitution of Faustin (Soulouque) of 1849. A modification of the constitution by Geffrard (1860) provided for the naturalization of foreigners but did not otherwise alter this provision. Salnave revised the constitution in 1867; Domingue in 1874, Salomon in 1879, and Hippolyte in 1889.[3] But each of these revisions left intact the prohibition of ownership of real property by aliens. As a matter of common practice, this prohibition had been circumvented in a scheme whereby a foreigner purchased land in the name of a Haitian citizen and took from him a mortgage, a practice very largely engaged in by the Germans. But the provision against foreign ownership of property had remained intact in the law for 113 years.

While this feeling against allowing foreigners to own land in Haiti is perhaps largely traditional, there undoubtedly exists a fear that the agricultural lands, which constitute practically the only known resource of the Republic and its people, may pass into the hands of foreigners. Agriculture in Haiti, with the exception of the few foreign enterprises, is almost entirely peasant agriculture, the one ambition of the peasant being to own and cultivate his little "garden," ill cultivated as a rule, but sufficient for his needs. All the coffee and cacao, most of the cotton, and all the vegetables are produced in these little plots, by far the greater number of which are located in the hills on land that would not be suitable for intensive cultivation by modern methods, and which therefore are in little jeopardy of being acquired by foreigners.

As a matter of fact, the peasants, over ninety-five per cent of the people, are now infinitely safer in relation to the

THE OCCUPATION

tenure of their property than ever before in the history of Haiti. The great areas of land which were intensively cultivated in the colonial times and have largely reverted to bush, are generally owned by people living in the towns who have never made any attempt at agricultural development and who, as a rule, have never set foot on their properties. While in some of these areas primitive cultivation is carried on by peasant farmers, much of the potentially most valuable land can be made productive only by costly irrigation or drainage projects. Great areas of such land have remained practically uncultivated for generations and, in so far as one can judge from the present situation, would so remain indefinitely if its development were left to the present owners. The possession of this land does little or no good to the owners. It is now of no benefit to the state, and adds nothing to the prosperity of the people. Such areas can be made profitable only by intensive methods of cultivation, involving three things which are woefully lacking in Haiti: money, constructive enterprise, and trained energy.

This same argument has been repeated by both of the chief executives who have held office since the American intervention, and is generally recognized as sound by all progressive Haitians. That this has been recognized by many thoughtful Haitians is well known. The feeling against foreign ownership of land is not by any means universal. In June, 1911, a United Committee of Finance and Justice and Public Works reported to the Chamber of Deputies in part as follows:

> We have been for a long time habituated to the discussion of Article VI of the Constitution [old constitution], some demanding that it be abrogated because the circumstances were not the same to-day, and because it is, moreover, detrimental to the economic growth of the country; others defending traditions, in restating the same

reasons which had inspired them since 1804. . . . Since 1804, what have we done except to lament upon lack of capital which causes the greater part of our lands still to remain virgin?

In the form in which it was passed, the 1918 constitution gives to foreigners who are residing in Haiti, and to companies formed by foreigners, the right to own land for the purpose of residence, and for agricultural, commercial, industrial, or educational purposes; this right to terminate five years after such foreigners shall have ceased to reside in Haiti, or when the activities of these companies shall have ceased.

It should be added, while this subject is being considered, that in July, 1920, after very unfortunate disagreements between the Haitian government and the financial adviser, a decree was promulgated by President Dartiguenave which practically nullified this provision and gave to foreign landowners a year in which to dispose of their holdings.

The American minister immediately notified the Haitian government that the American legation could not give its approval of "this project of law," which he stated was "an erroneous interpretation of Article 5 of the Constitution, absolutely contrary to the spirit thereof, of a nature to discourage the investment of capital in Haiti, and a hindrance to the attainment of the aims of the treaty of September 16, 1915."

He followed this protest by a letter in which he stated that this "law, having been passed without the approval of this legation in violation of the agreement of August 24, 1918, is not recognized as law by my government; I have therefore to demand its immediate repeal."

While this law remained in the statutes until February, 1925, it was never enforced, and on February 13, 1925, it was abrogated by a new law setting forth a restored basis of more liberal conditions under which the right of ownership of real property is now granted to foreigners in Haiti. This latter law, which remains in effect to-day (1928), while it is not wholly satisfactory, does grant practically unrestricted rights to corporations formed in Haiti under Haitian laws.

This law provides that foreigners may acquire real property in Haiti only for the needs of residence, or for agriculture, commercial industries, or educational enterprises, and then only if the holder has established a residence. An uninterrupted absence of five years forfeits the right to maintain ownership, and the land is sold by the state and the proceeds paid to the owner. Foreign corporations may, subject to the approval of the President, obtain authorization to transact business in Haiti and may acquire real property for the needs of residence, and for their agricultural, commercial, industrial, or educational enterprises. Corporations formed under Haitian law having their main place of business in Haiti may enjoy all the rights attached to Haitian citizenship with respect to ownership of real property.[4]

CHAPTER V

THE CACO UPRISING

THE need of highways in Haiti, not only for military purposes and economic development, but also to bring the people of the South and North into closer social relations, was realized by the Americans from the very beginning of the occupation. No adequate funds were available for this purpose, so in 1917 the commander of the *gendarmerie* revived a law, dating from 1864,[1] requiring citizens to work on roads in the communes in which they lived. This revival of the *corvée* law, or rather the manner in which it was abused, has been described by perhaps the most able investigator who has visited the island since the American occupation as the "biggest blunder we have made in Haiti."[2]

There was no question as to the need of roads, there being practically no highways in the Republic. To reach Cap Haitien, the principal commercial centre of the North, from the capital, was impossible for wheeled vehicles, and few Haitians had ever made the overland trip except to engage in one of the recurrent revolutions. Nor was there any question of legality in requiring men to work on the construction or repair of roads and trails in their own communes.

The Haitian peasant is accustomed to obey without protest the orders of any person who appears to be in authority. In the beginning no protest was made, and it is doubtful if any serious objections would have materialized if the *gendarmerie* had kept within the legal limits of the *corvée* law. Between July, 1916, and March, 1918, ap-

THE CACO UPRISING

proximately 470 miles of road were built, or rather rebuilt, as the work consisted chiefly in repairing the old roads of French colonial times. The then chief of the *gendarmerie* has stated that the cost of these roads was about $205 a mile, representing a certain amount of hired skilled labour to build culverts, the cost of cement, tools, etc., and the cost of feeding the *corvée*.

The fundamental trouble with the *corvée* was not with the law itself, but with the manner in which it was executed. Orders were issued that no inhabitant should be compelled to perform *corvée* work outside of his own district, or should be forced to exceed the period of labour required by law. But in many cases this rule was not observed. Much of the road constructed ran through districts that were sparsely populated, and even in settled districts the inhabitants quite naturally avoided the *corvée* if possible. The official system issued cards notifying the people that on a certain date they must report for road work or pay a tax. When their three days' work had been completed these cards, endorsed by the *gendarmerie* officers of the district, were supposed to be evidence of adequate performance and to exempt the holder from further work. In some districts, however, the system was disregarded, and it is claimed that in many instances cards which had been endorsed were destroyed by *gendarmes*. Certainly a great many men were retained in the *corvée* for a much longer time than provided by law, and many of these were compelled to work outside of their own districts.

One of the principal difficulties with which the American officers, who organized the *gendarmerie*, had to contend, was the time-honoured idea among the Haitians that a military policeman, *and practically all policemen had been military*, was licensed to ill-treat prisoners. This has been corrected to a degree highly creditable to the officers of the *gendarmerie*, but in the early days it was impossible for a native *gendarme* to appreciate how times had changed. In practice the men required for the *corvée* were secured through the local *chef de section,* usually a man of many years' experience in local affairs, who saw little difference between the *corvée* and the old system of securing "recruits" for the army. The *gendarmes* charged with recruiting the *corvée,* and with the duty of guarding the gangs collected, were often unnecessarily rough, treating the labourers as if they were criminals.

In the beginning, however, there was little opposition to the *corvée,* and no adverse criticism even by the most ardent opponents of the occupation. But as reports of mistreatment and abuse of the *corvée* labourers, generally greatly exaggerated, were spread through the country, many of the natives took to the hills. This afforded an excellent opportunity for the old caco leaders, and for the politicians opposed to the government and to the American occupation, to spread propaganda that the *blancs* were reestablishing slavery. Persistent complaints resulted in orders to stop the *corvée* on October 1, 1918, about two years after the system had been revived. Unfortunately these orders were disregarded in certain sections of the North, districts which for years had been the centre of caco activities. And before this illegal *corvée* was finally stopped, a strong anti-American feeling had been engendered in that section of Haiti from which for generations the caco armies had been recruited.

Within a year after the intervention the country had apparently been completely pacified, and excepting for a few cases of banditry, which were handled by the *gendarmerie,* no military movements were necessary. But in the summer of 1918 Charlemagne Peralte, a caco chief of Hinche, who had been convicted by a provost court and was working as a prisoner on the streets of Cap Haitien, escaped to the hills, taking his *gendarme* guard with him, and, collecting a

THE CACO UPRISING

few of his old followers, began a caco uprising. Resentment against the *corvée,* and especially against its illegal continuance, made recruiting easy in the North, and Charlemagne was soon joined by other leaders whose bands of professional cacos were supplemented, as usual, by inhabitants forced into their service.

This outbreak was in character as much organized banditry as it was revolutionary, acts of violence being committed against innocent natives, and whole districts being systematically looted. There was, however, a distinct anti-American feeling which, intensified by propaganda from the cities and highly exaggerated accounts of oppression by the Americans, soon led to a very serious situation. The caco movement was at first opposed only by the *gendarmerie,* but in the spring of 1919 it was estimated that over five thousand cacos were in the field in the northern and central districts of Haiti, and the marines were ordered to suppress them.

The cacos, ill equipped and with few effective weapons and little ammunition, could not face the marines in actual battle, but the difficulty of overcoming them is inconceivable to one unfamiliar with the country. The serious problem confronting the military forces of the United States in Haiti was to restore peace and order in the central and northern mountain sections. It proved impossible to engage any large body of cacos, for, knowing the country and accustomed to long marches over difficult trails, they easily kept out of range of the troops sent against them. The marines therefore adopted the only practicable method of operations, that of constantly patrolling the mountain country in small detachments of twenty to forty men. More difficult service could hardly be imagined, and regardless of the widespread accusations of unnecessary cruelty and "atrocities," it is beyond question that this campaign reflected the utmost credit on the officers and men of the ma-

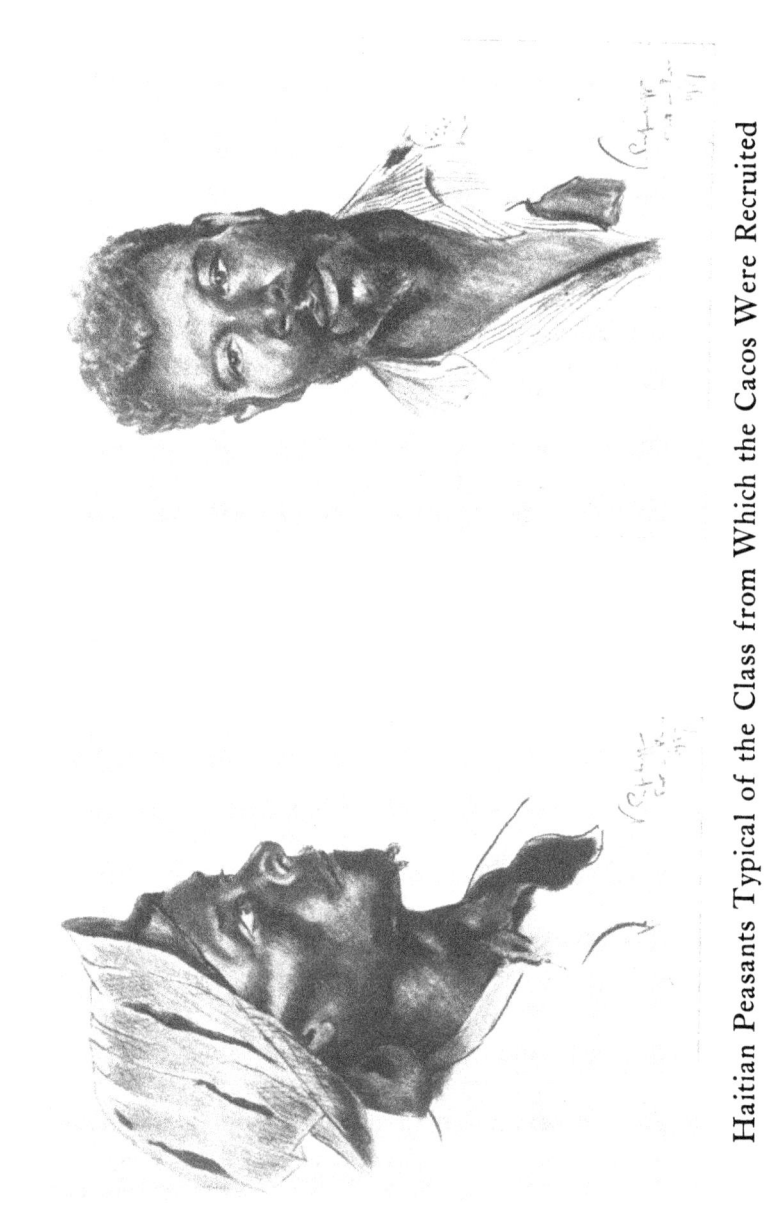

Haitian Peasants Typical of the Class from Which the Cacos Were Recruited
Reproduced by the courtesy of the artist, Vladimir Perfilieff

rine corps who were engaged for over eighteen months in guerilla warfare.

All through the year 1919 the marines, supported by the *gendarmerie,* were employed in pursuing and attacking bands of cacos, sometimes numbering as many as five hundred or more. This campaign was conducted in most difficult mountain country under a tropical sun; and the marines, totally unaccustomed to such conditions, suffered cheerfully hardships which it is difficult to overestimate.

In the fall of 1919 the situation in the northern interior of Haiti became extremely serious. Charlemagne was a clever and resourceful leader, a member of a family for generations very influential in the central plain, and to a lesser degree throughout the North. He had by this time come out openly against the occupation and had organized a "government," created a cabinet, and was commissioning "generals" and other officers to fight *"against the Americans."* His avowed object was to overthrow the *de facto* government and drive the Americans from Haiti, and through a well-organized system of espionage and propaganda he was endeavouring to attach to his cause all the leaders of the North and the disgruntled politicians of the cities and towns. It seems improbable that Charlemagne seriously thought he could succeed in driving the marines from Haiti by force. His field tactics indicated as much. But he evidently hoped to create a political situation which would result in the downfall of the government and the withdrawal of the occupation. It is estimated that at this time he had between five and six thousand men in the field, about three thousand under his immediate command in the north-western mountains and plains, two to three thousand under his first lieutenant, Benoit Battraville, and scattered bands under minor leaders. In addition there were several thousand who were not actually in the field but were available when needed. It has been estimated that in all Charle-

THE CACO UPRISING
magne had at his disposal between fifteen and seventeen thousand men.

In October, 1919, the number of marines in Haiti was 1,253; this force was reduced in January to only about 1,000 officers and men, and as it was necessary to garrison the principal cities and coast towns, maintain the brigade organizations, transport, quartermaster, and aviation units, there were never more than a few hundred marines available for actual field operations. The *gendarmerie* consisted of about 130 officers, mostly United States marines, and something over 2,000 enlisted Haitians; but this organization was nominally an urban and rural police force, and at no time during the caco uprising could any large body of *gendarmes* be spared for field duty.

The events leading to Charlemagne's death on the night of October 31, 1919, were as dramatic as any in the history of this war-torn land. Hearing that the caco chief, accompanied by about 1,200 outlaws, was in the neighbourhood of Cap Haitien for the purpose of capturing the town of Grande Rivière, two enlisted men of the United States marine corps, holding commissions in the *gendarmerie,* Captain Hanneken and Lieutenant Button, blackened their faces and, disguising themselves and twenty picked *gendarmes* in old civilian clothes, marched for many hours over the mountains, which were at the time alive with the 700 or more cacos advancing on Grande Rivière toward the enemy camp. The Americans knew the countersign and that Charlemagne would expect a detachment of his men to bring him news of their victory. Impersonating these messengers, the party of disguised *gendarmes* succeeded in passing five of the six outposts guarding the caco's head-quarters. The last outpost was but thirty paces from the chief's person, and here they were stopped abruptly by guards who handled their rifles with a threat, while Charlemagne, thinking the new-comers were his messengers, awaited their advance. Seeing that his time was limited, Hanneken opened fire on the chief while Button turned a machine gun on the caco guard, who were already seeking cover. Charlemagne and about nine of his personal body-guard fell before this surprise attack. The little detachment made good their return to Grande Rivière next day, meeting and dispersing a number of bands of outlaws returning from their unsuccessful attack.

The death of Charlemagne was a serious blow to the cacos. Not only had they lost by far the cleverest of their leaders, but Charlemagne had claimed that he was immune from bullets, and the report that two white men, supported by a few *gendarmes,* had succeeded in penetrating through thousands of the best caco troops and killing their invincible leader completely demoralized his immediate following. After a short intensive campaign by marine patrols, the caco movement of the North collapsed and many prominent chiefs surrendered. The remaining cacos chose Benoit as supreme head, thus transferring the caco activities to the mountain district of Mirebalais farther south. The efforts of the marines in this district were redoubled, and Benoit, realizing that the end was in sight and fearing to surrender, resorted to the old caco methods of recruiting by force, and in conjunction with certain people in the capital planned an attack on Port-au-Prince.

Except for the effect on commerce resulting from a decrease in the consumption of imported goods, and practical suspension of production in the comparatively small territory infested with cacos, this uprising had not seriously affected the people of the coast towns; while the South and East were scarcely affected at all. It was known that certain politicians in Port-au-Prince were in communication with the caco chiefs, but no one of any intelligence doubted that the marines, if they were not withdrawn from Haiti, would ultimately disperse the bandits. Even when a small band of

THE CACO UPRISING

cacos actually succeeded in entering Port-au-Prince in November, 1919, and three Haitian engineers of prominent families were killed by cacos in the plain of the Cul de Sac, there was little apprehension of serious danger from an attack on the capital. The death of Charlemagne had been generally accepted as a death-blow to cacoism. In the early morning of January 15th, however, sounds of shots in the city, followed by the burning of a poorer section of the town known as Belair, caused intense excitement in the capital. For a while it was feared that one of the old-time revolutionary proceedings would be repeated. But if any plans had been made for an uprising in the city they failed to materialize, and a handful of marines quickly dispersed a large band of cacos, either killing or capturing them, or forcing them back into the hills. It has been impossible definitely to determine the number of cacos who entered Port-au-Prince, but it is estimated that over three hundred were killed or captured, and an active pursuit by marine and *gendarme* patrols resulted in the surrender, within the next few weeks, of over 3,200 more.

In May, 1920, Benoit was killed in the field, and after his death the remaining caco chiefs, realizing that the end had come, surrendered to the military forces of the occupation, and by the midsummer of 1920 the country was completely freed from caco activities. While official reports estimated the total number of Haitians killed in the various campaigns at 2,500, it is believed that this is very decidedly an overestimate. The Senate inquiry disclosed that reports of casualties were often guesses made in the field and very often greatly exaggerated. The report of the Senate committee states as a fair estimate of casualties about 1,500.[3]

It has been asserted that many innocent natives were killed by the marines, and it is probable that some who had no direct connexion with the cacos were killed. Military operations are never accomplished without the suffering of innocent people; moreover, in this campaign it was most difficult for the marines to distinguish innocent people from the enemy. A peasant might well be an active caco up to the time of the arrival of a marine patrol and, simply by hiding his arms, become to all appearances an innocent bystander. In some instances caco bands were surprised in settlements or villages where, either out of sympathy or from fear, they were harboured by the inhabitants. When such bands were located they were instantly attacked, and in the engagements innocent people very probably were killed. Although it was well known that peasants, particularly the market women, habitually carried messages and even ammunition from Port-au-Prince to the cacos in the fields, there is no record that any of them were unduly punished.

In October, 1920, a naval court of inquiry was convened in Washington to inquire into the conduct of the personnel of the navy service which had served in Haiti since 1915.

The occasion for this court was the publication, in the American press, of lurid accounts of atrocities alleged to have been committed by marines in Haiti.[4] These articles were inspired by a most astonishing letter from the major-general commandant of the marine corps to the brigade commander at Port-au-Prince, which had inadvertently reached the press. In this extraordinary letter, marked confidential and personal, the major-general commandant stated that "the court martial of *one private* for the killing of a native prisoner brought out a statement *by his counsel,* which showed me that practically *indiscriminate killing* of natives has gone on for some time." *

This indictment of a brigade of the United States Marine by the highest officer of the corps, although based on no other evidence than a statement of counsel for a defendant in a court martial, was a newspaper "story" of the first importance; but it is extremely doubtful if it would

* The major-general commandant later testified to this effect.

～ *Left:* A Peasant ～
～ *Right:* A Caco ～

THE CACO UPRISING

have received anything like the publicity that immediately followed if it had not also been good political propaganda, and if it had not been that in the United States a national presidential campaign was then in the stage where anything detrimental to the party in power was eagerly seized upon by the opposition. In newspapers all over the United States there appeared most sensational and usually absurdly exaggerated accusations against the marines and the American occupation in Haiti; and as a result several investigations were immediately ordered.

Early in October the major-general commandant who had succeeded the author of the above-mentioned letter returned from an investigation of conditions in Haiti and reported that he had found the marines in Haiti in a highly efficient condition and that he was proud of the "intelligent, zealous, efficient, and courageous service" which this organization was giving to its country and to the Republic of Haiti.

A naval court of inquiry, consisting of two admirals and a major-general of the United States marine corps, after a thorough investigation of the records in Washington and a visit to Haiti, submitted the following conclusions:

> Referring to paragraph 2 of the precept, it is the conclusion of the court that there have been no proper grounds for the statement that "practically indiscriminate killing of natives has been going on for some time," as alleged in the letter from Brig. Gen. George Barnett, United States Marine Corps, to Col. John H. Russell, United States Marine Corps.
> Referring to the amendment to the precept, calling for the conclusions of the court as to the general conduct of the personnel of the naval service in Haiti since July 28, 1915, the court does not consider that the small number of isolated crimes or offences that have been committed by a few individuals of the service during the period in question are entitled to any considerable weight

in forming a conclusion as to the general conduct of such personnel. It was inevitable that some offences would be committed. However, considering the conditions of service in Haiti, it is remarkable that the offences were so few in number and that they all may be chargeable to the ordinary defects of human character, such defects as result in the commission of similar offences in the United States and elsewhere in the best-regulated communities. . . .

After a careful study of the matters in issue, based not only on the evidence in the record but also other original and reliable sources of information, and the court's own observations, while in Haiti, the court regards the charges which have been published as ill considered, regrettable, and thoroughly unwarranted reflections on a portion of the United States Marine Corps which has performed difficult, dangerous, and delicate duty in Haiti in a manner which, instead of calling for adverse criticism, is entitled to the highest commendation.

The record of the proceedings of this twenty-first day of inquiry was read and approved, and the court, having finished the inquiry, then, at 11 o'clock A.M., adjourned to await the action of the convening authority.

This report has been characterized as "a liberal coat of whitewash," but while it is generally conceded that additional "acts of violence" other than those established before the naval court were committed, it is unfair to question the legitimacy of this court or the general integrity of its findings. The United States marine is a fairly typical American. It is absurd to suggest that a short stay in Haiti could radically alter his character, or create, out of a normally decent citizen, the brute beast so luridly described in some of the articles which, largely owing to a presidential campaign in the United States, received such widespread publicity.

Delegates of the *Union Patriotique d'Haïti,* an organization founded in Port-au-Prince in November, 1920 (Exhibit E), visited Washington in the spring of 1921 for the

THE CACO UPRISING

purpose of presenting a memoir to the President of the United States, to the Department of State, and to Congress, in the conclusion of which the salient aspirations of the Haitian people are summarized as follows:

1. Immediate abolition of martial law and courts martial.
2. Immediate reorganization of the Haitian policy and military forces, and withdrawal within a short period of the United States military occupation.
3. Abrogation of the Convention of 1915.
4. Convocation, within a short period, of a constitutional assembly with all the guarantees of electoral liberty.

This memoir, which was printed in full in the *Nation*, New York, May 25, 1921, concluded as follows: "But the Haitian people desire too strongly the friendship of the great American people, and are too anxious for their own material, intellectual, and moral development not to wish and bespeak for themselves the impartial and altruistic aid of the United States government. They have urgent needs, vital to the development of the natural resources of the country and essential to the full expansion of its agricultural, industrial, and commercial activity. The satisfying of these needs is absolutely necessary for the continued progress of the Haitian community.

"Nothing would serve better to bring about the speedy re-establishment of normal conditions between the two countries than the friendly aid of the United States government in the economic prosperity and social progress of the Haitian Republic." *

This memoir, which recited about the same charges against the American occupation as had caused the investigation by the naval court, was presented to the Depart-

* See Exhibit E.

ment of State and the Foreign Relations Committee of the Senate on May 9, 1921, and on the same day the Secretary of the Navy stated that the Navy Department welcomed any investigation that Congress might care to make. The Secretary is quoted as saying, "The marine corps did a splendid work there [in Haiti] as humanely as it was possible to do it." The Secretary also stated that when he visited Haiti recently * on a tour of inspection he saw evidence on every hand to convince him that the continued presence of American marines in Haiti was desirable.

Pursuant to a resolution of the United States Senate (S. Res. 112, Sixty-seventh Congress) authorizing a special committee to inquire into the occupation and administration of the territories of the Republic of Haiti and the Dominican Republic, a "Select Committee on Haiti and Santo Domingo—United States Senate" met on August 5, 1921. After holding sessions in Washington, from August 5 to November 16, 1921, during which comprehensive statements, memorials, and documents were placed on record and many witnesses were heard, the committee adjourned to meet at Port-au-Prince, Haiti, on November 29, 1921. The Senators (McCormick, Oddie, Pomerene, and Jones) arrived at Port-au-Prince on the morning of November 29, 1921, and were met with a reception which must have very seriously prejudiced the case of the Patriotic Union, which was admittedly responsible for this demonstration.

A procession made up largely of people hired for the occasion, carrying banners with such legends as "SHALL HAITI BE OUR CONGO?" "SHALL HAITI BE OUR BELGIUM?" paraded the streets from the dock to the American legation.

The committee opened the session on Haiti on November 30th, and after calling the committee to order the chairman stated: "There was published in Port-au-Prince, on the

* March, 1921.

THE CACO UPRISING

24th of November, a communication which appeared in both English and French, and which in part reads as follows: 'It is not necessary to state that a committee of the Senate is the judge of the character and competence of the testimony which it admits to its records. The committee seeks the calm and reasonable judgment of those who come before it competent to offer opinions upon the problem which it is studying, and, under oath, an unbiassed and unclouded statement of substantiated and proven facts by those who desire to state such facts.' The committee deems it unnecessary any further to assure the security of witnesses conforming to these standards, as it does to deny that it would in any degree condone perjury."

At the second session of the committee, the principal witness was the "Delegate Administrator" of the *Union Patriotique,* who had, in a short session on the previous day, practically accused the "military occupation" of intimidation and of preventing witnesses from coming to Port-au-Prince to testify. That the Senators did not credit this, and that they were not favourably impressed by the *Union Patriotique's* contention, is apparent from the following excerpts from the record of the hearing:

THE CHAIRMAN: When was the *Union Patriotique* organized?
DR. SYLVAIN (Delegate): November of last year. . . .
THE CHAIRMAN: How many members are there in this Union?
DR. SYLVAIN: We may estimate the number at 10,000 adherents throughout the country.*
THE CHAIRMAN: On what do you base that estimate?
DR. SYLVAIN: Because we have committees in nearly all

---

* The delegate of the *Union Patriotique* who presented the memoir to the committee a few weeks before had stated the Union "has at least 20,000 members."

BLACK DEMOCRACY

communes of the country. These committees constitute the directing element.

THE CHAIRMAN: How many members are there in Port-au-Prince?

DR. SYLVAIN: The population may say in its generality that the membership is unlimited.

THE CHAIRMAN: I am not asking what the population say. I want your knowledge.

DR. SYLVAIN: One may have an idea of the numerical importance of our adherents by the manifestation which was organized yesterday entirely by the *Union Patriotique*.

After several public hearings and much private investigation by individual members of the committee, a number of hearings were held at points in the interior.

As the investigation progressed it became increasingly evident that much of the testimony before the committee was most unreliable, and evident that some of it, at least, was inspired by no other purpose than to create sentiment antagonistic to the existing government and the American occupation.

In summing up the results of the naval court of inquiry which had investigated much of the same matter, the Judge Advocate in an oral argument had said that had the court been sitting within the territorial jurisdiction of a Federal Court, there would have been means whereby perjury committed by a witness could have been properly punished, but for perjury committed in testifying before the court of inquiry in Haiti he knew of no method of reaching the perjurers. The Senate committee was confronted by a similar situation, and much truth which might have been of interest was so obscured in a tissue of falsehood as to be totally inadmissible.

On the return of this committee to the United States in

THE CACO UPRISING

December, 1921, the chairman issued a preliminary summary of the committee's views which read in part as follows:

> The Marines in Haiti were as necessary to the peace and development of the country as are the services to the Haitian Government of the American officials appointed under the Treaty of 1915. There can be no abrogation of the treaty and at this time no diminution of the small force of Marines. . . . It is important that steps should be taken forthwith to co-ordinate the labours of the representatives of the United States Government in Haiti and of the so-called American treaty officials. There should be appointed a special representative of the President, a high commissioner, in whom should be vested the usual diplomatic powers of an envoy extraordinary, and to whom, furthermore, all the American officials appointed under the treaty, as well as the commandant of the Marine brigade, should look for direction and guidance. . . .
>
> The chairman of the Committee has ventured to point out the very great importance of carefully choosing for service in Haiti, in civil or military capacities, officers who are sympathetic with the Haitian people, who will seek to establish cordial relations with the Haitians. Officers of the Marine corps going to Haiti should understand that in order fully to discharge their duty to the United States and to deserve the commendation of their superiors they must consider the dual responsibilities of their duty. They should be selected not only because of their capacity to command troops, but to command them in Haiti and among the Haitian people. Conversely, the most intelligent and active elements of the Haitian people must appreciate that since American forces are to continue in Haiti for the maintenance of peace, and that since under the existing treaty American officials are to remain to help the Haitian Government to carry out necessary reforms, the greatest measure of service to Haiti with the smallest degree of friction will require a spirit of accommodation and co-operation not only on the part of the American officials, but also on the part

of those in Haiti who are active in the life of the capital and of the other principal centres.

After a number of additional hearings the Committee submitted its final report on April 20, 1922 (Senate Report 794, Sixty-seventh Congress, Second Session). In connexion with the charges of military abuses, this report presented the following summary of facts:

(1) That the accusations of military abuses are limited in point of time to a few months and in location to a restricted area.

(2) Very few of the many Americans who have served in Haiti are thus accused. The others have restored order and tranquillity under arduous conditions of service, and generally won the confidence of the inhabitants of the country with whom they come in touch.

(3) That certain caco prisoners were executed without trial. Two such cases have been judicially determined. The evidence to which reference has been made shows eight more cases with sufficient clearness to allow them to be regarded without much doubt as having occurred. Lack of communications and the type of operations conducted by small patrols not in direct contact with superior authority in some cases prevented knowledge of such occurrences on the part of higher authority until it was too late for effective investigation. When reported, investigations were held with no apparent desire to shield any guilty party. Such executions were unauthorized and directly contrary to the policy of the brigade commanders.

(4) That torture of Haitians by Americans has not in any case been established, but that some accusations may have a foundation in excesses committed by hostile natives or members of the *gendarmerie* without knowledge of the American officers. Mutilations have not been practised by Americans.

(5) That in the course of the campaign certain inhabitants other than bandits were killed during operations

THE CACO UPRISING

against the outlaws, but that such killings were unavoidable, accidental, and not intentional.

(6) That there was a period of about six months at the beginning of the outbreak when the *gendarmerie* lost control of the situation and was not itself sufficiently controlled by its higher officers, with the result that subordinate officers in the field were left too much discretion as to methods of patrol and local administration, and that this state of affairs was not investigated promptly enough, but that it was remedied as soon as known to the brigade commander. That the type of operations necessarily required the exercise of much independent discretion by detachment commanders.

(7) That undue severity or reckless treatment of natives was never countenanced by the brigade or *gendarmerie* commanders and that the investigation by naval authority of charges against members of the Marine Corps displays no desire to shield any individual, but on the contrary an intention to get at the facts.

(8) That the testimony of most native witnesses is highly unreliable and must be closely scrutinized and that many unfounded accusations have been made. It is also felt that in the case of accusations of abuses committed two years ago now made for the first time, the delay has not arisen through any well-grounded fear of oppression by military authority, but that many of those accusations in affidavit form, now forthcoming, are produced at this late date because it is thought by those who are agitating for the immediate termination of the Occupation that such accusations will create in the United States a sentiment in favour of such termination. In such cases the delay in making the charges and in presenting the evidence weighs heavily against the truth of the charge. All such charges, however, require full investigation. The Committee feels certain that the necessary investigation by the Navy Department will be thoroughly conducted, that the rights of those accused will be respected, and that there will be no suppression of facts. When collected the facts so obtained may be weighed with the facts alleged in the accusation. If, when all such evidence is in, the Com-

mittee has any reason to change any of its conclusions, it will submit with the evidence as printed such revision of this report on the alleged military abuses as may be required.

The Committee believes that an important lesson may be learned from a study of this bandit campaign and the subsequent grave charges of misconduct. The lesson is the extreme importance in a campaign of this kind for higher command to require daily operation reports to be prepared by patrol leaders. In the early days of the outbreak such reports were not systematically required. Small patrols would be out of touch with the rest of our forces for days or weeks under distressing conditions of service. There is no complete record of the places they visited or when the visits were made or who was in command. If such reports or records were in existence, innocent individuals could instantly be cleared of unfounded charges, and guilty individuals could be identified with certainty. Such reports would have been a safeguard to the inhabitants and to the reputation of the Americans.

In summing up the record of the failure and achievements of the American occupation in Haiti, the Senate committee stated that it was impossible not to condemn the blunder committed when, under the *corvée,* labourers were carried beyond their own districts and forced to work under guard in strange surroundings. This the committee held to be an error of commission "like those of omission arising from failure to develop a definite and constructive policy under the treaty; to centralize responsibility for the conduct of American officers and officials serving in Haiti"; blunders partly due, the committee held, to the failure of the departments in Washington to appreciate the importance of selecting for service in Haiti, whether in civil or military capacities, men who were sympathetic to Haitians, and able to maintain cordial personal and official relations with them.

THE CACO UPRISING

In this conclusion the committee voiced the opinion of many competent observers who had investigated conditions in Haiti under the occupation. Perhaps the most difficult aspect of the American intervention, on which its success or failure may ultimately depend, arises from the racial antagonisms inherent in both whites and blacks, which are intensified in this black man's country by the fact that the executive departments and the expenditures thereof are largely directed by Americans, and such Haitians as hold official positions are generally subordinate to white men. The fact that such governmental agencies as that of Finance, Public Works, Sanitation, and Public Safety are indisputably much more efficiently administered than ever before in the history of the Republic, and that graft and corruption have been largely eliminated from public service, while public funds are expended for the benefit of the people, does not overcome the repugnance of the political classes of Haiti to white administration of the offices which for generations they had considered their natural prerogative.

Unfortunately the attitude of many of the American officials has unnecessarily, and even perhaps gratuitously, wounded the very real sensibilities of their Haitian collaborators and subordinates. The purely social relations between Americans and Haitians, both official and unofficial, have been equally unfortunate. Americans in Haiti have been too prone to see and emphasize the "funny" side of many phases of the political history and social life of the Haitian people, and while most Haitians will cheerfully admit the national shortcomings, they very naturally hate being laughed at, and resent exaggeration or misrepresentation of things which involve their dignity, either national or personal.

After reviewing the material benefits which in their opinion might be credited to the American occupation—sanitation, roads, the stabilization of finances, the assurance of peace and order, etc.—the Senate committee cited particularly the highly creditable achievement of the marine officers who were responsible for the organization and administration of the *gendarmerie* of Haiti. In summing up "What Must Be Done," the committee submitted that the American people would not consider their duty under the treaty discharged "if in addition to what has been accomplished there are not placed within the reach of the Haitian masses justice, schools, and agricultural institutions." The Senators realized that these things, so absolutely necessary to the progress of Haiti, were not mentioned in the treaty, and that no means were provided in this instrument for their accomplishment. But they made certain recommendations as to the procedures whereby such things might be brought about. Some of these improvements have been inaugurated, in spite of a very definite opposition from a certain element in Haiti. Others are planned or contemplated, but in justice to the American officials it should be pointed out that practically every program submitted by them, designed to benefit the Haitian people, has been opposed by the Haitian press and the opponents of the Government, *i.e.*, a majority of the articulate Haitians who are not "in" the Government. While some of this opposition is doubtless sincere expression of disapproval of the projects in question, it is generally inspired by a spirit of hostility to the Government and particularly to the American intervention, and by bitter opposition to any increase in the powers of the treaty officers or further so-called "encroachments" by them.

A recommendation that the marine forces be gradually withdrawn from all outposts and reduced in number, and that ultimately the preservation of peace and order should be entrusted to the *gendarmerie,* has been met partly by the concentration of the remaining marine force in Port-au-

THE CACO UPRISING

Prince and Cap Haitien, and by a decided increase in the efficiency of the *gendarmerie*.

While recognizing the original necessity for the declaration of martial law, the committee stated, was conditional courts, the committee recommended that the system under which offences by the press against peace and order were tried by provost courts should be abolished. This has been done, and such offences are now prosecuted by Haitian courts under a recently adopted "press law." Martial law is still in effect, and apparently must be so long as the United States maintains a military force in Haiti. Provost courts, however, do not in any way infringe on the liberties of the Haitian people, but are confined to trying offences against the United States military establishment. The final abolition of martial law, the committee stated, was conditional on certain precedent steps, among them the reform of the courts of first instance, which, with all other intelligent observers of the situation in Haiti, the committee held to be of urgency and importance.

In concluding, the committee stated that along the lines suggested by them there could be "rapid development in Haiti, moral, social, political, and economic, *always provided that American policy be marked by continuity and the spirit of service.*" "Not only," they said, "have certain American officers and officials been chosen for service in Haiti who were unsuited to their task, but men have been transferred from responsible posts before they could very well have learned the duties to which they had been appointed." The committee further cited that during the six years of the occupation there had been half a dozen chiefs of the Latin-American division of the United States Department of State and many changes in the office of chief of the *gendarmerie* of Haiti. This might well have been elaborated to include a discussion of the question as to the advisability of assigning officers of the navy limited to short tours of duty to such positions as engineers in the Department of Public Works. Since the organization of the Direction General of this department in 1917, three United States Navy officers have held the position of chief engineer. That the present chief engineer and his predecessor were men of exceptional ability and devoted to their work is generally recognized; yet it seems obvious that changes in the personnel of such important positions every three years are detrimental to efficiency. This is especially true under the peculiar conditions existing in Haiti, where the chief object of the American officials is, or should be, to develop, in so far as possible, a permanent organization and to train men ultimately to take over the administration of the various departments.

The report concludes: "On the part of Haitian officials and the literate element of the Haitian people there must be co-operation with the American officials. Haitians must candidly realize the meaning of the unhappy events of the last twenty years and appreciate that in collaboration with America under the treaty Haiti can develop the wealth necessary to progress, provide for general education of her people, and establish a more truly representative system of government than she has ever known. There are certain elements in Haiti which can baulk and perhaps delay the rehabilitation of the country. They cannot prevent it. They can do much to further it. The obvious duty of patriotic Haitians is to uphold their own government in effectively co-operating with that of the United States under the treaty, and so hasten the day when Haiti can stand alone. The alternative to the course herein suggested is the abandonment of the Haitian people to chronic revolution, anarchy, barbarism, and ruin."

One pathetic aspect of the situation is that the majority of this same "literate element" which is thus warned by the Senate committee is, or at least pretends to be, in favour

THE CACO UPRISING

of the immediate withdrawal of the American occupation, and apparently prefers to face the dark picture of chronic revolution, anarchy, etc., rather than to countenance the present régime. And unfortunately the masses who have profited most by the American intervention are absolutely inarticulate, have never heard of the Senate committee, or of the Senate, or for that matter of the United States of America, and have only a vague conception of their own government. Such, however, is the existing situation, which is still further complicated by the lack of any apparent constructive effort to solve the long-deferred problem of giving to the Haitian people political autonomy. This is the most legitimate and by far the most vital of the complaints of the still resentful and disgruntled political class which represents the only articulate public opinion in Haiti.

CHAPTER VI

NATIONAL ELECTIONS

UNDER the Constitution of 1918 the national sovereignty is vested in the legislative, the executive, and the judicial power; "each power is independent of the other two in its functions, which it exercises independently" (Art. 128).

The executive department by law consists, under its terms, of the president, elected for four years, who is eligible for re-election but may not serve more than two consecutive terms, and a cabinet of five members appointed by the president. The constitution provides for two legislative houses—the Chamber of Deputies with 36 members * elected by the people, and the Senate of 15 members, representing the five "departments," who are elected by "universal and direct suffrage." These two Houses constitute the National Assembly, whose prerogatives are, first, to elect the president of the Republic; secondly, to declare war; thirdly, to approve or reject all treaties and international conventions. Such is the organization provided for in the permanent articles of the constitution, but, the legislative bodies having been dismissed in 1917 and not since reconvened, a very different organization has actually functioned since that time.

Some of the most strenuous criticism of the present régime in Haiti has been directed against the failure to take any steps towards the re-establishment of so-called repre-

---

* Pending a census of the population, when the number of deputies is to be fixed at one deputy to each 60,000 inhabitants.

~ Louis Borno, President of the Republic of Haiti ~

NATIONAL ELECTIONS

sentative government. It is frankly admitted by Haiti's best friends that nothing approaching a truly representative form of government has ever existed in Haiti or can possibly exist while ninety-five per cent of the population remains as it is now—illiterate, inarticulate, and completely unaware of the sources or functions of government. Haiti as a nation has been run by and for the benefit of some 30,000 articulate persons and especially in behalf of about 2,000 *élite* of the political class. The utter disregard for the great mass of the people of the peasant class is, and always has been, an unfortunate tradition of the realities of Haitian government.

It is natural, however, that the small body of the aristocracy of Haiti, unfortunately the only class that is heard, bitterly resents the suppression of the legislature, not only because of the humiliation, but because the greater part of the income of this class, prior to the American intervention, was derived from political jobs. Moreover, the substitution of a small appointive council of state for the Senate and Chamber of Deputies has deprived a considerable number of them of one of their few recognized means of gaining a livelihood. The legislature has been twice dissolved since the American intervention on the ground that this body was dominated by a spirit of hostility and obstruction towards the executive, the treaty, and the program agreed upon between the representatives of the United States and of the Haitian government.

The Constitution of 1918 provides (Article D) that "a council of state, consisting of twenty-one members apportioned among the different departments, shall exercise the legislative power until a duly elected legislative body shall have been constituted, at which time the council of state shall cease to exist." The preceding article provides that the next elections of senators and deputies after the adoption of this constitution could be held only after the presi-

BLACK DEMOCRACY

dent had fixed the date for such election. These two articles were obviously drafted for the express purpose of enabling the president to proceed with the program agreed upon between the two governments, unhampered by a hostile legislature.

The reasons for the establishment of the council of state and the provisions for its continuation were considered imperative. It was abundantly evident that with the immediate reconvocation of a national assembly through a so-called popular election, there would recur the same obstructive tactics which had resulted in its dissolution. The President was also influenced by a very definite fear that a legislative body, so elected at that time, would proceed to impeach him, a proceeding practically unknown in Haiti, where simpler and more forceful means of removing a president had long been in vogue.

It may as well be honestly conceded that an elective legislature, in the sense in which such a body is elsewhere understood, could at the moment contribute very little to the betterment of Haiti. As a matter of fact, the legislators have never been elected by the people but have, to all intents and purposes, been chosen by the leaders in power. Just how casually these executives themselves secured their power should never be ignored when discussing the realities of Haiti. In one hundred and eight years, prior to the American intervention, twenty-four executives held office. Seventeen of the twenty-four were deposed by revolutions; five died in office, one it is said by poison, one in the explosion of the national palace, one on the eve of his overthrow by revolutionists. Two only of the twenty-four were allowed to retire peaceably from office; eleven of the twenty-four served for less than one year each. The six immediate predecessors of President Dartiguenave, elected in 1915, averaged only a little more than six months each, and his immediate predecessor was murdered by a mob. Never in the

NATIONAL ELECTIONS

history of Haiti has the great mass of the common people had any voice in the government of its country or in the selection of its rulers.

In spite of the fact that the majority of the executives of Haiti have been overthrown by so-called revolutions, there has never been a revolutionary movement which originated with the common people, or an election in which the people as a whole participated.[1] Revolutions have resulted from the desire of the politically influential "outs" to supersede the momentarily powerful "ins," and until the American intervention change of administration never favourably affected the condition of the common people in whose name revolutionary propaganda was invariably initiated. There has never been a "free" election, and there exists no general idea of popular suffrage.

Firmin, one of Haiti's most eminent publicists, in a letter from St. Thomas, where he was in exile, wrote: "For one hundred and three years, by disguising ourselves with a republican system—except for two inconsistent or burlesque attempts at an improvised monarchy—and by making a display of democratic institutions copied from the most beautiful precepts of rational policy, we have been living with immunity in the face of the whole world, for we have carefully conserved ignorance at the foundation of our social organization and made it the basis of all our constitutional and legal juggling. Such a persistent and systematic lie has not only corrupted intellects and perverted the best conceptions of true democracy, but has even influenced, in the most unfortunate way, the idea of sovereignty and the functioning of the national organism. Authority which must reside, in fact and by right, in law and reason, has lost among us all moral prestige, all solid basis, and has been transformed into ephemeral, malevolent, sanguinary, or grotesque preponderance."

An appointive council of state is admittedly an unsatisfactory substitute for a representative legislative body in a country where the people are *capable of exercising suffrage,* but it has certain very definite advantages under the actual and not theoretical conditions which exist in Haiti to-day, where the executive has usually controlled all elections, including the primary assemblies, until he was overthrown by armed force. The difference now is that the manner of selection of the legislative body is *openly and frankly appointive.*

It is pertinent also to point out that a council of state in Haiti is an institution as old as the proclamation of independence. Three executives have been elected and three constitutions drafted by councils of state.*

First Election by the Council of State

One of the principal criticisms of the Haitian government as constituted, and particularly as to the perpetuation of the council of state as a legislative body, other than the claim that the latter had no power to act as a national assembly, has been that the control of the council of state through the power of appointment and removal would inevitably result in the re-election of the executive then in power. That this natural supposition was not necessarily true was proved at the first presidential election at which the council of state functioned as an electoral body. The term of office of Dartiguenave, elected by the national assembly in 1915 for seven years (old constitution), expired in May, 1922. As Dartiguenave had not promulgated a decree fixing the day for legislative elections, the council of state continued to function as the legislative body, and on April 10, 1922, the date fixed in the constitution for presidential elections, this body, notwithstanding that Dartiguenave was an active candidate, elected Louis Borno, a

* See Exhibit I.

NATIONAL ELECTIONS

former Minister for Foreign Affairs, to the presidency for a term of four years (new constitution).

President Borno was inaugurated on May 15, 1922, on which day the Haitians witnessed the, to them, unique spectacle of the peaceful transfer of office from a president to his successor. During his first term, which expired on May 15, 1926, President Borno refrained from fixing a date for the election of a legislature.

The position of the present Haitian government as to holding national elections was clearly presented just before the expiration of President Borno's first term in the executive's letter to the prefects of *arrondissements*. In this letter President Borno quoted extensively from an official statement made by President Dartiguenave in August, 1916, in which the former chief executive pointed out that the national assembly, which he had recently dissolved, had ratified three *coups d'état* by electing successively three revolutionary chiefs, and that while the American intervention was certainly a sacrifice of national self-respect, "between this sacrifice and the life of shame, misery, and ignominy from which it had rescued us, no citizen having a true sense of national honour could hesitate."

President Borno, in this letter, then reviewed innumerable benefits which had resulted from the American intervention, and stated: "Nevertheless, if the general situation offers so much satisfaction, how can it be denied that the work accomplished until now is but a beginning, when one considers all that is still left to be done to assure the continued development of agriculture, commerce, public education, health, seriously to guarantee public peace, public and private property, the home, and the security of all against any possible return to our evil past, our past of bloody and destructive revolutions, scandalous pillage, and the persecution and exploitation of the peasants by military satraps, masters of life and property?

BLACK DEMOCRACY

"And before this immense task which solicits, urges, and demands an active coalition of all good wills, what do we see to-day? Groups of politicians at bay, scattered through different parts of the country, pretend to oppose the civilizing progress of the Government by exerting themselves to create and to develop an agitation purely political under the lying pretext of 'restoring democratic institutions,' that is to say, to be exact, to replace the present legislative council of state by a chamber and a senate!"

The President assured the prefects that it was the firm intention of the present government to "realize fully the constitutional provision for the election of the two legislative chambers," but pointed out that the constitution had made dependent upon a special convocation by the president of the Republic the time when such elections should be held, and he added:

"This is the whole question between the Government and its adversaries. These latter say, immediately; that is to say, on January 10th next. But the Government, which has no thought of deceiving itself or of deceiving anyone else, replies, No, the Haitian people are not ready. Democracy is the government of the people by conscious, popular suffrage, practised with the greatest possible liberty; we have that liberty. Never in any period of our history, for more than a century, has there been in Haiti as much liberty as at the present moment. The liberty of circulation is absolute; without any passport one crosses the country in every security. The freedom of holding meetings is subject only to a previous notification to the local police. The freedom of the press, which is, when summed up, the expression of all the others, is absolute; the law which governs it is made only to suppress abuses, defamation, outrage, provocation to crime, all those intolerable excesses by which the old revolutionary demon, impatient to break his chains, manifests himself from time to time.

NATIONAL ELECTIONS

"We have liberty. But where, then, is our *popular conscious suffrage?*

"Our rural population, which represents nine-tenths of the Haitian people, is almost totally illiterate, ignorant, and poor; although its material and moral situation has been appreciably bettered in these last few years, it is still incapable of exercising the right to vote, and would be the easy prey of those bold speculators whose conscience hesitates at no lie.

"As for the urban population, one-tenth of the total population, those of its members who are capable of expressing an intelligent vote—a little progressive minority formed of peaceful men, business men, artisans, citizens of different professions, belonging to different social classes—have for a long time, for the most part, renounced their electoral rights, disgusted by the immoral and insolent frauds which render and would still render illusory their efforts as intelligent electors. The remainder is the small group of professional politicians, with their followers of every sort, who are mainly illiterate.

"This is the present electoral body; it is characterized by an absolute lack of organization as to the little number of its useful elements, and, for the rest, by a flagrant inability to assume, in the decisive period through which we are passing, the heavy responsibilities of a political action.

"Popular suffrage has not its *raison d'être* if it can only serve to elect individuals and nothing else. True democratic suffrage should serve, primarily, to elect individuals, definite principles, programs of action, and methods of government.

"All this amounts to saying that the rational and necessary foundation of democratic suffrage is, in a conscious electoral body, the organization of practice with platforms.

"Our national history has presented up to now only two real parties—the National party, which extols the principle of a strong executive authority, and the Liberal party, enthusiastic about parliamentarism. Both have disappeared from the political scene through lack of interior discipline and of support by a real public opinion.

"The Government is working to prepare the way to the intelligent and disciplined democracy, to the solid organization thereof. The present electoral law is recognized by all as incompatible with the sincere expression of popular will. A new law, now in the course of preparation, will be presented at the next ordinary session; it will offer all the possibilities for the full functioning of political parties, and for the constitution of an intelligent electoral body, capable of exercising, without danger to the Republic, the sovereign attributes of universal suffrage.

"And when the hour shall have struck, an hour which will be hastened, let us hope, by the wisdom of our citizens, the president of the Republic will be proud to put into operation the solemn prerogative which the constitution has consigned to his patriotism, his judgment, and his conscience, to fix the date of the legislative elections." *

On April 10, 1926, no Chamber of Deputies or Senate having been elected, the Council of State, functioning as a national assembly, met as an electoral body and re-elected Louis Borno for a term of four years. His election naturally was highly satisfactory to the American advisers of the Haitian government. President Borno is an able lawyer and a man of wide diplomatic and administrative experience, and notwithstanding bitter and even rabid criticism

---

* In the second annual report of the American High Commissioner (December, 1923), he stated: "While it is desired that Haiti should have a duly elected legislative body at as early a date as possible, the actual situation must be given due consideration. Until the American Intervention and for over 100 years, Haiti has been nothing more or less than a military oligarchy of the most severe type. Ninety-five per cent of its people were and are illiterate and a large per cent unmoral. Under such conditions the word 'democracy' has but an empty sound."

NATIONAL ELECTIONS

had loyally and consistently given most intelligent co-operation and support to the program agreed upon between himself and the American officials. The re-election of Mr. Borno assured an orderly and progressive continuation of this program.

The procedure under which a president was elected by twenty-one men over whom he exercised the right of appointment and dismissal very naturally gave rise to much adverse comment. The usual accusations of official pressure and graft materialized. On election day an abortive attempt to create a riot was quickly suppressed without bloodshed, and on May 15th President Borno inaugurated his second term of four years.

Thus, since the adoption of the constitution in 1918, the even-numbered years, 1920, 1922, 1924, and 1926, years in which an election for senators and deputies might legally have been held, passed without such elections, and during that period the Council of State had functioned as the legislative body of Haiti and twice elected Louis Borno to the presidency.

The next following date on which elections of senators and deputies might legally be held was January 10, 1928, and then only if the President exercised the power granted to him under the transitory provision of the constitution, and three months prior to that date issued a call for such elections.

President Borno made no such call, but while maintaining his position that the people of Haiti are "flagrantly unable to assume, in the decisive period through which we are passing, the grave duties of a political action," he sent to the Council of State a series of thirteen amendments to the constitution, which, to become effective, must be adopted by the majority of the entire electorate of the Republic.

It is difficult to convey to American readers an idea of the situation which has developed in Haiti since the ratification of the Haitian-American Treaty. This treaty, obviously a compromise, pledged the United States to very definite obligations but failed to provide proper machinery for the accomplishment of these pledges.

It was the old story of honest, blundering "Uncle Sam" rushing into a situation long anticipated but for which no adequate preparation had been made.

The political element in Haiti, seeing no personal profit in affiliation with the American-controlled régime, had from the beginning opposed practically every program designed by the President and his American advisers to secure the accomplishment of the objects expressed in the treaty.

It was the obstructive tactics of this element that forced the administration to choose between the abandonment of plans for the development of an agreed program, and the adoption of such drastic steps as the dissolution of the legislature in 1917.

It is equally unfortunate that the constitution of 1918, said to have been drafted by the then Assistant Secretary of the United States Navy,[2] should have been so inadequately drawn as to necessitate at this late date (January, 1928) the choice between the serious curtailment of plans for constructive development, and the resort to the somewhat extraordinary procedure of again amending the constitution.

Embarrassing as it must have been to the President and his American advisers, they chose to close up the gaps left open in the treaty and the constitution, notably in connexion with the reorganization of the judiciary, rather than to see some of their most cherished plans for betterments seriously imperilled.

To cause the election of a senate and chamber of deputies to consider these proposed amendments would have meant the organization of a few hundred active obstructionists, and the decision was taken to have the desired amend-

NATIONAL ELECTIONS

ments passed by the amenable Council of State and then submit them to the (constitutionally required) vote of the electorate for approval.

It must be admitted that while this mode of obtaining sanction to these amendments was perhaps the only course left open, it was an unfortunate and embarrassing expedient. If the Haitian electorate is, as the President and the Americans in authority have so convincingly stated, ill qualified to elect representatives in congress, it can hardly be claimed to be qualified to pass intelligently on intricate and vital amendments to the constitution of the Republic.

The thirteen amendments submitted by the President were adopted by the Council of State on October 8, 1927, and ratified by "popular" vote on January 10, 1928.

From the text as given below it will be seen that five of the thirteen amendments contain the dynamics of the changes desired, the remaining eight being devoted to comparatively innocuous administrative adjustments.

LAW

Borno, President of the Republic, in accordance with Articles 128 and D of the Constitution, and with the approval of the Council and of Secretaries of State, has proposed, and the Council of State has adopted, the following amendments to the present constitution.

First Amendment

Article 2 is changed to read: "The territory of the Republic is divided into Departments. Each Department is sub-divided into *arrondissements,* and each *arrondissement* into communes.

"The number, the limits, the organization, and the functions of the administrative divisions and subdivisions are determined by law."

BLACK DEMOCRACY

Second Amendment

Article 16 is modified as follows:
"Freedom of the press is guaranteed, subject to conditions determined by law."

Third Amendment

Article 19 is modified as follows:
"Trial by jury is established in criminal prosecutions, in those cases specified by law."

Fourth Amendment

Article 36 is modified as follows:
"The Senate is composed of fifteen Senators. Their term of office is four years, and begins the first Monday in April of an even year. They may be re-elected."

Fifth Amendment

Article 37 is modified as follows:
"The Senators represent the Departments. They are elected by direct universal suffrage by the primary assemblies of the different Departments, in the manner determined by law.
"The candidates who obtain the largest number of votes in their Departments will be elected."

Sixth Amendment

Article 72 is modified as follows:
"Subject to the following conditions, the President of the Republic is elected for six years; he cannot be a candidate for immediate re-election.
"He assumes office the fifteenth of May of the year in which he is elected, unless he is elected to fill a vacancy; in such a case he shall take office immediately upon his election, and his term shall expire six years after the fifteenth of May immediately preceding his election.
"A citizen who has served as president can be re-elected only after an interval of six years since the expiration of

NATIONAL ELECTIONS

his first term. And if he has been elected president twice, and has served his term of office, he shall be ineligible for this office."

Seventh Amendment

Article 77 is modified as follows:
"In case the office of president falls vacant, the executive power is temporarily vested in the Council of Secretaries of State.

"It shall immediately convoke the National Assembly for the election of the President of the Republic.

"If the legislative body is in session, the National Assembly shall be convoked without delay. If the legislative body is not in session, the National Assembly shall be convoked in accordance with Article 45."

Eighth Amendment

Article 83 is modified as follows:
"The Secretaries of State shall be five in number. The President of the Republic may, if he deems it necessary, add to them Under-Secretaries of State whose powers shall be determined by law.

"The Secretaries of State and Under-Secretaries of State shall be divided between the different ministerial departments as required by the needs of the state.

"A decree shall fix this division according to law."

Ninth Amendment

Article 89 is modified as follows:
"The judiciary power shall be exercised by a supreme court and lower courts, whose number, organization, and jurisdiction shall be determined by law.

"The President of the Republic shall appoint all judges. He shall appoint and recall the officers of public ministry in the supreme court and other courts, the justices of the peace, and their assistants.

"The judges of the supreme court are appointed for ten years, and those of other permanent courts, with the exception of justices of the peace, are appointed for seven years.

"Once these judges have been appointed, they are not subject to recall by the executive. However, the judges continue to be subject to the conditions of Articles 100, 101, and 102 of the Constitution and to special legislation which will determine the causes for removing them from office.

"A judge of the supreme court who has served as judge for twenty-five years or more, at least eight years as judge of the supreme court, shall be irremovable, subject to the above reservations."

Tenth Amendment

Article 109 is modified as follows:
"Taxes for the benefit of the state and the communes shall be levied only by law."

Eleventh Amendment

Article 118 is modified as follows:
"A public force, subject to the conditions fixed by law, is established to guarantee the interior and exterior security of the Republic, the rights of the people, maintenance of order, and to police the cities and country. This shall be the sole armed force of the Republic.

"Regulations for the maintenance of discipline and for the punishment of offending members of this organization shall be established by the executive power. They shall have the force of law. These regulations shall provide for the establishment of courts martial, shall prescribe their power, and shall define the duties of their members and the rights of persons brought to trial before them.

"The decisions of the courts martial are subject to revision only by the supreme court, and then only when questions arise as to jurisdiction or possible excess of the court's powers."

Twelfth Amendment

Article E is modified as follows:
"For a period of twelve months following the adop-

tion of these amendments, the executive power is authorized to make changes in the present personnel of the courts which he may deem necessary.

"Those judges who are retained shall be given commissions of the same kind as those given new appointees; the date of these commissions shall mark the time from which their term of office shall be measured, as provided by Article 89.

"In order to establish a periodic succession of judges, the executive power is authorized, in making his first nominations, to appoint some judges for shorter terms than those mentioned above. A law shall determine the conditions under which these nominations shall be made."

Thirteenth Amendment

The following articles of the present Constitution are suppressed: 90, 91, 92, 93, 95, 104, 105, 106, 119.

The second and third amendments modify somewhat drastically the freedom of the press. The constitution itself is rather exuberant on this point. Article 16 says, for instance:

> Everyone has the right to express his opinion on all matters and to write, print, and publish his thoughts. Writings shall not be submitted to previous censorship. Abridgment of this right shall be defined and punished by law, without thereby abridging in any way whatever the freedom of the press.

Abuse of the freedom of the press in Haiti has been flagrant, scandalous, and at times beyond all bounds of fairness and decency. There have been, on the other hand, attacks on the Government of which the very logic and address constituted their offence. The present régime in Haiti has been in a serious quandary as to where to draw the line. The loose terms of the constitution of 1918 have admittedly not been lived up to, recalcitrant editors have been held in gaol for months at a time without trial, and this has resulted in much adverse criticism of the Government and the American officials. But it is difficult, under the circumstances, to see that any other method could have been adopted to curb the scurrilous and utterly irresponsible editorial policy of certain newspapers, some of which have devoted practically all their space to atrocious attacks on the Government and absurd and utterly unfounded charges against American officials. One particular article directed against President Wilson was so salacious as to be unprintable in a country where offences against decency or defamation are enforceable. Such attacks, although intensely annoying to President Borno and to his American advisers, who were earnestly striving to give their best efforts to the work to which they had been assigned, were ignored until patience ceased to be a virtue, and a well-justified feeling that such half-veiled suggestions as that the president of the Republic might be poisoned and open accusation that the chief of the American occupation had tried to embezzle a large sum of money * were incitement to riot and bloodshed and dangerous to the peace, led to the arrest of several editors. Some editors were arrested for the publication of much less vicious articles than those cited above. While opposition papers in Haiti have gone to extremes, it is also true that some of their published criticism has been

---

* During the war General Russell, then the commander of the United States forces in Haiti, administered a "flour fund" authorized by Washington to secure wheat flour for the benefit of the people of Haiti. The settlement of this operation showed a credit balance of some $74,000 which Washington decided should be paid over to the Haitian government. Owing to red tape in Washington, there was some delay in transferring this balance to Haiti and one of the opposition papers charged that General Russell had tried to embezzle the money and had been forced to refund by the Department of State. Instead of gratitude for the most able administration of a program which resulted in an ample supply of one of the necessities of life at the lowest possible cost, the chief of the occupation was charged with the meanest sort of criminal graft.

This $74,000 has since been expended on a hospital in the Central Plain.

NATIONAL ELECTIONS

justifiable. Many well-intentioned and honest critics of the present régime have held that such offences should have been tried, as provided in the constitution, by a jury. But anyone familiar with the situation is aware of the utter futility of submitting to a Haitian jury a libel suit in which the plaintiff is a Haitian government official or an American, or for that matter any foreigner. It is not only that prejudice against the government and the American officials would inevitably result in immediate acquittal, regardless of the evidence, but it is a well-established fact that all foreigners are held to be fair game. The only libel suits in Haiti in which judgments for damages are likely to be rendered are cases instituted by Haitians against foreigners for defamation of character or damages claimed in connexion with arrests made by the police on information laid by foreigners accusing Haitians of crime.*

The danger and annoyance of such suits is to-day a discouragement towards the legitimate investment of foreign capital and a definite impediment to the economic development of Haiti. It must be remembered that no such thing as freedom of the press ever existed in Haiti, where in spite of constitutional immunity no editor who valued his life dared to publish articles derogatory to the executive. No press law was necessary in a country where the will of the executive was supreme.†

---

* One typical example of such suits is that of a Syrian merchant, an American citizen, who imported two dozen very expensive silk shirts and found on delivery from the customs that four shirts were missing.

On the same day that he made a complaint to the customs collector, he met a custom house employee wearing one of these shirts. As this man refused to tell how the shirt had come into his possession, he was arrested. The court refused to hold him, and later the Syrian merchant was forced by a court decision to pay heavy damages for "defamation of character."

† *La Plume*, a newspaper of Port-au-Prince, printed in November, 1914, an extraordinary, courageous editorial from which the following excerpts are translated: "What is our army? A band of armed people who pretend that the soldier must not fight. What is our justice? Judges poorly

BLACK DEMOCRACY

The freedom from danger of summary execution, assassination, or deportation, guaranteed by the American intervention, coupled with the certainty that no Haitian jury would convict, resulted in licence to publish any libel, no matter how atrocious.

The new amendment affecting the freedom of the press is, in a sense, a means of giving the Haitian government the power to protect itself in a situation from which some amelioration was absolutely necessary. It provides quite simply that "the freedom of the press is guaranteed subject to conditions determined by law." And the subsequent amendment, the third, pointedly omits free-speech cases, for which trial by jury was before stipulated in Article 19 of the constitution, from this mode of judgment. Rather fatuously, "political offences" were also guaranteed trial by jury in the 1918 document. These also disappear in the current change.

Undoubtedly the broad purpose of these amendments is to square the law with the necessary reality of life in Haiti. But the discretion the government allows itself is very wide. The guarantee of the freedom of the press is to be "subject to conditions determined by law," says the new amendment. And the recently enacted press law not only gives the government the right to forbid writings that may incite to violence, but allows it to suppress with equal severity "attacks" on the president, on the Haitian government, and on the armed forces and the government of the

---

paid, trembling before the man in power and obligated to trade with their power in order to earn a living. What is our public education? A make-believe pretext, as are many others, to loot the public treasury. What of our men of letters? Hunger-stricken devils persecuted if they do not consent to keep silent. *What of our press? . . . Bought and paid for, taking money with one hand and offering the incentive of flattery with the other.* What of our parliament? A band of men subservient to power and strangely taking responsibilities in antipatriotic acts provided they are ordered to do so."

NATIONAL ELECTIONS

United States. It is also pertinent to point out that the present law-making body is appointed by the president.

This would seem to provide just as loose a forbidding injunction as the former law was loosely permissory. Under the peculiar existing conditions, however, it is probable that if wisely and temperately administered the proposed legal check on published attacks on the government may have a salutary effect on the whole situation. Certainly life will be much less trying for the president of the Republic and his American advisers.

The purpose behind the ninth and twelfth amendments is to bring the courts of Haiti into a closer harmony with the present régime.

To elucidate the motive for these proposed changes in the constitution, it is necessary to review briefly the progressive steps, since the intervention, to create agencies through which, in the opinion of the American officials, the aims and objects of this convention may be best accomplished.

In Chapter IV the installation of the American treaty officials was reviewed and some of their problems were briefly indicated.*

In this connexion it is essential to keep in mind that although these officials were entrusted with grave responsibilities and were expected to achieve radical reforms, they were from the very beginning handicapped by lack of funds, a deplorable absence of any well-defined general policy, and, for many years, more definitely by the distinctly antagonistic attitude of the government officials who were pledged to co-operate with them.

It was not until after the election of President Borno, in 1922, that the "efficient aid" of the Haitian government guaranteed in the treaty of 1915 was extended to the Ameri-

* The present administration and activities of these officials are reviewed at length in Chapter VII.

can officials. By supplementary agreements and by accepted interpretations ("encroachments" the opposition calls them), the powers of the treaty officials have been greatly enlarged, so that most of the functions of the government, including practically all the disbursing agencies, are now under the direction of Americans appointed by the President of Haiti on the nomination of the President of the United States.

The treaty, as now interpreted, gives the command of the armed forces of the Republic, the collection and disbursement of revenue, the administration of public works and public health, and, by recent supplementary agreement, the direction of agricultural and vocational training, to American treaty officials. But two vitally important departments were utterly ignored in the treaty—those of education and the judiciary.

Notwithstanding the fact that the national school system is a miserable farce and the lower courts are notoriously corrupt, venal, and inefficient, there has been strenuous opposition to any attempt to reorganize the department of education or change the condition of the judiciary along lines proposed by the Americans.

The pressing need for complete reform in each of these departments has been obvious from the beginning. The organization of the *Service Technique* of the Department of Agriculture under an American director in 1922 was a step towards reorganization of the educational system. But it has seemingly been impossible to devise a method for the reformation of the courts other than by revising the constitution.

It is generally admitted that the judges of the lower courts, with some conspicuous exceptions, are incompetent or venal or both. Haitian courts are generally highly partisan, anti-foreign, and particularly anti-American, and this has led to a definite realization by foreigners of the expediency of "settlement out of court."

In such settlements, unfortunately, the implication of bribery is not lacking. Haitian lawyers of the better class usually recommend to their foreign clients the early settlement of claims or damage suits by agreement out of court regardless of any element of justice. Innumerable cases might be cited of court decisions against foreigners so absolutely contrary to the fact and law as to be almost incredible, and recapitulation of cases where foreigners have paid considerable sums of money in settlement of alleged damages rather than face a partisan and unfriendly court is one of the principal topics of conversation when foreigners forgather in Haiti.

There are probably more lawyers in Port-au-Prince than in any city in the world of like population, and while there are a number of able and honourable lawyers, the majority are of the class known in the United States as "ambulance chasers."

This criticism of the judiciary does not apply to the supreme court, the judges of which are generally recognized as able and honourable jurists.*

Numerous occasions have arisen when the financial adviser has refused to allow the payment of awards by the supreme court against the state.

That the position taken by the financial adviser has occasionally saved the Haitian government some money is undoubtedly true, but regardless of whether or not such judgments were, in the opinion of the financial adviser, fair to the state, it is obvious that the principle thus established

---

* "In general terms, it may be said that the Court of Cassation, while underpaid and somewhat unwieldy, enjoys the confidence and respect of foreigners as well as Haitians."—Second annual report of the American High Commissioner.

is a dangerous one and not conducive to the establishment of that respect for the law which is one of the essentials of good government.

Haitian judges, independent of the executive and of the American officials, because prior to the recent amendments to the constitution they could not be recalled, have taken positions which are held by the supporters of the present régime to be deliberately obstructive. The judges of the supreme court, however, pass only on questions of law. They have maintained a dignified silence as to their procedures, and their supporters contend that they have consistently rendered judgments in conformity with the law.

The situation is complicated by the fact that Haitian law and legal procedure are based on the French system of jurisprudence, a system much more complicated and less direct than American procedure. While it is not to be questioned that the refusal of American officials to respect court decisions has been inspired by an honest regard for the welfare of the Haitian people and considerations of substantial justice, it is doubtful whether any individual, no matter how able or sincere, should be permitted to occupy a position of arbitrary power to decide whether or not judgments of the highest courts of the land should be recognized.*

The twelfth amendment temporarily suspends the immunity of judges from removal,† and the executive is authorized during twelve months to make such changes in the present personnel of the courts as he deems necessary.

---

* "But we cannot feel that a system of arbitrary personal government, directed by a personal judgment of what ought to be done, is good preparation for the constitutional law-abiding government that Haiti needs to develop."—Report of Committee of Six. (See Exhibit H.)

† Article E of the constitution of 1918 provided that for a period of six months the constitutional provision against the removal of judges by the executive was suspended. While President Dartiguenave made no attempt at a complete reform of the judiciary, he did exercise the right so conferred to the extent of removing a number of "objectionable" judges.

NATIONAL ELECTIONS

The independence of the judges is further nullified by the ninth amendment, which provides that judges "shall be subject to special legislation which shall determine the causes for removing them from office." Heretofore they have been irremovable save for derelictions of duty under which judges may be removed in any country.

Although, if wisely directed and administered, this special legislation may have a decidedly beneficial effect on the whole judicial system in Haiti, it will certainly be looked on by Haitians with considerable anxiety. While these changes will not alter the Haitian system of jurisprudence or of Haitian reasoning, they may perhaps, and probably will, remove a definite impediment to the consummation of the program of the present government and facilitate the steps which the President and his advisers deem necessary for the country's progress.

Here again, the President, by wise administration of the extraordinary powers given to him, may mitigate the objectionable features of these amendments. This procedure was undoubtedly considered necessary by the President and by the United States Department of State. It is, however, unfortunate that at this time, when a conciliatory policy is so obviously called for, further drastic action, clearly dependent on the existence in Haiti of outside force, should have been necessary.

The sixth amendment increases the president's term to six years. President Borno is not a beneficiary under its terms, for it expressly provides that a president who has served two terms shall be ineligible for another election. The eleventh amendment is a concession to Haitian sensibilities in changing the designation of the armed forces of the Republic so that they will no longer be known as the *gendarmerie*. The discipline of this force, and the power of its own courts martial, are further defined. The other amendments, readjusting the administrative divisions of the Republic, arranging for the election of senators (in the future) to conform with these changes, and adapting the above capital amendments to other purely routine phases of the constitution, are mainly alterations in the interest of convenience and simplification.

CHAPTER VII

HAITI TO-DAY—WHAT IS BEING DONE

THE foregoing review of the political phase of the present régime in Haiti reflects but one side of the Haitian question, and by no means the most admirable aspect of the American intervention.

Administrative reforms instituted and directed by the American officials have begun a new life for the Haitian people. The responsible American officials who have undertaken these reforms started with, and have had to contend against, staggering handicaps. Haitian precedents were overwhelmingly against them. Traditional modes of government and of political administration, so dramatically suspended in 1915, had by time-honoured use been tolerated by the Haitian people. The peasant class plodded along with no hope of amelioration for their condition, and the more enlightened of the literate class, much as they might desire the reformation of their government, were powerless against the military oligarchy which had seized the reins of government.

The events which led to the American intervention have been reviewed in Part II of this volume with an endeavour to divorce from their consideration the romantic and picturesque appeal so ingeniously emphasized by Haitian politicians and their American supporters. Actually the Haitian government for some years prior to the American occupation was shamelessly incompetent and corrupt. Three of the presidents to hold office during the six years that preceded the American intervention had been convicted of the crime of embezzlement. Public works, sanitation, and public welfare were neglected. In former days President Hippolyte and other able executives built bridges and roads and markets which still exist to do them credit. But during the period of ephemeral government, public works, although paid for, were rarely completed. The customs service was so notoriously riddled with graft that the immensely greater amount of coffee that was received in France compared with the record of exports from Haitian custom houses had ceased to cause comment.

A not unfairly typical example of corruption of the school system was that of the *lycée* at Gonaives, whose principal was discovered to be able neither to read nor write, while the medical director could not name the simplest drugs nor the music instructor read a note of music. Salaries were low under the old administration, but a large part of the country's revenue, some even say over half, was dissipated in private corruption of one sort or another. The proportion is unimportant—no one will ever know it accurately—but the practice was universal, perennial, and a most unhappy extravagance for poor Haiti.

Even during the worst periods, some of the leading families in Haiti continued to live useful and honourable lives uninterrupted by and contemptuous of the prevailing political debauch. But the common people were not so fortunate. No man in those times ventured on the public roads for fear of being drafted in a revolutionary or, perhaps worse, a governmental army. They stayed in their hills, and all marketing to the towns was done by the women. Numbers were killed in each revolution, towns looted and sections burned, and no life was safe and no justice existed once the government in power marked a man as its enemy and could lay hands upon him.

Generally speaking, it may be said that the system carried within itself the seeds of its own destruction and was

~ Place d'Indépendance, Port-au-Prince ~

HAITI TO-DAY—WHAT IS BEING DONE

bound to fall. Its fall brought with it a vast relief to many of the better-class Haitians, despite the blow to their pride.

The reforms in administration following the assassination of President Sam and the intervention of the United States were not so swift or so complete as planned by the Americans or anticipated by the better element among the Haitians. Considering the actualities of Haiti's political past as outlined above, however, the betterments achieved since the American intervention have been very considerable. In some directions, as for instance in the rehabilitation of the finances, constructive betterments were delayed, perhaps unnecessarily; in others, such as public works and sanitation, the achievements would have been creditable to any administration in the world.

American intervention in Haiti was improvised as time went on. No adequate policy was determined in the beginning, nor has any definite constructive policy been followed. Under the circumstances, the wonder is that the responsible officials of the intervention have made so few mistakes and have so admirably succeeded in certain constructive achievements.

The organization of responsible American officials in Haiti functioning to-day is as follows:

(a) A High Commissioner with the rank of ambassador, a *chargé d'affaires* in charge of the American legation, and consular officials.
(b) A military force consisting of one skeleton brigade of the United States marine corps under the command of a colonel, attached to which are an aviation unit, motor transport corps, quartermaster department, etc.
(c) Under the provisions of the Haitian-American treaty, certain American officials appointed by the President of Haiti on the nomination of the President of the United States. These officials, who are

~ Peasant Women Going to Market ~

under the direction of the American High Commissioner, include:
A Financial Adviser and General Receiver of Customs;
a Chief Engineer of Public Works;
a Chief Sanitary Engineer;
a Chief of the *Gendarmerie* of Haiti;
a Chief Agricultural Engineer.

Under each of these officials are employed a number of American assistants, some of whom are civilians, and others officers or enlisted men in the United States Navy or marine corps, who draw extra pay from the Haitian government. The total number of Americans in all departments, including both military men (other than the marine corps brigade) and civilians, is about two hundred and fifty.

In the beginning these officials were subject to no superior control in Haiti, and after they began to function the necessity for definite co-ordination of their activities became increasingly apparent. Until 1922 they worked more or less independently of one another and reported to a number of different departments in Washington. There was little co-ordination at either end, and friction often developed among themselves and with the Haitian government. The situation was complicated by the fact that there were three government organizations in Haiti:

A. The Haitian government: President, Council of Secretaries of State, and Council of State.
B. The treaty officials "appointed by the President of Haiti on the nomination of the President of the United States," and as a matter of fact appointed by the American State or Navy Department.
  1. The Financial Adviser, responsible to the State Department.
  2. The Receiver-General, responsible to the State Department.

HAITI TO-DAY—WHAT IS BEING DONE

3. The Chief of the *Gendarmerie,* responsible to the Navy Department.
4. The Chief Sanitary Officer, responsible to the Navy Department.
5. The Chief Engineer, responsible to the Navy Department.

The receiver-general was also to some extent under the supervision of the Bureau of Insular Affairs (War Department), and the chief of the *gendarmerie* is an officer of the marine corps (Navy Department).

C. The Military Occupation directed by the marine officer in command of the expeditionary forces of the United States operating in Haiti.

This situation was unfavourably commented on by many observers who visited Haiti and by foreigners engaged in business there, and the preliminary statement of the committee of United States Senators which investigated conditions in Haiti, published in December, 1921, strongly recommended that there should be appointed, as special representative of the President of the United States, "a high commissioner in whom should be vested the usual diplomatic powers of an envoy extraordinary, and to whom, furthermore, all the American officials appointed under the treaty, *as well as the Commandant of the Marine brigade,* should look for direction and guidance." *

The Senate committee, in making this recommendation,

---

* Many competent witnesses before the Senate committee testified to apparent lack of any definite policy in Washington, and it was quite obvious that the members of the Senate committee fully agreed with them. Not only did the American treaty officials have to contend with the actively obstructive tactics of Haitian government officials and lack of co-operation among themselves, but during the first five years of the intervention five different men acted as chiefs of the Latin-American Division of the Department of State.

evidently contemplated the appointment of a civilian to the office of High Commissioner.

The chairman of the committee stated, at one of the public hearings, that he had taken occasion to express to the Department of State his judgment that civil functions are better performed by men trained to civil rather than military functions.*

A prominent Haitian lawyer, in discussing this proposed appointment at a public hearing of the Senate committee, prophesied that this office would be filled by a military officer, stating that in his opinion it would be impossible to secure the appointment of a civilian with functions superior to the brigadier-general then commanding the marines in Haiti.†

Four months later, in June, 1922, Brigadier-General John H. Russell, U.S.M.C., then serving his second tour of duty as brigade commander in Haiti, was appointed by the President of the United States High Commissioner to Haiti with the rank of ambassador.

Regardless of any difference of opinion as to whether or not the American intervention should be withdrawn prior to the expiration of the treaty in 1936, the great majority of people who have investigated the situation in Haiti have agreed that the military aspect of the intervention should be reduced to the smallest proportion consistent with the situation, as rapidly as possible. It is perfectly obvious that military control of civil affairs, particularly in Haiti, where the chief evils have arisen from a practically continuous series of military autocracies, is not good policy.‡

In particular, it has been pointed out that the creation of the position of High Commissioner was inspired or at least recommended by the Senate committee primarily for

* *Senate Hearings*, p. 1476.
† *Ibid*.
‡ See Exhibit H.

HAITI TO-DAY—WHAT IS BEING DONE

the express purpose of ending the friction and lack of friendly relations between Americans and Haitians which had resulted, at least partly, from a strong feeling that military control by purely civil functionaries could not secure the spirit of "co-operation and accommodation" recognized by the Senate committee as essential.

It was further held that the appointment of a military officer who had been so closely identified with the past régime would not tend to achieve the ends contemplated in creating this position.

There can be no question, however, that the appointment of a High Commissioner was a decidedly beneficial measure. President Borno, from the very beginning of his first term, displayed an attitude of sincere and intelligent co-operation, and General Russell, during his long service in Haiti as commander of the United States military forces, had gained the respect of the Haitian people and earned a reputation for absolute integrity.

This co-operation between the President and the High Commissioner has resulted in a certain amount of constructive legislation and orderly development of a program of political and economic reform.

But the feeling has persisted that, ably as the present High Commissioner has performed his manifold and onerous duties, the time is overripe for the subordination of the military to a civil administration, and for the appointment to this high office of a man trained to civil rather than military functions.

Financial Adviser-General Receiver

Prior to the appointment of the financial adviser-general receiver in 1924, at which time the two offices were combined, three men held the office of financial adviser. In justice to these three men, who have been very seriously criticized for lack of achievements, it should be remembered that until the inauguration of President Borno in May, 1922, the policy of the Haitian government was one of more or less open non-co-operation. Such accomplishments as were effected were brought about in spite of the passive resistance or, in some instances, the active opposition of the president of Haiti or his ministers.

The lack of definition of the powers of the financial adviser and general receiver made it essential that in order to exercise real authority they should have not only the active and prompt support of the government of the United States, but the co-operation of the executive, legislative, and judicial branches of the Haitian government. Without the co-operation of the executive and legislative branches it was impossible to change existing laws, and without the co-operation of the judicial branch it was impossible effectively to enforce legislation.

Support of the government of the United States to this end was often slow in materializing, and not in accord with any continuous policy. Plans of the financial advisers tending to secure the expenditure of public funds exclusively for public purposes often met with determined opposition from the Haitian officials. It was not until 1918, three years after the intervention, that the authority of the financial adviser and general receiver over expenditures was established. In spite of the handicap under which these officials laboured, achievements were gradually accomplished. The currency was stabilized, the budgetary requirements closely analysed, and expenditures co-ordinated in logical relation to the revenues and the needs of the people.

There has been such a mass of necessary reconstruction in every department of the government, and such a small revenue available, that the estimates of expenditures have generally been in excess of estimated revenues. From the beginning the financial advisers have maintained a policy

~ New Palace of Finance ~

HAITI TO-DAY—WHAT IS BEING DONE

of careful examination and scrutiny of the estimates of the spending departments of the government, and have excluded from such estimates all items not deemed of urgent necessity. A previously unheard-of proportion of the revenue, meanwhile, has been devoted to expenses for public works, public health, and public safety.

The chief aims of the treaty were to maintain tranquillity and to remedy the condition of the revenues and finances of the Republic, and to carry out plans for economic development.

At the time of the American intervention, the financial situation in Haiti was almost as deplorable as was the political condition. The Haitian-American treaty specifies that the United States "will by its good offices aid the Haitian government in the establishing of the finances of Haiti on a firm and solid basis." While there has been much possibly justified criticism of unnecessary delays in achieving this end, and of an unfortunate lack, for several years, of a continuity of policy, the present fiscal position of the government testifies that very material progress has been made.

The public debt has been reduced from $30,772,000 to $19,369,000.* A mass of claims against the government, totalling $40,000,000 and settled by the claims commission for $3,500,000, have been paid or funded. The currency, formerly subject to violent fluctuations, has been stabilized, and all government paper money has been retired and a reserve fund created for the nickel subsidiary currency. The unsecured government currency has been replaced by National Bank notes secured by a reserve.

The interest and amortization of the public debt, including all expenses, now absorb about thirty-seven per cent of the revenues as compared to about seventy-six per cent prior to the intervention.

The budget has been balanced, and in spite of large ex-

* As of November 30, 1927. See note 1.

~ *Above:* Telephone and Telegraph Building ~
~ *Below:* New School Building ~

penditures of funds for public improvements, current expenses are kept within the current revenue, and cash reserves have been created as a precaution against bad times.[2]

A modern system of government accounting has been instituted. A complete revision of the archaic import customs tariff has been prepared and put into effect. Custom houses have been greatly improved, graft largely eliminated, and inefficiency greatly reduced. The internal-revenue service has been placed under control of the general receiver, and new administrative laws have been enacted, with the result that the internal revenue was increased from a little over $100,000 in 1916 to $831,000 during the fiscal year ending September 30, 1926. This increase of over seven hundred per cent was accomplished primarily by increased honesty and efficiency in collection and not materially by any additional legislation.

Complete records of government revenues and expenses, and of the imports and exports of Haiti, are promptly published in a monthly bulletin in French and English, together with a monthly summary of activities of the services under the direction of the treaty officials.

Public Works

The productive period of the Department of Public Works dates from July, 1920, when a public-works law, prepared by the engineer-in-chief and approved by the Minister of Public Works, was first enacted. This law organized a corps of engineers and put under the engineer-in-chief the control of construction and maintenance of public utilities, the operation of telegraphs and telephones, and the water services of towns and communes, irrigation projects, and the supervision of all concessions.

Since the intervention about 1,200 kilometres of national highways have been built, and many secondary roads and

HAITI TO-DAY—WHAT IS BEING DONE

trails rebuilt or repaired. In 1915 there were only two or three automobiles in Haiti and no place for them to go. To-day there are more than 2,600 motor vehicles in Haiti. Commercial trucking, hitherto unknown in Haiti, is rapidly becoming an important factor in the commercial development of the country, and passenger busses are developing an interurban communication which is most beneficial to the people of Haiti both socially and economically. In 1915 there were three lighthouses for about 1,100 kilometres of coast line. There are now fifteen lighthouses in operation, and in the principal harbours wharves have been improved and buoys installed for the aid of navigation.

A definite building program has been adopted and followed; hospitals, schools, docks, and other necessary buildings have been constructed, or remodelled, and an extensive program of construction of necessary buildings for the *gendarmerie* service and the *Service Technique* of the Department of Agriculture has been inaugurated. A decided improvement in the streets of the towns is very noticeable, and both municipal water-supply systems and sanitation works have been materially improved.

While no large irrigation systems have yet been developed, much has been already done to supply irrigation water to certain areas, and surveys have been completed and studies made of such great irrigation projects as the Artibonite Valley, where a contract has been entered into for the development by irrigation of some sixty thousand acres of rich alluvial soil. Other projects have been studied and will undoubtedly be developed.

Under existing conditions, an active program of public works is a paramount necessity. Except at Port-au-Prince, where very decided improvements have been made, housing of government activities is generally inadequate. Except in a few favoured localities which are now more or less adequately supplied, municipal water-supply systems are badly needed. The telephone and telegraph systems have been very greatly improved but further communication facilities are required.

From an economic standpoint the present expenditures for public works could well be more than doubled. But even with the limited funds provided, the scope of the activities of the *Direction Générale des Travaux Publics* has been systematically and effectively extended, and the value of its operations is apparent to even the most disgruntled critic of the occupation. Expenditures for this service during the fiscal year ending September 30, 1927, were over $1,400,000.

Public Health

When the Americans first entered Haiti, it was immediately discovered that the *Jury Médical,* the Haitian public-health administration, virtually existed in name only. One of the first acts of the new régime was to assign a corps of able medical officers of the United States Navy to this vital service.

The country was divided into sanitary districts with a public-health officer in charge of each, and the quarantine service of the open ports taken over. Sanitary rules and quarantine regulations were adopted and have been vigorously enforced. The existing hospitals were taken over and have been gradually improved. The Haitian general hospital at Port-au-Prince has been developed into an institution capable of treating the sick not only of the capital, but chronic cases from all over the country. It is a standing testimonial to the efficiency of the men who have directed the public-health service.

Ten major hospitals have been constructed or remodelled; thirty rural dispensaries are in operation, and over one hundred free rural clinics are held weekly in over one hun-

Above: A Ward, General Hospital in Port-au-Prince
Below: A Rural Clinic

HAITI TO-DAY—WHAT IS BEING DONE

dred different places treating about fifty thousand people monthly. A modern public-health laboratory has been created, the services of which are available to every physician in the Republic.

Inspection of public markets, house-to-house sanitary inspection, removal of garbage and disease-spreading filth, cleaning of streets and elimination of mosquito-breeding areas by drainage, filling and spraying with oil, measures which were hitherto absolutely neglected in Haiti, have been thoroughly organized and most effectively administered. Research work in connexion with the determination of certain diseases most prevalent in Haiti has been carried on with definitely important results; and in collaboration with the International Health Board of the Rockefeller Foundation, a medical survey of Haiti has been made.

This development in the medical attention afforded the people of Haiti, aside from its actual medical importance, has had a most salutary educational effect on living conditions and the general well-being of the people. The devotion of the American Navy doctors to their work, and the admirable manner in which they have generally conducted themselves towards the Haitian people, have created, especially in the rural districts, a lasting friendship for this service, and have been of real assistance in establishing a feeling of confidence in "the Americans."

The directors of this service have not lost sight of the fact that the ultimate object of the treaty, under which they are acting, is to create an organization to which the public health of Haiti may be entrusted at the expiration of the convention.

The continued policy of co-operation with Haitian physicians and extension of all facilities for medical investigation and research work, at first hardly appreciated, has done much to win the confidence of the Haitian medical fraternity.

∽ *Above:* New *Gendarmerie* Head-quarters, Port-au-Prince ∽
∽ *Below:* Review of *Gendarmerie*, National Palace ∽

BLACK DEMOCRACY

The medical school at Port-au-Prince has been reorganized and is now installed in an adequately equipped building constructed for this purpose; a training-school for Haitian nurses, of whom there were none in Haiti, has been organized under the direction of American Red Cross nurses, and graduates each year a number of trained nurses. Through the aid of the International Health Board a number of Haitian physicians are sent each year to the United States and to Europe for postgraduate training in order that they may more adequately fill their positions as instructors in the medical school.

The total annual appropriations for this service, which is responsible for the health and sanitation of about 2,500,000 people, is only about $690,000 per annum, and of this amount less than one-half is available for hospitals.

While the amount of money devoted to public-health work is pitifully small compared with the population served, the budget allots to the public-health service an unusually large proportion of the total income of the state.

The state now bears practically the whole burden of measures for public health and the relief of suffering. Neither individuals nor charitable organizations in Haiti are financially or technically able to be of material assistance, and for some reason difficult to understand no aid has been given by American organizations except some slight help rendered by the American Red Cross and the survey made by the International Health Board.

The public-health service is facing many problems of vital importance for which adequate funds are not available, problems which are most intimately associated with the well-being of the Haitian people and therefore with the attainment of the objects of the intervention. The rapidly increasing faith in this service is resulting in an equally rapid increase in the number of applicants for medical treatment. An appalling proportion of the people are suffer-

HAITI TO-DAY—WHAT IS BEING DONE

ing from syphilis, hookworm, and malaria, which might be brought under control or greatly alleviated if facilities were available. The problem of caring for the insane, for lepers, paupers, and orphans has been treated with intelligence and energy in so far as available funds allowed, but such funds are inadequate.

Haiti and the American intervention in Haiti have been investigated and reported on by all sorts of American organizations, but so far, with the exception of the cases cited above, there has been no attempt by American organizations to extend greatly needed assistance to the vitally important and commendable work which is being done by the public-health service. Such assistance should be forthcoming.

The Gendarmerie

The organization and training of the *gendarmerie* of Haiti, the constabulary provided for in the treaty, has proceeded efficiently since the old picturesque but worse than useless army and police of Haiti were abolished early in 1916.

The enlisted personnel of the *gendarmerie* was drawn almost entirely from the lower class. It was difficult in the beginning to recruit a sufficient number of men who could read and write to supply material from which to develop the necessary number of non-commissioned officers. This difficulty has since been largely overcome by the enlistment of a better class of men attracted by the increasing popularity of the service.

The old army was recruited largely by the simple method of impressing men into the service. During the revolutionary periods, especially the years preceding the intervention, the men of the peasant class seldom ventured into town for fear of being captured and forced into the army. The pay of the private soldiers under the old régime, when they were paid at all, was about twenty cents a week for rations and the same amount per month for pay. Their living conditions were extremely bad, and medical attention negligible. Enlistment in the *gendarmerie* is entirely voluntary. The enlisted personnel is housed in clean barracks, provided with proper bedding and serviceable and attractive uniforms, paid $10 per month (United States currency), allowed a ration, and given a liberal clothing allowance.

Nothing more clearly visualizes the improvement in the police force of Haiti since 1915 than the weekly review of the Port-au-Prince battalion of the *gendarmerie,* in which the officers and men, all Haitians, compare very favourably in military bearing and general fitness with the police or troops of any country.

An inspection of the prisons gives another outstanding visualization of the efficiency of this organization. When taken over by the *gendarmerie,* the Haitian prisons were totally unfit for human habitation and prisoners were treated with a disregard for humanity which is almost unbelievable. Food was supposed to be supplied by contract, but unless friends on the outside brought food to a prisoner he got very little to eat, and prisoners received practically no medical attention. The prisons are now absolutely sanitary, clean, healthy places, the food is infinitely better than the rations of the average peasant, and efficient medical inspection and adequate hospital facilities are provided. A general workshop is maintained in the larger prisons where prisoners are not only taught useful trades but allowed a certain payment for their work. All this is open to inspection, and a visitor at Port-au-Prince may view the prison where in August, 1915, after an atrocious massacre, the gutters were running blood, and find conditions which compare favourably with those of correctional establishments in the United States.

Flagrant graft and inefficiency in the administration of

HAITI TO-DAY—WHAT IS BEING DONE

communal affairs, and the obstructive tactics of the communal officials, many of whom considered it a "patriotic duty" to oppose the present régime, have led to the assignment of district and sub-district *gendarmerie* officers as "advisers" of the elected communal officials.

As communal advisers these officers audit expenditures, and assist in preparing communal budgets and in supervision of schools. It is natural that complaints have been made that these supervisory powers have been abused, and it is possible that these young officers, predominantly American commissioned or non-commissioned officers in the marine corps, have at times exceeded their authority. But there is no question that communal administration has been greatly improved and that a very material saving in communal funds has been effected.

Throughout the Republic, *gendarmerie* stations have been constructed or improved, and an elaborate program for further improvements is well under way. The *gendarmerie* maintains its own medical department, with a hospital and dispensary service covering all its posts. In addition to the medical care of the personnel of the organization, this service is charged with the sanitation of prisons and care of sick prisoners. The reduction of prison mortality is one of the outstanding achievements of the American intervention.

The present *gendarmerie* force consists of a major-general (commandant), a brigadier-general (chief of staff), 177 commissioned officers, of whom thirty per cent are Haitians, and an enlisted force numbering 2,571. All the officers (excepting the medical department) are commissioned or non-commissioned officers of the United States marine corps, or Haitians who have graduated from the *gendarmerie* officers' school.

Article X of the treaty provides that the American officers shall be replaced by Haitians as they are found to be qualified to assume such duties. In the early days it was extremely difficult to secure material from which commissioned officers could be developed. The service was not then popular, and the ideas of most of the applicants for commissions regarding military service were totally at variance with those of their American instructors; and a considerable percentage of these first applicants were either discharged or resigned within a few months.

The prejudice of the upper-class Haitian against any form of manual labour, even to the care of his own horse, and a disinclination to leave the towns, where practically all of the *élite* of Haiti are gathered, added to the difficulty in securing and training young Haitians of the better class for this service. However, although after ten years only fifty-four Haitians hold commissions in the *gendarmerie*, the service is becoming more popular and the number of cadet officers is gradually increasing.

Out of a total of fifteen districts, two are commanded by Haitian captains, and of the forty-two sub-district commanders twenty are Haitians. It has been made quite evident that the enlisted personnel of the *gendarmerie* prefer to serve under American officers, and also that the Haitian people as a rule have greater confidence in American district and sub-district commanders. A number of efficient Haitian officers, however, have been developed. During the caco uprising several Haitian commissioned officers distinguished themselves in the field. But cases have also developed where Haitian officers have displayed a strong disinclination to take over independent commands, especially in districts in which they have lived. It is not that such officers fear to exercise their purely military duties, but they apparently are loath to assume the responsibilities of the administrative functions attached to such positions in communities where friends and relatives may bring pressure to bear on them.

~ *Above:* *Gendarme* Rifle Team Which Won Second Place at Olympic Games ~
~ *Below:* American Marines, *Gendarmerie* Head-quarters Staff ~

HAITI TO-DAY—WHAT IS BEING DONE

The gradual replacement of American officers by trained Haitians is, however, absolutely essential, and the best method of accomplishing and at the same time maintaining an efficient organization is one of the vital problems of the present government.

Communal fire departments are under the control of the *gendarmerie*, as is also the rural police, composed of 551 chiefs of sections. In the Olympic games of 1924 a *gendarmerie* rifle team, composed of one Haitian officer and four Haitian sergeants, tied with France for second place, being defeated only by the United States.

The *gendarmerie*, so far as personnel is concerned, is probably the most adequately equipped branch of the public service, and its buildings and other facilities are being rapidly improved. As the terms of the treaty assure Haiti from danger of foreign aggression, the duties of the *gendarmerie*, although a military organization, are confined to the preservation of internal peace and order. The Haitian people are not given to acts of violence, and as the old tendency towards recurrent revolutionary outbreaks has been pretty well eliminated, the present organization is quite adequate and is developing into a decidedly efficient military police force.

The advantages of the military organization of the *gendarmerie* are many and obvious. First is the superior discipline that could not be maintained in a civil force; second, the advantage of having under one head a unified urban and rural police and the administration of the correctional institutions; and third, the fact that the possession of arms in the Republic is subject to the regulations of this organization.

The cost of maintaining the *gendarmerie* organization is approximately $1,285,000 per annum, or about fifteen per cent of the total revenue of the state.

Above: Rural Farm School
Below: Boys' Industrial School

BLACK DEMOCRACY

Agricultural Service

While the economic future of Haiti is obviously in the development of its agricultural resources, the Department of Agriculture, prior to the intervention, did little or nothing except to support a ministry and hold a yearly agricultural *fête*.

Practically the whole income of the Haitian people and the revenue of the government were, and are, derived from agricultural production. Agriculture in Haiti is conducted in a most primitive and inefficient manner; and the necessity for a constructive program of agricultural education and research is obvious. However, it was not until over six years after the intervention that anything was actively initiated in this connexion.

In 1922 the *Service Technique de l'Agriculture* was established by law, and in the following year an agricultural engineer to direct this service arrived in Haiti.

In 1924 a plan of organization of this department and of agricultural and vocational education was enacted into law. In addition to research and demonstration, this department is charged with agricultural and vocational education. A central school for training teachers for farm and industrial schools, agricultural advisers, and research workers has been established near Port-au-Prince. Over fifty rural farm schools have been established and many more are planned.

Estimating the population of Haiti at 2,500,000 and the population of the principal cities and towns at 200,000, it is seen that over ninety per cent of the people of Haiti live in rural districts and are directly dependent on agriculture. The distribution of the population is influenced very largely by the productivity of the soil, and in some favoured districts the population averages over 300 to the

HAITI TO-DAY—WHAT IS BEING DONE

square mile, while large areas of arid land are practically uninhabited.

Haiti is an extremely mountainous country, and many of the more fertile agricultural districts are distant from towns, the most important of which are situated on the coast. These isolated districts have never been provided with anything like adequate schools; not even such poor facilities as were provided in the towns were available to the people in the hills, and as a result the percentage of illiteracy is appalling.

The treaty, for reasons best known to the framers thereof, failed to include any provision for American supervision of education, and it is only recently that, under the clause wherein the United States is to "assist in developing agricultural, mineral, and commercial resources," the *Service Technique* has taken over a program of elementary education in connexion with its farm schools.

Ultimately, it is proposed that experienced farm advisers be placed in charge of rural districts to advise farmers as to methods of planting and cultivation of crops and caring for livestock, as well as to keep the department informed of crop conditions. A beginning has been made towards the establishment of co-operative demonstration farms in various parts of the country. Recognizing that coffee is, and will for many years be, the principal source of revenue, efforts have been made to increase coffee planting and to improve both production and quality by instructing the peasants in better methods of production and preparation of the product for market. A system has been inaugurated under which bonuses are given for new coffee planting.

A veterinary staff gives instruction in the care and treatment of animal diseases, and animal clinics are held at various stations throughout the country; and stock-breeding stations have been established.

BLACK DEMOCRACY

A department of forestry is making a survey of forestry conditions, has established a small forestry nursery, and is distributing useful trees. A forestry law has been enacted. Experiments have already demonstrated that conditions of soil and climate are favourable to the commercial production of sisal, and a number of commercial sisal enterprises have been started in Haiti.

The *Service Technique* has effectively co-operated with the Department of Public Works in studies of areas which may be intensively developed by irrigation, and in this connexion has issued a report on the potentialities of the Artibonite Valley, the largest irrigable area in Haiti for which ample water is available.

That there is a wide and fundamentally important field for this organization is beyond question. The control of diseases of plants and animals has been practically unknown in Haiti. No systematic attempts were ever made to ascertain the economic products, both vegetable and animal, which are best suited to Haitian conditions. No attention had been given to establishing proper methods of handling, preserving, and marketing the products of Haiti, and as a result Haitian coffee, cotton, cacao, honey, and other products command prices materially lower than their potential value.

The program adopted for the organization and the administration of the school system of the *Service Technique* has been bitterly criticized. It has been claimed that the program was initiated too quickly, that the peasant class is too ignorant to profit from such instruction, and that the young men of the educated class who have been induced to attend the normal schools are as a rule so opposed to rural life, and so prejudiced against any profession other than law or medicine, that they will not continue in the service after having been graduated.

It is generally felt that something of this kind should have

HAITI TO-DAY—WHAT IS BEING DONE

been instituted many years ago and that, once instituted, the program should move more slowly and that recruits for the farm-school instructors should be selected from the more intelligent boys of the country districts who have had some primary education in the schools conducted by the Brothers of Christian Instruction or in the national schools.

The American officials feel, with justification, that the teaching most urgently needed in Haiti is instruction in agricultural production and training which will assist the peasant class to raise their standard of living and produce more foodstuffs for their own miserably undernourished bodies and for sale in the market. But the problem of how to secure the proper material for such a program is a serious one which will be solved only with the sincere co-operation of the people of Haiti. It is generally felt in Haiti that some revision or modification of the present plans will be necessary.

The present annual expenditure of the *Service Technique* of the Department of Agriculture is about $500,000, but of this amount a large proportion is expended in connexion with agricultural and industrial educational work.

It is here pertinent to point out that the common conception of the average American, that "Uncle Sam" is digging down into his own pocket and spending America's money for the benefit of Haiti, is quite erroneous. The funds expended under the direction of the American administrators in Haiti are provided solely from the revenues of the Haitian state.

Even to the casual visitor to Haiti, the very definite achievements of the departments directed by the American officials are obvious. Anyone who has been familiar with the very real problems which these officials have had to face, and the handicaps under which they have laboured, must perforce acknowledge that these men appointed by the

BLACK DEMOCRACY

President of Haiti on the nomination of the President of the United States have given to their work a devotion which has been highly commendable.

However, it is difficult not to feel that the desire to get results quickly has overshadowed the primary reason for their being in Haiti, *viz.*, the organization of the collecting and disbursing departments of the Haitian government in such a manner that Haitians may be fitted to take up the administration of public funds effectively for the public welfare after the United States withdraws from Haiti, presumably in 1936.

It is generally conceded that if the American intervention were withdrawn to-day a very large part of the good which has been accomplished would almost immediately be wiped out and the graft and inefficiency which had characterized Haitian administrations prior to the intervention would be resumed and the old conditions, which led to the intervention, would again materialize. The United States contracted with Haiti to *assist* in the reorganization of its finances and the development of its resources. Very definite accomplishments have been achieved towards these ends; but there is nothing in the treaty to indicate that we are to continue to direct the agencies created for these purposes. To admit that no Haitian personnel can be developed to carry on the work thus inaugurated, is to confess fundamental errors in the original treaty and the futility of the intervention itself. While it seems highly improbable that material is lacking in Haiti from which to fill positions now held by Americans, it is quite obvious that with such conspicuous exceptions as that of the public-health service, this vitally important aspect of the situation has unfortunately been neglected.

It is undoubtedly true that the American treaty officials have found it difficult to secure the services of Haitians competent to fill the more important and responsible administrative positions. It may be conceded that from a purely

~ *Above:* National Palace, Port-au-Prince ~
~ *Below:* Champ de Mars, Port-au-Prince ~

HAITI TO-DAY—WHAT IS BEING DONE

economic standpoint the desire of these Americans to get the greatest possible results from the very inadequate amount of money at their disposal to some extent justifies, or at least explains, their disinclination to substitute Haitians for their more highly trained and efficient American employees. But even at the expense of a certain amount of efficiency it would seem to be a much wiser policy to give more attention to the creation of a Haitian personnel, even if it were necessary to sacrifice a definite amount of actual physical accomplishment.

The adoption of such a policy in every department of the government now controlled by Americans would not only tend towards the ultimate good of the Haitian people, through the creation of Haitian administrators prepared to function after the withdrawal of the Americans, but would go a long way towards allaying the present discontent and towards the creation of more cordial relations.

∽ *Above:* A Residence in Port-au-Prince ∽
∽ *Below:* Dock at Port-au-Prince ∽

CHAPTER VIII

WHAT SHOULD BE DONE

THERE are three possible policies which might be adopted by the United States in relation to the Haitian problem:

First: Abrogate the treaty, withdraw completely, and wash our hands of further responsibility.

Second: Continue the intervention indefinitely, leaving open the question of ultimate withdrawal.

Third: Announce definitely that we will withdraw at the expiration of the treaty in 1936, and adopt a definite program designed to prepare the Haitian people, in so far as possible, to take over and administer an efficient independent government.

The first procedure would be not only a humiliating confession of incompetency and an admission of fundamental error in our policy towards Haiti from the very beginning, but would probably lead to immediate catastrophe.

The second is equally untenable. While it is possible that we could let things continue as they are, and later secure by pressure an agreement from the Haitian government again extending the treaty, it is extremely doubtful if such an extension would be ratified by the United States Senate. It is certain that such an arrangement would be hotly contested in both countries and would reflect most disastrously on our relations with Latin-American peoples in general and the Haitian people in particular. There exists a well-defined fear in Haiti that this *will be* our policy, and so long as this fear remains there is no possibility of securing the confidence

WHAT SHOULD BE DONE

and friendly relations which are so essential to the successful outcome of the intervention.

Many well-informed people hold that the only honourable and logical procedure is to announce definitely, in no equivocal terms, that we propose to live up to the spirit of the treaty and such supplementary agreements as have been made, that we will not seek to renew the treaty or in any other manner perpetuate our control, and that in the meantime we will honestly and diligently strive to prepare the Haitian people to run their ship of state independently and effectively, confident, if they succeed, of the friendly assistance of the United States and, through its protection, secured from foreign aggression.

Mr. Charles E. Hughes, in defining the position of the Department of State towards Haiti, said, "The government of the United States is seeking to make its relation to Haiti beneficial to the Haitian people. It has no other aim but to establish peace and stability. It does not seek to acquire or control the territory of Haiti, and it will welcome the day when it can leave Haiti with the reasonable assurance that the Haitians will be able to maintain an independent government competent to keep order and discharge its international obligations."

It is hard to understand how any American who is conversant with the situation can question that Mr. Hughes expressed honestly and sincerely the sole aim of the American intervention in Haiti. It is, however, possible to question the adequacy of the methods and policies which have been pursued towards preparing for the day when the United States can leave Haiti with reasonable assurance that the Haitians will be able to maintain a competent government.

The conditions which forced the election of six presidents in four years have been, for a time at least, corrected. Since the suppression of the caco uprising, tranquillity has been maintained in the Republic. The finances of the government have been stabilized, medical and sanitary conditions have been very greatly improved, important public works have been completed, and definitely beneficial steps taken towards the economic development of Haiti and the welfare and prosperity of its people. These betterments have been accomplished without in any manner jeopardizing the ultimate independence of the Haitian nation or the integrity of its territory. But to the all-important question as to what has been accomplished towards the assurance that the Haitian people will be able to maintain a competent government after the withdrawal of the United States, presumably in 1936, a less satisfactory answer is forthcoming.

A prominent Haitian, one of the best-educated men on the island, a man who has never been in political life, told Dr. Carl Kelsey in 1920: * "Those of us who have been trained have never been trained to work physically; we do not believe in it; we have no respect for it. We have got to go into the government service; that is the only outlet for any large number of us. It does not make any difference whether the lowest type of man gets into office or the highest type in this country; the moment he gets in and appoints his assistants, there are many more disappointed people than satisfied ones. And the disappointed ones immediately begin to counsel together to know how they can get rid of him. That has been true all through our history."

Politics has not only been the principal occupation of the *élite* of Haiti, but, excepting law and medicine, the only recognized profession for the *élite*. The majority of upper-class Haitians were dependent on incomes derived from political sinecures, which have been at least temporarily abolished. This class is now suffering acutely both in pride and pocket as a result of the intervention. The actual control of the government of Haiti has for the time being passed from

* See Exhibit F.

Above: Royal Bank of Canada and Banque Nationale
Below: Street in Port-au-Prince

WHAT SHOULD BE DONE

this class, and the administration of governmental activities is now vested, to a large extent, in the hands of Americans appointed by the President of Haiti on the nomination of the President of the United States.

It is true that the class which dominated the affairs of Haiti had failed to establish or maintain a competent government, and that the record of the ephemeral governments which preceded the American intervention had demonstrated that without outside aid the Haitian people were unfitted to maintain a government which could keep order at home or discharge its international obligations. But regardless of this conspicuous failure, it is evident that the only individuals in Haiti capable of maintaining any government at all are of the class which for lack of a better term has been referred to in this book as the *élite*.

A prominent Haitian has been quoted as saying that two thousand men controlled Haiti absolutely and that from the beginning of the history of free Haiti the upper class constituted a self-appointed oligarchy.

It is unquestioned that this class, for generations, has completely dominated the political life of Haiti and for many years to come must be the only medium through which public opinion in Haiti can find expression. From this class therefore must be chosen the executives and legislators, the officers of courts and of the police. Granted that they have abused their privileges, the fact remains that they are the natural leaders of the people, and the co-operation of this literate minority is essential to any permanent betterment in conditions. Without such co-operation nothing that the intervention has accomplished will be of lasting benefit. We have built public works and public buildings and reorganized administrative procedures, but there is no way for us to keep these structures in repair after we have left Haiti, nor can we prevent the complete disorganization of the administrative departments, except through the willing efforts of

~ *Above:* Typical Peasant Home ~
~ *Below:* Haitian Peasants ~

BLACK DEMOCRACY

the Haitians who will occupy the public offices after our withdrawal. Such efforts, to be effective, must be inspired by a feeling of responsibility to the public and maintained by public opinion. The only articulate public opinion in Haiti is voiced by the *élite,* who by this time must surely have come to a realization that the old methods of government are no longer tenable.

Although the Haitian people are of one race and only a few generations removed from a condition of slavery, class lines are clearly defined and pride of caste exists to an extraordinary degree. There is no large middle class in Haiti, and practically no planter class, which in other West Indian islands originates and contributes so materially to the wealth of the community. Haitians of the upper class have become doctors, lawyers, or politicians, or some few, merchants, but until recently few have studied mechanics or agriculture or the arts and trades which create and sustain a middle class and on which the prosperity of any country essentially depends. Skilled labour in Haiti in 1915 was practically non-existent, and even to-day an operation requiring skilled labour is performed by foreigners.

The great mass of the people are essentially inarticulate. It is not only that the peasants cannot read and write and have no knowledge of the elements of democracy, but they are completely indifferent to all matters which do not directly and obviously affect their own immediate communities. A vast majority are concerned only in maintaining their existence. They have never been allowed to think for themselves in terms of politics or given any part in the affairs of their country or voice in the government of their nation. It is only recently that the peasants have begun to realize that some power, which they are totally unable to define but which they vaguely attribute to the presence of the *blancs,* has very materially benefited their condition.

They are by no means a stupid people, and no people in

Above: Haitian Market
Below: Petit Commerce

WHAT SHOULD BE DONE

the world are more kindly and courteous to one another or to strangers. One of the most interesting of the many picturesque scenes encountered in the rural districts is that of an old village patriarch instructing children in "deportment." Children of from five to ten years take an active and responsible part in *petit commerce*, the trade of the little wayside shops which are found on trails and roadsides throughout the Republic. While these people have come to realize, now that the caco troubles are over, that the Americans are friends, they are still, and must remain to a large extent, subservient to the literate class to whom they have looked for leadership for more than a century.

Haitians of every class throughout the country have seen United States marines, and most Haitians have seen United States battleships. The American flag still flies over the marine barracks just behind the national palace. The peasants have come to respect the *blanc* doctors who wear the uniform of the United States Navy. They have gradually learned that they may look for justice from the white officers of the national police who wear the uniform of the *gendarmerie* of Haiti. But of the tremendous power of the United States very few Haitians of any class have the faintest conception. A very distinguished Haitian, on his return from a recent visit to the United States, told the writer that he found it absolutely impossible to convey to his friends his impressions of the vastness of the United States or its tremendous financial and economic power. "Mr. Davis," he said, "your country is overwhelmingly formidable." If it were possible to convey to the Haitian people a conception of the comparatively infinitesimal importance of the Haitian Republic in the minds of the American people, much of the propaganda against the American intervention would be killed by a realization of its utter absurdity.

It is perfectly true, as Dr. Kelsey has stated, that our

duty to the people of Haiti is not fully met by accepting at its face value all the statements emanating from its upper classes. But it is equally true that the bitterness which inspires statements so derogatory to the present government and to Americans is not wholly without justification, and it is evident that every cause for such bitterness should be investigated and so far as possible removed or alleviated. Dr. Kelsey,* in describing the upper-class Haitians, said: "Go into any gathering of the upper class, shut your eyes and listen, and you will believe yourself in a cultured European gathering. In bearing and courtesy, in interest and appreciation of art, music, and literature, in ability to sing, play, dance, or discuss, the American finds that he has no advantage."

Many Haitians of the upper class have been educated in France, and their traditions, culture, and language are French, not African. They respond at once to courteous treatment and are equally quick to resent condescension and any evidence of the feeling of racial superiority which many Americans find it so difficult to conceal. The mistake of employing in Haiti Americans who have strong racial prejudices against the Negro has been stressed by almost every observer who has visited Haiti since the intervention. Haitians of the upper class are fully aware that such racial prejudices are much stronger in the United States than in any European country, and this very fact entails a definite obligation on the part of Americans in Haiti. No American who does not care to maintain a certain amount of ordinary social intercourse with Negroes should be sent to a Negro state.

Mr. Hughes, in an address to the delegates to the Conference of the Central American Republics (December, 1922), said:

* See Exhibit F.

WHAT SHOULD BE DONE

The government of the United States has no ambitions to gratify at your expense, no policy which runs counter to your national aspirations, and no purpose save to promote the interests of peace and assist you, in such manner as you may welcome, to solve your problems to your own proper advantage.

This was doubtless a sincere expression of the policy of the Department of State towards Latin America. But the majority of literate Haitians passionately insist that the policy of the United States in relation to Haiti has been counter to their national aspirations, and it is futile to deny that even to those Haitians who welcomed the armed intervention of the United States in 1915, the manner in which the United States has so far attempted to solve their problems has been far from welcome.

The Haitians do not believe that the Department of State has been guided solely by motives so altruistic. Under the circumstances it would be rather extraordinary if they did so believe. Since the beginning of the intervention they have been told by American critics of the foreign policy of the United States that they were a greatly abused people, informed that the policy of the United States in Haiti was dictated from "Wall Street," and urged to organize to protect their sovereignty.

It is undoubtedly permissible to criticize the policy of our government or the acts of its agents, but reckless statements based on hearsay evidence or on conclusions arrived at without a reasonable amount of careful investigation not only are unintelligent, but defeat their own ends by widening the breach between the Haitians and the Americans, who must co-operate if the problems of the intervention are to be solved.

Failure to define a clear policy and to announce a definite program has been a contributing cause of much of the muddle in which we find ourselves in Haiti. John Hay once said that American diplomacy, so far as he had practised it and learned it from his predecessors, told squarely what we wanted, announced early in the negotiations what we were willing to give, and allowed the other side to accept or reject it.

While it is futile to question the good faith of the American government in its relations with Haiti, it is obvious that these practical and highly commendable axioms of sound diplomacy have not been followed. Unless we are to register a failure in Haiti which will seriously reflect on our whole Latin-American policy, it is high time for a thorough elucidation of the situation and the adoption and public announcement of a definite program in such terms that no one can further question our good faith. There are difficulties which will require investigation and thought by the best procurable American brains. We have blundered into complications from which no mere amount of good will and honest intention will extricate us. We should first convince the Haitians and Latin America in general that we intend to live up to the spirit and the letter of the treaty and of such supplementary agreements as have been made. We should send to Haiti a civilian High Commissioner, a man of recognized ability, to devise and put into execution a constructive policy designed to attain the ends contemplated in these agreements. The apparently hopeless tangle in Santo Domingo was settled in a manner highly satisfactory to both parties by a civilian commissioner acting as special representative of the President of the United States.

Our problem in Haiti is largely psychological. To convince the Haitian people that such a program has been definitely adopted, and to secure the absolutely essential co-operation of the upper-class Haitians, it is necessary to separate the military from all civil functions and reduce to

WHAT SHOULD BE DONE

a minimum the armed forces of the United States in Haiti.

Any readjustment of our policy should include the reduction of the marine forces in Haiti to an organization sufficient only to form the nucleus of an expeditionary force in the improbable event that such a force will become necessary.*

That a genuine and efficient democratic government can be established in Haiti before the expiration of the treaty is improbable. But regardless of the concrete results which have been achieved towards efficiency, it is clear that our present program has not tended towards the establishment of a Haitian democracy.

Before we leave Haiti it will be necessary that a parliamentary form of government be restored. Just when congressional elections may wisely be held will be one of the serious problems of the Haitian government and its American advisers. But that a Haitian senate and chamber of deputies should be elected, and should function before our withdrawal, is as obvious as is the necessity for definite steps towards the gradual replacement of Americans by Haitians in all administrative departments.

The writer is thoroughly convinced that many of the critics of the American intervention in Haiti who have urged immediate abrogation of the treaty, including some of the ablest Haitian opponents of the present régime, would welcome the program outlined above, particularly if this program should be irrevocably adopted, and the status of the intervention determined, by congressional action. That discussion in Congress of the intervention might result in the adoption of a very different program is possible,

* Paul H. Douglas, in a paper on the American occupation in Haiti (*Political Science Quarterly*, September, 1927), said: "It is highly important to convince the Haitians of our good faith, and it is difficult to do this so long as there is a military commander of the occupation and a considerable military force. Despite General Russell's sincerity it would be better to replace him by an equally able citizen."

but it would seem to be highly desirable that our policy in Haiti should be determined by Congress rather than left solely to the executive departments of the government.

NOTES

NOTES

PART ONE

CHAPTER II

1. Cap Français, or Cap François (old spelling), became the centre of the most prosperous community in the French colony. After the revolution the name was changed to Cap Haitien. On the coronation of Christophe as Henri I, the King renamed this city Cap Henri, and on his death and the incorporation of the North with the Republic, the former name of Cap Haitien was resumed. Cap Haitien is now the second in importance of the commercial centres of the Republic, and from an historical standpoint the most interesting town in Haiti.

2. The census reports of the slave population of St.-Domingue are, owing to fraudulent returns, quite unreliable, but from official memoirs presented to the ministers of marine it is possible to make a comparatively accurate estimate of the number of slaves in St.-Domingue and the number imported into the colony.

When d'Ogeron, the first governor of the French West India Company, assumed control of Tortuga in 1664, it was stated that the settlers, not including filibusters, numbered not over 400. The census of 1681 gives the slave population at 2,000. Figures presented in official reports to the minister of marine estimate the slaves in 1701 at 20,000 and in 1754 at 230,000; a very conservative estimate for 1798 would be not less than 450,000. As over 1,000,000 slaves were imported into St.-Domingue in a little over one hundred years, it would seem that the mortality was abnormally high.

Stoddard * states that the annual excess of deaths over births was fully two and one-half per cent.

"The continual dying out," he says, "of the slave population in a favourable climate excited much comment at the time, and many reasons for it were given. In 1764, a governor attributes it to improper food, undue labour imposed upon pregnant women, and a very high infant mortality. The general opinion seems to have been

* Bibliography.

that the Negroes were worked too hard, and Hilliard d'Auberteuil asserts that this was often deliberately done, as many masters considered it cheaper to buy slaves than to breed them. A colonial writer lays much of the trouble to immorality among the Negroes, and to the ensuing ravages of venereal disease.

"Modern writers have advanced further reasons. Peytraud, perhaps the ablest student on the subject, thinks that much stress should be laid on the great nervous strain imposed by the sudden change from the careless indolence of savage existence to a life of continuous labour. His contention seems to be sound. It was apparently this more than anything else which killed off the enslaved Indian population; if the Negro, less nervous and more robust, survived, it was only after a costly process of natural selection.

"Leroy-Beaulieu holds that, by some fundamental law of nature, slavery hinders man's reproduction, as captivity does that of wild animals. Certainly the sterility of the slave population was not confined to San Domingo; it was common to the other West Indian islands without distinction of nationality. Wallon pithily sums up the matter. 'Slavery,' he says, 'like Saturn, devours its own children.' "

It is obvious that to cover an annual deficit of two and one-half per cent, and to provide a steady increase as well, the yearly importation of Negroes must have been progressively large. The statistics, however, are both insufficient and faulty. No record was kept of the smuggled Negroes, whose number is put at fully 3,000 a year. The official estimate for 1754 is 10,000, and that for 1766 is 13,000. An official memoir on the state of French commerce with St.-Domingue estimates the importation of Negroes for the year 1787 at over 40,000. This is probably the approximate figure for 1789.

At the outbreak of the revolution, the slave trade was a highly organized industry. In 1787 ninety-two ships were employed in supplying the French colonies with Negroes, and in 1788 the number had risen to one hundred and five. The slave traffic was extremely lucrative, and was one of the greatest sources of prosperity of the French maritime towns.

A chain of slave "factories" had been established from the Senegal coast around the Cape of Good Hope to Mozambique. The slaves procured at these factories were exposed to great hardships. The average death-rate during the voyage to St.-Domingue was from seven to eight per cent, and the horrors of the "middle passage" were such that in spite of enormous profits from such traffic, many captains refused a second voyage.

NOTES

3. Captain Marcus Rainsford * says, in his *Historical Account of the Black Republic:* "Flushed with opulence and dissipation, the majority of the planters in St. Domingo had arrived at a state of sentiment the most vitiated, and manners equally depraved; while injured by an example so contagious, the slaves had become more dissolute than those of any British island. If the master was proud, voluptuous, and crafty, the slave was equally vicious, and often riotous; the punishment of one was but the consequence of his own excesses, but that of the other was often cruel and unnatural. The proprietor would bear no rival in his parish, and would not bow even to the ordinances of justice. The creole slaves looked upon the newly imported Africans with scorn, and sustained in turn that of the mulattoes, whose complexion was browner, while all were kept at a distance from an intercourse with the whites; nor did the boundaries of sex, it is painful to observe, keep their wonted distinction from the stern impulses which affect men. The European ladies too often participated in the austerity and arrogance of their male kindred, while the jet-black beauty among slaves, though scarcely a native of the island, refused all commerce with those who could not boast the same distinction with herself."

4. Bryan Edwards * said: "In countries where slavery is established, the leading principle on which government is supported is fear, or a sense of that absolute coercive necessity, which, leaving no choice of action, supersedes all questions of right.

"The great and, I am afraid, the only certain and permanent security of the enslaved Negroes is the strong circumstance that the interest of the master is blended with, and, in truth, altogether depends on the health, strength, and activity of the slaves. This applies equally to all the European colonies in America; and accordingly the actual conditions of the Negroes in all those colonies, to whatever nation they belong, is, I believe, nearly the same.

"I have, therefore, only to observe in this, that in all the French islands the general treatment of the slaves is neither much better nor much worse, as far as I can observe, than those of Great Britain. If any difference there is, I think that they are better clothed among the French and allowed more animal food among the English. The prevalent notion that the French planters treat their Negroes with greater humanity and tenderness than the British I know to be groundless; yet no candid person who has had an opportunity to

* Bibliography.

see the Negroes in the French islands, and of contrasting their condition with that of the peasantry in many parts of Europe, will think them by any means the most wretched of mankind."

CHAPTER IV

1. The significance of these negotiations was apparent to Jefferson, then President of the United States, who realized that a change of ownership of the Louisiana Territory from Spain, under Don Carlos, to France, ruled by Bonaparte, then scheming to acquire a colonial empire, might well seriously affect the American Union. Jefferson apparently had no idea of acquiring the Louisiana Territory from France, but he instructed his minister to France, Robert Livingston, to impress upon Bonaparte that if France took possession of Louisiana, at least New Orleans and the Floridas should be ceded to the United States.

This suggestion was ignored by Bonaparte, who proceeded to press Don Carlos for the delivery of Louisiana, and finally, in October, 1802, the transfer was effected. The failure of Bonaparte's campaign in St.-Domingue resulted in an abrupt change in his plans for a colonial empire in the Americas, and in the spring of 1803 he proposed to sell Louisiana to the United States. The first price named was 100,000,000 francs, and to this offer Livingston replied that the United States did not desire the Louisiana Territory but would consider the purchase of the island of New Orleans and the Floridas. In April, 1803, after prolonged negotiations in which James Monroe, as Special Envoy, took part, the Louisiana purchase was consummated; the United States agreeing to pay to France 60,000,000 francs and to assume certain American claims against France amounting to about 20,000,000 francs, a total, if all these claims were valid, of less than $16,000,000.

2. Donatien Rochambeau was a son of General Comte de Rochambeau, who commanded the French forces in the American Revolution and who rendered such effective help at the battle of Yorktown. Charles Mackenzie,* the first British Consul-General to Haiti, in his *Notes on Haiti,* published in 1830, says of Rochambeau: "By enormities that rivalled those of Dessalines, he soon alienated the few blacks and coloured partisans of France. . . . The memory of Rochambeau in Haiti is associated with all that is infamous."

* Bibliography.

NOTES

Rochambeau, after his capture by the British at Cap Haitien, was sent as a prisoner of war to England, where he remained until exchanged in 1811. He was killed at the battle of Leipzig in 1813.

3. For details of the arrest, deportation, and death of Toussaint, see *La vie de Toussaint l'Ouverture, Chef des noirs insurgés de Saint-Domingue,* by J. F. Dubroca (Paris, 1802), a brief in support of the Leclerc expedition; *Toussaint l'Ouverture,* by Cragnon Lacoste (Paris and Bordeaux, 1877), extremely prejudiced in favour of the black chief; *St. Domingo, or an Historical, Political, and Military Sketch of the Projected Black Republic,* by Captain Marcus Rainsford (London, 1802), a prejudiced account of the wars in St.-Domingue by a former British officer; *Vie de Toussaint l'Ouverture,* by M. Saint Rémy, a mulatto who did not love the black chief; *Toussaint l'Ouverture: A Biography and Autobiography,* Boston, Mass., U.S.A., 1863, edited and published by James Redpath. The biography was republished from *The Life of Toussaint l'Ouverture,* by the Rev. John Beard. The autobiography is taken from *Mémoires de la vie de Toussaint l'Ouverture,* edited by M. Saint Rémy. Both show decided partisanship and are not, by the author of this book, considered reliable.

So much has been written of the "First of the Blacks," and from such divergent angles, that any true estimate of the character of Toussaint is now impossible.

The author has, in his library, a biography, an autobiography, histories, essays, pamphlets, tracts, and poems about Toussaint, and even a novel of which he is the hero, and has faithfully but vainly endeavoured to reconcile the conflicting opinions of the writers thereof.

The zeal of antislavery propagandists has created a Toussaint so sublime as to be absolutely incredible. One can hardly accept seriously the following tribute of Wendell Phillips, an ardent antislavery advocate:

"I would call him Napoleon, but Napoleon made his way to empire over broken oaths and through a sea of blood. This man never broke his word. 'No retaliation' was his great motto and the rule of his life; and the last words uttered to his son in France were these: 'My boy, you will one day go back to St. Domingo; forget that France murdered your father.' I would call him Cromwell, but Cromwell was only a soldier, and the state he founded went down with him into his grave. I would call him Washington, but the great Virginian held slaves. This man risked his empire rather than permit the slave-trade in the humblest village in his dominions.

"You think me a fanatic to-night, for you read history, not with your eyes, but with your prejudices. But fifty years hence, when truth gets a hearing, the Muse of History will put Phocion for the Greek, and Brutus for the Roman, Hampden for England, Fayette for France, choose Washington as the bright, consummate flower of our earlier civilization, and John Brown the ripe fruit of our noonday, then, dipping her pen in the sunlight, will write in the clear blue, above them all, the name of the soldier, the statesman, the martyr, TOUSSAINT L'OUVERTURE."

The following description of Toussaint is by an officer in the army of France in St.-Domingue: "He has a fine eye, and his glances are rapid and penetrating; extremely sober of habit, his activity in the prosecution of his enterprises is incessant. He is an excellent horseman and travels on occasion with inconceivable rapidity, arriving at the end of his journey alone or almost unattended, his aides-de-camp and domestics being unable to follow him in journeys often extending to fifty or sixty leagues."

4. On June 22, 1802, Leclerc issued the following decree:

"Head-quarters at the Cape, June 22, 1802.

"In the name of the French Government, the General-in-chief, Captain-General, decrees as follows:

"In the French part of St.-Domingue, the administration of the quarters and communes is confined to military commandants and councils of notables; the commandants to have the jurisdiction of police in their respective districts, and the chief command of the *gens d'armerie;* the councils of notables to be composed of proprietors or merchants, and to consist of five members in the towns of Port Républicain,* the Cape,† and Les Cayes, and of three members in other communes; the members to be appointed by the colonial prefect; and everyone so appointed to be compelled to accept the office. The military commandants are charged with the delivery (granting) of passports for travelling in the colony, the suppression of vagrancy, the care of the police, the maintenance of cleanliness and health, the care of citizens newly arrived, the police of prisons, and the regulation of weights and measures, in concurrence with the council of notables. Except in the case of flagrant crimes,

* Port-au-Prince.
† Cap Haitien.

NOTES

the military commandants cannot arrest any citizen without an order from the commandant of the quarter. The communes to provide for their own expenses; the sums to be regulated by a decree of the general-in-chief, with the advice of the colonial prefect. No military commandant can put in requisition the labourers or cattle of any plantation; the general-in-chief reserves that power to himself. The councils of notables to provide for the expenses of the commune and for the imports adopted by the commander-in-chief with the advice of the colonial prefect; those councils alone to deliberate upon the communal interests; all other assemblies of citizens are prohibited, and shall, if attempted, be considered seditious and dispersed by force. The councils to correspond immediately with the sub-prefects, by whom their members may be suspended, and finally dismissed by the colonial prefect. There shall be in each parish a commissary to register the public acts."

CHAPTER V

1. Haiti, or Hayti, signifying high or mountainous land, was the name given to this island by the aborigines; another name used by the natives was Quisqueya, meaning great country or mother of nations. This latter name was more commonly used in the eastern part of the island, now the Dominican Republic.

2. The nature of these events is shown by a letter of a French officer secretly in Port-au-Prince at the time, who himself escaped by a miracle to the lesser evil of an English prison in Jamaica. "The murder of the whites in detail," he writes, "began at Port-au-Prince in the first days of January, but on the seventeenth and eighteenth of March they were finished off *en masse*. All, without exception, have been massacred, down to the very women and children. Madame de Boynes was killed in a peculiarly horrible manner. A young mulatto named Fifi Pariset ranged the town like a madman searching the houses to kill the little children. Many of the men and women were hewn down by sappers, who hacked off their arms and smashed in their chests. Some were poniarded, others mutilated, others 'passed on the bayonet,' others disembowelled with knives or sabres, still others stuck like pigs. At the beginning, a great number were drowned. The same general massacre has taken place all over the colony, and as I write you these lines I believe that there are not twenty whites still alive—and these not for long."

BLACK DEMOCRACY

This estimate was, indeed, scarcely exaggerated. The white race had perished utterly out of the land, French St.-Domingue had vanished for ever, and the black state of Haiti had begun its troubled history.

3. *Massacre of the Whites.*—The massacre was executed with an attention to order which proves how minutely it had been prepared. Precautions were taken that no other whites than the French should be included. In the town of Cap Français, where the massacre took place on the night of the twentieth of April, the precaution was first taken of sending detachments of soldiers to the houses of the American and English merchants, with strict orders to permit no person to enter them without the permission of the master of the house, who had been previously informed of what was about to happen. This command was so well obeyed that one of these foreigners was able to preserve the lives of a number of Frenchmen whom he had concealed in his house, and who remained there until the massacre was over.

Priests, surgeons, and some artisans were preserved from destruction, probably in all about one-tenth of the French residents. The rest were massacred without regard to age or sex. A witness of the night of terror has stated that "at every moment of the night the noise was heard of axes, which were employed to burst open the doors of the neighbouring houses, of piercing cries followed by a deathlike silence, soon, however, to be changed to a renewal of the same sounds of grief and terror, as the soldiers proceeded from house to house."

4. At the end of the prosperous colonial period, there were in operation over three thousand sugar estates and almost as many coffee "places," but in bulk and value sugar was by far the most important source of revenue. Since the insurrection, coffee has continued to be the most important product, contributing from sixty to eighty per cent of the total revenue of the people of Haiti. Although for years after the expulsion of the whites some sugar was shipped, it was not until after the American intervention that sugar again became one of the important exports.

CHAPTER VI

1. "The repossession and recultivation of this island [St.-Domingue] appear to have been favourite objects with a considerable number of leading men of the nation [France]; and in the hope

NOTES

of effecting this, the French cabinet, though placed in circumstances which prevented the total rejection of the African slave trade, yet refused an immediate relinquishment of that abominable traffic, and stipulated for its continuance for five years, promising, by treaty, its definitive cessation at the end of that period. Five years they thought would be sufficient to supply the plantations of St.-Domingue with as many cargoes of slaves as should be wanted, in addition to the myriads of Negroes and mulattoes who have again to be brought under the yoke."—*Edwards.**

2. Haiti gave a hearty welcome to Simon Bolivar, Commodore Aury, and the many Venezuelan families whom the successes of the Spaniards had compelled to leave their country. At the end of December, 1815, Bolivar arrived at Cayes, in which port were anchored, on January 6, 1816, ten men-of-war commanded by Commodore Aury, who had been forced to evacuate Carthagena. The embarrassed circumstances in which the Republic found itself did not prevent Pétion from extending all the help he could to the sailors and the Venezuelan families, who, owing to their hasty flight, were in the greatest state of indigence. He was most kind to Bolivar, requesting only, in return for the unselfish assistance given to the latter's cause, that slavery be abolished. Bolivar promised to proclaim general freedom in Venezuela province and all other provinces which he should succeed in winning over to the cause of independence. He received from the president of Haiti four thousand rifles, powder, cartridges, and all kinds of provisions, even a printing-press. Pétion did not content himself with furnishing these articles; he was peacemaker between Bolivar and his two companions, General Bermudes and Commodore Aury, who had quarrelled, thus dispelling for the time being the misunderstanding which was about to set them at variance. Haitians were authorized to join in the expedition. In the following letter, written on the eighth of February, Bolivar expressed his intense gratitude to Pétion:

MR. PRESIDENT:

I am overwhelmed with your favours. In everything you are magnanimous and kind. We have almost completed our preparations and in a fortnight we may perhaps be ready to start; I am only awaiting your last favours. Through Mr. Inginac, your worthy secretary, I take the liberty to make a new request. In my

* Bibliography.

proclamation to the inhabitants of Venezuela and in the decrees I have to issue concerning the freedom of the slaves, I do not know if I am allowed to express the feelings of my heart toward Your Excellency and to leave to posterity an everlasting token of your philanthropy. I do not know, I say, if I must declare that you are the author of our liberty. I beg Your Excellency to let me know his will on the matter.

Pétion refused to be designated as the author of the independence of Venezuela, and made the following answer to Bolivar:

Port-au-Prince, February 18, 1816,
the 13th year of the Independence.

GENERAL:
Your kind letter of the 8th instant reached me yesterday. You know my regard for the cause you are defending and for yourself; you must, then, be convinced how great is my desire to see freedom granted to all those who are still under the yoke of slavery; but out of deference for a power which has not yet openly declared itself an enemy of the Republic, I am compelled to ask you not to mention my name in any of your documents; and for this purpose I reckon on the sentiments which characterize you.

After leaving Cayes on the tenth of April, 1816, Bolivar landed at Carupano on May 31st. Defeated on the 10th of July by the Spanish General Morales, he fled again to Haiti. Pétion once more gave him his sympathy and assistance, furnishing him with large supplies of arms, ammunition, etc. On the 26th of December, 1816, Bolivar left Haiti and this time succeeded in ridding his country of Spanish domination. He expressed his gratitude once more in the following letter, which he wrote before embarking, to General Marion, Commandant of the *arrondissement* of Cayes:

Port-au-Prince, December 4, 1816.

GENERAL:
On the point of starting with a view to returning to my country and strengthening its independence, I feel that it would be ungrateful of me were I to miss this opportunity of thanking you for all your kindness to my countrymen. If men are bound by the favours they have received, be sure, General, that my countrymen and I shall for ever love the Haitian people and the worthy rulers who make them happy.

NOTES

One of the most prized exhibits in the historical collection of the author is a very beautiful court sword which was presented to Pétion by Bolivar, shortly after his final success, in testimony to his gratitude.

3. "Appended to the order for the creation of the new nobility there were minute instructions as to the costume of the black court. The princes and dukes were required to wear a white tunic reaching below the knees, and over this undergarment there was to be thrown a black cloak descending to the calf of the leg, with red facings embroidered with gold, and connected at the neck by a gold button. The legs were to be clothed in white silk hose, and the shoes to be of red morocco, fastened with square gold buckles. A gold-hilted sword, and round Spanish hat with red and black plumes, completed this court attire. The counts were habited like the princes and dukes, except that their cloaks were to be blue instead of black, and to be faced with white instead of red, while the barons and chevaliers were dressed in simple coats, which for the latter were blue and for the former red, their hats being decorated with plumes, the colours of which were white and green. The knights of St. Henry bore for a decoration a large gold cross set with brilliants and suspended from the neck by a ribbon. Upon one side of this cross there was engraved the image of Christophe, with the words, *Henry fondateur, 1811,* and upon the other a crown of laurel with a star, and the device, *prix de la valeur.*"
—*Brown.*

CHAPTER VII

1. Opposition of Senators and Representatives of the Southern, slave-owning States blocked the recognition of Haiti by the United States government. Haiti was not recognized by the United States until 1864.

2. Indemnity was finally paid to a great many of the former colonial proprietors, and the records of such payments, with the accompanying descriptions of properties, which have been preserved, are the most authentic basis of land titles in Haiti.

3. In a message of abdication read to the Senate on March 4, 1843, Boyer said: "The efforts of my administration have always been to economize the public funds. At the present moment there are nearly a million piastres [dollars] in the national treasury, besides certain sums in France held in deposit for the Republic. In

submitting myself to voluntary exile, I hope to annihilate all pretext for civil war on my account."

Léger * says: "In 1843 Boyer was deposed from power by a political party composed principally of the young, active, and ambitious men of the island, some of whom, having been educated abroad, really desired to see the island improved, while others, however, ruined by a course of reckless extravagance and debauchery, hoped to better themselves by the change. But this was effected under the plea that Boyer had made no advance in twenty-five years; that he had not given education to the people, that he had maintained the military system, which retarded the progress of civilization, and aided him to violate the laws."

4. The strategic importance of the island of Haiti in relation to the trade routes from the United States to the South and Central American Republics, and between the Atlantic and Pacific coasts of the United States, has long been recognized by American statesmen.

President Grant, in a message to Congress in 1871, recommending the annexation of the Dominican Republic, said:

> The acquisition of St. Domingo is desirable because of its geographical position. It commands the entrance to the Caribbean Sea and the Isthmus transit of commerce; it possesses the richest soil, best and most capacious harbours, most salubrious climate, and the most valuable products of the forest, mine, and soil of any of the West Indies Islands. Its possession by us will in a few years build up a coastwise commerce of immense magnitude, which will go far toward restoring to us our lost merchant marine. It will give to us those articles which we consume so largely and do not produce, thus equalizing our exports and imports. In case of foreign war, it will give to us command of all the islands referred to, and thus prevent an enemy from ever again possessing himself of rendezvous upon our coast. At present our coast trade between the States bordering on the Atlantic and those bordering on the Gulf of Mexico is cut in two by the Bahamas and Antilles twice. We must, as it were, pass through foreign countries to get by sea from Georgia to the west coast of Florida. . . . The acquisition of St. Domingo is an adherence to the Monroe Doctrine; it is a measure of natural protection; it is asserting our just claim to a controlling influence over the great commercial traffic soon to flow from west to east by way of the Isthmus of

* Bibliography.

NOTES

Darien; it is to build up our merchant marine; it is to furnish new markets for the products of our farms, shops, and manufactories; it is to make slavery insupportable in Cuba and Porto Rico at once, and ultimately so in Brazil; it is to settle the unhappy condition of Cuba, and end an exterminating conflict.

Much unfriendly feeling was aroused in Haiti by the proposal to annex the Dominican Republic. Samuel Hazard, a newspaper correspondent who accompanied the commission sent by President Grant to investigate conditions in Santo Domingo, reported to the American Journal which he represented that the feeling among the Dominicans was strongly in favour of annexation. He also wrote that he was convinced that much of the opposition to annexation originated and was maintained in Haiti.

The American government had made repeated representations to the Haitian government to the effect that any interference in the matter would be resented, and had called on Haiti to keep its hands off. In February, 1871, Hamilton Fish, then Secretary of State, wrote to the American minister at Port-au-Prince, intimating that the promises of the Haitian government to respect this demand were not being fulfilled. In March, 1871, American commissioners sent by President Grant to report on conditions in the Dominican Republic in support of his policy of annexation arrived at Port-au-Prince and conferred with President Saget. The following extract from the report of his commission is enlightening:

> The commissioners, of course, felt a deep interest in the experiment of self-government which the blacks are trying in Haiti. They certainly wished it all success.
> They could not understand how any new and close relations between St. Domingo and the United States could affect that experiment otherwise than favourably. They felt that it would be unjust to our government to suppose that it contemplated any action injurious to it. They had too much faith in the virtue of our institutions to doubt that the form established of similar institutions in a neighbouring land must act favourably upon republicanism and progress in Haiti. The only force to be exerted would be a moral one, the force of example. They knew of no valid claim that Haiti had against St. Domingo, nor of any rights or interests which could be endangered by the extension of our institutions over the western end of the island. Nevertheless, they desired to give to the government, and to intelligent citizens, an opportunity of stating their views.

BLACK DEMOCRACY

Moreover, they desired, in the most friendly spirit, to make the same observations and study of Haiti and its inhabitants as they had made of the Dominican Republic. They intimated to the President and his council their dispositions and desires. They stated even that they should be glad to be put in the way of ascertaining what were the views and wishes of the Haitian people with respect to any changes that might be brought about in the neighbouring republic. But they received no encouragement to pursue their inquiries. They asked verbally, and through our minister in writing, for permission to explore the interior of the island, but this was met in a spirit equivalent to a refusal.

They contented themselves, therefore, with taking such testimony and gathering such information upon matters bearing upon the question of annexation as they could without giving offence. In reviewing the whole field of their investigations, looking to the interests of both divisions of the island, they are firmly persuaded that the annexation of Santo Domingo to the United States would be hardly less beneficial to the Haitian than to the Dominican people. This benefit would arise first from the example which would doubtless be afforded of a well-regulated, orderly, and prosperous state, the great need of that part of the world, and which it has as yet never seen; a second and more direct benefit would arise from the equitable establishment of a boundary line between the French-speaking and the Spanish-speaking nations upon that island, and its guarantee by a strong power. This would end the exhausting border warfare which has been one of the greatest curses of Haiti as well as St. Domingo, and would enable both to devote their energies thenceforward to the education of their people and the development of their resources.

Charles Sumner, who strongly opposed the treaty of annexation in the United States Senate, is still regarded by the Haitians as one of the benefactors of their country. A street in Port-au-Prince is named after him, and his portrait still adorns the hall of the Haitian national assembly. The Negro writer and orator, Frederick Douglass, at one time United States minister to Haiti, although an ardent supporter of Senator Sumner, differed radically with him on the question of annexation of Santo Domingo. In this connexion Mr. Douglass said:

> The reasons in its favour were many and obvious; and those against it, as I thought, were easily answered. To Mr. Sumner, annexation was a measure to extinguish a coloured nation, and to do so by dishonourable means and for selfish motives. To

NOTES

me it meant the alliance of a weak and defenceless people, having few or none of the attributes of a nation, torn and rent by internal feuds and unable to maintain order at home or command respect abroad, to a government which would give it peace, stability, prosperity, and civilization, and make it helpful to both countries. . . . Santo Domingo wanted to come under our government . . . and for more reasons than I can stop here to give, I then believed, and I do now believe, it would have been wise to have received her into our sisterhood of States.

5. In connexion with the negotiations for the lease of Mole St. Nicholas, Mr. Douglass, in an article published in the *North American Review,* September, 1891, stated:

This position of Mr. Firmin's was resisted by Admiral Gherardi [special commissioner of the United States], who contended, with much force, that while there was no formal agreement consummated between the two governments, Haiti was nevertheless bound, since the assistance for which she asked had made Hippolyte president of Haiti. Without intending to break the force of the Admiral's contentions at this point, I plainly saw the indefensible attitude in which he was placing the government of the United States in representing our government as interfering by its navy with the affairs of a neighbouring country.

These negotiations completely failed of their purpose. Léger, in reviewing this matter, said:

From his flagship, the *Philadelphia,* Rear-Admiral Gherardi addressed his demand to the Haitian government, his letter containing the following proviso: "So long as the United States may be the lessee of the Mole St. Nicholas, the government of Haiti will not lease or otherwise dispose of any port or harbour or other territory in its dominions, or grant any special privileges or rights to use therein, to any other power, state, or government."
Rear-Admiral Gherardi was in so great a hurry to win what he imagined would be an easy success, that he did not think it necessary to secure the co-operation of Mr. Frederick Douglass, who was at that time United States minister at Port-au-Prince; he alone signed the letter.
Mr. A. Firmin, then Haitian Secretary of State for Exterior Relations, availed himself at once of the blunder to request the credentials of the Rear-Admiral, who, not being provided with any, was obliged to write to Washington for them. When Pres-

ident Harrison's letter appointing Bancroft Gherardi his Special Commissioner reached Port-au-Prince, public opinion was in such a state of excitement by the protracted sojourn of the powerful white squadron in Haitian waters, that it would have been impossible for President Hippolyte even so much as to attempt to grant the slightest advantage to the United States. The Secretary for Exterior Relations clung tenaciously to the Constitution, which forbids the alienation of any portion of the territory. Thus ended the matter.

PART TWO

CHAPTER I

1. *Cacos*.—Admiral Caperton, in his testimony at the Senate inquiry, stated: "The caco question will be the most difficult one for the United States to solve in Haiti, as these men have long been used to the wandering life of a bandit, and to a life without work. The caco question is a most serious one, and will probably not be successfully handled until a reliable constabulary is established and money comes into the country to provide work for these men."

This and somewhat similar comments by American officials appear to the writer to convey an erroneous idea of just what a so-called caco was, and give the impression that there existed in Haiti a very considerable number of bandits.

As a matter of fact, while the cacos did at times resort to banditry, and during an uprising all bandits became cacos, the fact remains that cacos were as a rule the profoundly ignorant and deluded tools of politicians. They fought because they were accustomed to obey their chiefs or because they dared not refuse.

Except in the section of the Central Plateau, near the Dominican border, there has never been much banditry, and at the present time there are probably fewer bandits in Haiti in proportion to the population than there are in a large American city. General Smedley Butler, the marine officer who organized the *gendarmerie* of Haiti, in defining the word "caco," said: "You can get fifty definitions. The one popularly given to me by the Haitians . . . was that the caco was a bird of prey that lives off the weaker fowl; it has a red plume and makes a sound like 'caco' as it is called, and these bandits live entirely off the weak, so they adopted that name. They wear a patch of red on their clothing . . . to indicate the fact that they are cacos."

NOTES

Here again no distinction is made between bandits and cacos. A better definition is that of General Waller, U.S.M.C.: "It must be explained that the cacos have been the controlling element in all revolutions; they were purchased by first one candidate and then another. Finishing a contract with one man, they, having put him in power, would immediately sell their services to the next aspirant and unseat the first." Later General Waller stated that the cacos were "the king-makers," that "an aspirant for political power, a man who wanted to be president, would go to the North and make an agreement with these caco leaders, and for a certain sum, to be paid by the Haitian treasury after he was successful, also the privilege of looting some of the towns on the way down, they would descend from the mountains and put the president in power."

As a matter of fact, the name "caco" was first applied to revolutionists in 1867 when the peasants at Vallières, near Cap Haitien, who had taken up arms against Salomon assumed the name of "cacos." The name at that time had no connexion with bandits, nor has it since been, in Haiti, synonymous with banditry.

2. *Gourde.*—The *gourde* (derived from the Spanish word *gordo,* an obsolete monetary unit of the Spanish-American colonies) is the Haitian dollar of 100 centimes. Its value fluctuated, during the ten eventful years prior to the American intervention, from 34 cents (United States currency) to less than 10 cents.

At the time of the intervention the *gourde* was exchangeable at about ten *gourdes* to the dollar. It was stabilized shortly after the intervention by agreement with the Banque Nationale at a ratio of five *gourdes* to the dollar gold. One *gourde* now equals 20 cents (United States currency), and the *gourde* is by law exchangeable on demand and without expense at the fixed rate of five *gourdes* for one dollar gold; accordingly, the value of Haitian currency is measured by dollars and does not fluctuate.

3. On November 12, 1914, Secretary of State Bryan cabled to the American minister at Port-au-Prince:

> If in your opinion the Government headed by Theodore is *de facto,* you are instructed to inform him that recognition by the United States will be granted him as provisional president when a commission to be named by the Haitian Government with full powers to act upon certain questions of interest to this government and to the Republic of Haiti is in position to give necessary assurances.

BLACK DEMOCRACY

The questions to be acted upon were a customs convention between Haiti and the United States, the settlement of matters outstanding between the government of Haiti and the National Railroad, the settlement of questions outstanding between the government of Haiti and the Banque Nationale, and an agreement by Haiti to give full protection to all foreign interests in Haiti.

4. The writer has been informed that on one occasion when President Theodore was compelled by lack of funds to refuse payment to certain chiefs who had visited the palace to collect, these men from the hills, seeing him surrounded with luxury and doubting his word, pointed out that no one who owned such magnificent trappings could be without money. Theodore in desperation remarked that what they saw was all that he possessed, and told them to help themselves. Followed the curious spectacle of caco generals departing from the palace with mirrors, pictures, and elaborate pieces of furniture on their heads.

5. When Admiral Caperton sailed with his flagship to Port-au-Prince, he stationed United States gun-boats in the ports of Gonaives and St.-Marc. In connexion with this procedure, the following testimony at the Senate inquiry is of interest:

> ADMIRAL CAPERTON: "I left them [the gun-boats] at the various ports and gave them orders to meet the General [Sam] outside of the city and make him again promise me that he would not loot or burn down the cities or fire in the cities, because I considered that not humane. The cities are all undefended, and they were poor people, generally speaking, and unarmed."
>
> THE CHAIRMAN: "These were campaign pledges you were exacting from him?"
>
> ADMIRAL CAPERTON: "Yes, sir. He gave me first one in Cap Haitien. That I was not satisfied with. I met him in each one, and so he finally laughingly said to me: 'I do not see how you know where I am going. Every time I go to enter a city, I find your representative outside with some question asking me to behave myself.' He promised to do so, and upon the whole he did very well, considering everything. He kept his word very well in that respect."

Unfortunately General Sam's reaction to this new style of personally conducted revolution cannot be ascertained. But the writer has been informed by one of Sam's officers in the campaign that this unusual and unconventional manner of conducting a revolution

NOTES

was equally puzzling to the caco army and the government forces.

6. In connexion with the arrival at Port-au-Prince of General Sam and the departure of Theodore, Admiral Caperton testified (*Senate Hearings*):

"Guillaume was a strong man, but feared by the better class of Haitians on account of his harsh methods and crooked tendencies. He had already served one year of a life sentence imposed for falsifying government financial statements and causing a large over-issue of bonds the proceeds of which he had appropriated to his own use.

"In view of the conditions in Haiti which I believed were unusually disturbed because of the excessive number of plots and counterplots among the Haitians, the excessive continuation of revolutionary movements and disorder throughout the country, the rapidly approaching fall of the Theodore Government, and the consequent chaotic conditions that would occur in Port-au-Prince, the approach of Vilbrun Guillaume with about fifteen hundred men, among whom were many cacos, the lawless men of the North who were very much feared; in view of the representations made by the United States with reference to the customs and other matters; in view of the possible violation of Haitian neutrality by belligerent ships of European powers; in view, further, of the unsettled condition of the bank question which, although assurances had been received that no forcible attempt would be made to remove funds, was yet far from settled owing to the breaking of the contract by the Theodore Government; the changing of the depository for customs receipts, and the action taken by the directors of the bank in connexion therewith; in view of the disturbed conditions in Santo Domingo; and *especially in view of my lack of knowledge of the policy of the United States government,* which without warning might demand of me to take prompt action in that vicinity, I requested that an expeditionary regiment of marines be sent to the naval station, Guantánamo Bay, Cuba, together with the necessary means of transportation to Haiti, and that both the marines and the transport be subject to immediate call.

"On February 18, the commanding officer of the *Des Moines* reported that St.-Marc was in the hands of the revolutionists; that about eight of them had taken the town during the night; that casualties were few; and that a number of the government forces were drowned while trying to get off to the *Nord Alexis;* and that Montplaisir, the Theodore Minister of the Interior, was reported dead. It was afterwards found out that Montplaisir had been stabbed in the back, presumably by one of his own men in the boat getting off to the *Nord Alexis.*

"In the midst of the foregoing events on February 8 the commander of the *Wheeling* reported that ex-Minister Bobo was on board the *Pacifique* going to Monte Cristi and Quanaminthe to organize and lead a new revolution.

"During this time Port-au-Prince was becoming more disturbed, but up to this date, February 18, 1915, there had been no outbreaks. On that day several changes were made by Davilmar Theodore in his cabinet, among which was the resignation of Mr. Borno, Minister of Foreign Affairs.

"At 7 P.M., Saturday, February 20, the commanding officer of the *Des Moines* reported that the Dutch steamer *Prins Frederick Hendrik* had arrived at St.-Marc from Cap Haitien with 70,-000 *gourdes* for Guillaume, and that all was quiet at Cap Haitien and Quanaminthe, and that the *Pacifique* had recently been at Puerto Plata.

"As I believed that Guillaume had the situation well in hand at St.-Marc and would preserve order, and as he now had received considerable money and had paid his troops, and as, therefore, the pressure on the customs money at St.-Marc was relieved, and as the situation was rapidly approaching a climax at Port-au-Prince, I decided to concentrate all my forces at Port-au-Prince, and accordingly ordered the *Des Moines* to that place.

"The arrival of the Dutch steamer *Prins Frederick Hendrik* had been expected for a day or so prior to arrival, and it was believed that President Davilmar Theodore would take passage on her, this being in accordance with the time-honoured custom of procedure in the abdication of Haitian presidents who were exiled.

"After the departure of President Davilmar Theodore on the *Prins Frederick Hendrik,* and after the occupation of Port-au-Prince by the Guillaume forces on February 23, a beneficent effect was noticeable. Business was resumed. Stores, which had been closed for several days, were reopened; the market reopened and the country people began bringing produce into the city; the water was turned on in the city again; and excellent order was preserved. It was reported to me by men who have witnessed these revolutionary movements for many years that this change of government in Port-au-Prince at this time had been occasioned by the least disturbance of any time for many years."

NOTES

Later the Admiral testified:

"At 11:45 A.M., January 22, Fort Alexander and the battery on the waterfront fired a salute, and Davilmar Theodore, accompanied by a guard, went aboard the *Prins Frederick Hendrik,* unoccasioned by disturbance of any kind. With him only went two or three of his cabinet."

THE CHAIRMAN: "Accompanied by whom?"

ADMIRAL CAPERTON: "Accompanied by the ex-Minister of War Vagues. I saw them with my glasses. They made quite an imposing march down the street and wharf with their long frock coats and silk hats. He was then going aboard the *Prins Frederick Hendrik,* leaving the country. He was accompanied by ex-Minister of War Vagues, as I said before, Locean Baptiste, Mr. Geradin Theodore, and two sons. I know it to be a fact that the old man, Mr. Davilmar Theodore, had hardly a sufficient amount of money to buy his ticket out of the country, as he appealed for money to help him to go where he wished to go, and as it turned out he only went to Santo Domingo."

THE CHAIRMAN: "Now, will you not move on to the events which led to the occupation? I think that is what we want."

ADMIRAL CAPERTON: "You wish to know how the President came in—how Mr. Guillaume Sam got in? The then president, as I have said before, Mr. Davilmar Theodore, left the country in the Dutch steamer."

THE CHAIRMAN: "In a plug hat, on a Dutch ship?"

ADMIRAL CAPERTON: "Yes, sir; leaving the city without any government whatever, and the only people with any authority whatever were those two officers, General Pradel and General Polynice, who appointed themselves a committee of safety, as they usually called themselves.

"The city became more quiet as soon as Theodore left, Generals Pradel and Polynice being in charge, working until the arrival of Vilbrun Guillaume Sam."

SENATOR KING: "Where were the revolutionary forces then— how near the city? Were they in the city then, some of them?"

ADMIRAL CAPERTON: "Not yet. About eight hundred revolutionists arrived in the city the following day."

SENATOR KING: "You said they had been firing?"

ADMIRAL CAPERTON: "Well, on the outskirts, a mile or so out, but there was some firing in the city. Everybody fires there on an occasion of this kind.

"The moment the President left, according to custom the government forces occupying the city usually turned over and joined forces with the new man coming in, because they wanted to be paid, and they would be paid under this procedure. The government had some forces at this time up in the north-eastern part of the island around Quanaminthe, where they went after Guillaume Sam proceeded around on this tour of his.

"On the afternoon of the twenty-third of February, about eight hundred troops of Vilbrun Guillaume's forces entered the city from the north. A committee of administration took charge, pending the arrival of Vilbrun Guillaume, and publicly assured peace and order.

"On the morning of the twenty-fifth of February, Vilbrun Guillaume entered Port-au-Prince with about two thousand men on foot and four hundred mounted. His entry was occasioned with no disturbance of any kind. It was now estimated that about five thousand troops were in Port-au-Prince. These men, or troops, had very few clothes. They were ragged, hungry, dirty, irresponsible, with no education, and simply did what they pleased in the city."

SENATOR KING: "The cacos constituted a large part of the troops, did they?"

ADMIRAL CAPERTON: "Yes, sir, they are all cacos; all the revolutionary fellows are cacos. They live in the northern hills, and they have chiefs, as I said, and they all come in to be paid by the new Government. I might say that in the course of a few days—not being on shore at this time, I do not know how many days it was—but in a few days they paid them off a few *gourdes,* five or ten each. Eight *gourdes* at that time were equivalent to our dollar. They pay these troops off, who generally turn in their rifles, and sometimes they pay them a *gourde* or two for a rifle, and then they proceed back to their hills again, waiting for the next presidential move."

CHAPTER II

1. *American Intervention in Haiti Prior to 1915.*—The United States had been compelled to send naval vessels to Haitian waters in the interest of law and order at intervals ever since the final expulsion of the French in 1802.

As early as 1799 the United States government intervened in Haiti. In June of that year President Adams issued a proclamation prohibiting American ships from entering the southern ports of Haiti, thus preventing the delivery of materials of war on which Rigaud depended to sustain his struggle against Toussaint.

During the reign of Faustin I (Soulouque), the emperor of

NOTES

Haiti attempted to regain the Spanish part of the island (Santo Domingo). France, England, and the United States jointly interposed to put an end to the war between Haiti and Santo Domingo which was devastating both countries.

Daniel Webster, then Secretary of State, instructed the American representative in Haiti to inform the Haitian government, in the event that the remonstrances of France and England should be disregarded, that more forceful measures would be taken by the three governments.

In 1870, during negotiations for the annexation of the Dominican Republic, the United States government warned the Haitian government to keep hands off Dominican affairs. Negotiations between the United States and the Haitian Republic for the acquisition of Mole St. Nicholas, in 1889–90, not only failed to secure this then much desired naval station, but created in Haiti an active spirit of unfriendliness to the American government. Hippolyte had undoubtedly been aided in his struggle for the presidency by the United States government; and it was later claimed by the representatives of the Department of State that Hippolyte and Firmin had made promises to the effect that support of Hippolyte would be repaid by the Mole concession. This was denied by the President and Firmin, then Minister for Foreign Affairs, and after prolonged negotiations the matter was dropped.

While it is certain that the United States did, at this time, endeavour to secure a lease of the Mole as a naval base, it is to be noted that the treaty of 1915 included no such provision, and it is certain that this harbour is no longer considered of military value by naval authorities.

A memorandum of the Navy Department prepared for the Senate committee investigating the American occupation in Haiti in 1921, after reviewing several incidents prior to 1866, states: "The secretaries' report shows that naval vessels visited Haiti in 1866 because of revolutionary movements and civil disturbances threatened to place in jeopardy the lives and property of American residents." In the next year the Secretary reported that naval vessels had visited Haiti, "a country afflicted with perpetual discontent and revolutions." Then follow visits in 1868, 1869, 1876, 1888, 1889, 1892, 1902, 1903, 1905, 1906, 1907, 1908, 1911, 1912, and 1913.

Returning to Port-au-Prince on the eighth of March, 1914, "because of political disturbances," the U.S.S. *South Carolina* "found it imperatively necessary to remain in that port until April 14,

BLACK DEMOCRACY

1914, while the U.S.S. *Montana* was also stationed at Port-au-Prince from January 25 to February 13, 1914." The U.S.S. *Washington* arrived at Cap Haitien on June 29, 1914, sent by the State Department to protect American and foreign interests, and remained there until relieved by the U.S.S. *South Carolina*, on July 8th. "Other naval vessels serving in Haitian waters during the political disturbances of 1914 were the U.S.S. *New Jersey*, U.S.S. *Georgia*, U.S.S. *Tacoma*, U.S.S. *Petrel*, U.S.S. *Nashville*, U.S.S. *Wheeling*, and U.S.S. *Hancock*."

In 1910, on the occasion of the reorganization of the National Bank of Haiti, a French institution, Secretary of State Knox had objected to the proposed contract as onerous on the Haitian people and also suggested that American banking interests should be represented in the reorganized bank, and for several years prior to the actual intervention the United States had endeavoured to persuade the Haitian government to come to some agreement which involved the American administration of the customs service.

2. "On the eve of the declaration of war between Germany and Russia, the U.S.S. *Connecticut* and the German cruiser *Karlsruhe* were both in the harbour of Port-au-Prince. On July 31, 1914, the *Karlsruhe* changed her position in order to screen the movements of her crew, and a number of boatloads of German sailors with small arms and machine guns left the *Karlsruhe* and proceeded to the wharf where they landed. When halfway down the wharf, the Germans turned about, returned to their boats, and went back to their ship.

"This mysterious action took place at dusk. Shortly afterwards the captain of the *Karlsruhe* came aboard the *Connecticut* and told the captain he had received orders to proceed to St. Thomas for coal and asked the captain of the *Connecticut* to protect German interests while he was gone. The *Karlsruhe* then steamed out of the harbour to begin her commerce-destroying cruise. Shortly afterwards the captain of the *Connecticut* was informed by wireless that war between Russia and Germany had been declared.

"There is reason to believe that the German landing party was turned back on the wharf by the German minister to Haiti pursuant to cabled orders to the *Karlsruhe* to leave Port-au-Prince at once. Thus the local situation was, by the outbreak of war, relieved of a conflict of interests which might have caused serious embarrassment."—*Extract from a letter from Hon. Robert Lansing, for-*

NOTES

mer Secretary of State, to the chairman of the Select Committee of the United States Senate, May 4, 1922.

CHAPTER III

1. *Haitian Finances in 1915*.—Admiral Caperton in this connexion testified at the Senate inquiry: "To explain the condition of Haitian finances at this time, I may say that last January the treasury service, by an arbitrary act, was taken from the National Bank of Haiti, the national treasury—this was done by the Guillaume Sam Government—and given to private banking firms, the principal one of which is Simmonds Frères. The Simmonds Frères is under no control which will safeguard public interests. They merely make collections of the revenues and receive a certain percentage as their fee and turn the rest over to whosoever may exercise sufficient force or persuasion in the name of a government or revolution to obtain it.

"The result is that considerable money is being thus forced from Simmonds Frères by the so-called revolutionary committees in various towns, and this money is being used to actively support revolutionary activity. I might add that in all these towns they have also a self-constituted 'committee of safety.'

"On account of military necessity, therefore, I this day, on the ninth, informed the committee in Port-au-Prince, Simmonds Frères, and the National Bank of Haiti that the treasury service would be resumed by the National Bank of Haiti. This bank is under legal and exacting contract for the handling of the treasury service for the Haitian government."

2. Martial law, established in 1915 and later further extended, has been continued ever since with the consent of the Haitian government. But since the very early days of the intervention martial law has seldom been invoked, and since the fall of 1920 provost courts have sat "only for trial of offences that are beyond doubt inimical to the United States or a violation of the customs laws." It is certain that until some radical changes are made in the Haitian courts, so long as the United States maintains a military establishment in Haiti, this right to invoke martial law, at present practically quiescent, should be maintained, and it is certain that for some time the Haitians, in this connexion, have had no cause of complaint. Brigadier-General Smedley D. Butler, U.S.M.C., testified (Senate inquiry): "If you raise martial law while there are any United

States troops in Haiti, you are going to have some of them murdered."

CHAPTER IV

1. Admiral Caperton, in his testimony at the Senate inquiry, stated: "In connexion with the approaching session of Congress, which was to assemble during the first part of April, campaigning was going on amongst the senators and deputies to embarrass the Government. This information came to me from various reliable sources. It was well appreciated that with the American forces present a revolution was impossible, so other means were adopted to force the Dartiguenave Government out, being planned somewhat as follows:

"When Congress met in April, if the enemies of the Dartiguenave Government were strong enough to do so, a vote of censure and lack of confidence in the Government was to be passed, and the President impeached. The charges were to be violations of the constitution." *

2. James Weldon Johnson, Secretary of the National Association for the Advancement of Coloured People, testified at the Senate inquiry that "the intelligent Haitians of all political parties that I talked with felt that the constitution which they had now was unconstitutionally adopted." See also memoir of the *Union Patriotique,* Exhibit E, and *Seizure of Haiti by the United States,* Exhibit G.

3. Mr. Léger, after remarking that "everything is made a pretext for turning Haiti into ridicule" and pointing out that "France enacted twelve constitutions in eighty-four years," states: "From 1804 to 1889 Haitians were under the successive rule of the constitutions of 1806, 1816, 1843, 1846, 1867, 1874, 1879, 1889; most of these constitutions proceeded from two prototypes: the constitution of 1816, which organized a strong Executive Power, and the liberal constitution of 1843. All others were modifications or adaptions which represented the reforms adopted or the progress realized. The people on each occasion issued the whole constitution for greater convenience, naming it after the year in which the change was made, and this has given the impression that each constitution was an entirely new one." †

* *Senate Hearings,* p. 415.
† Léger, J. N., *Haiti, Her History and Her Detractors.* See bibliography.

NOTES

4. Extracts from Law—Ownership of Real Property by Foreigners.*

Article 1. No foreigner may acquire real property in Haiti unless he has his residence in one of the communes of the Republic and unless it is for the needs of his residence or of his agricultural, commercial, industrial, or educational enterprises.

Article 2. No society formed under foreign laws may acquire real property in Haiti unless it has made election of domicile in one of the communes of the Republic. In the case of an anonymous society (corporation), the society must first obtain from the president of the Republic authorization to transact business in Haiti. This authorization will be accorded it only after examination of its articles of incorporation.

Article 3. No acquisition of real property, whether under a gratuitous or under a burdensome title, can be made by a society formed under foreign laws, except for the needs of its residence or for that of its personnel or for its agricultural, commercial, industrial, or educational enterprises.

Article 4. Anonymous societies (corporations) formed in Haiti under Haitian laws, having their main place of business in the country, shall enjoy without restriction all the rights attached to Haitian citizenship with respect to the ownership of real property.

Article 5. Every other society formed in Haiti under Haitian laws shall be deemed to be a foreign society unless at least one-half of its capital belongs to Haitians.

Article 6. In case of the death of a foreigner owning real property in Haiti, the respective rights of his heirs, devisees, or surviving spouses (sic) pertaining to such property shall be determined, if they are all foreigners, in accordance with the personal law of the deceased, subject to the provisions of the present law. The competent court shall be that of the residence of the deceased in Haiti. . . .

Article 8. Any foreigner who owns real property in Haiti and who leaves the territory of Haiti for an uninterrupted period of five years shall be deemed to have forfeited his ownership of such property. The property shall thereupon be turned over to the Service of Vacant Successions and sold in accordance with the provisions of Article 12 of the present law. The net proceeds of the sale

---

* This is believed to be a correct translation, but the author assumes no responsibility as to its accuracy.

shall be paid over to said foreigner or his duly authorized representative.

Article 10. In case of dissolution of a foreign society established in Haiti, the liquidators shall be required, within five years, to proceed with sale of the society's real property. At the expiration of this period, the said property shall be turned over to the Service of Vacant Successions and sold in accordance with the provisions of Article 12 of the present law. The net proceeds of the sale shall be paid over to the liquidators or their duly authorized representatives.

Article 13. In case of attachment against real property at the instance of a foreigner or of a foreign society, such foreigner or foreign society may be the successful bidder in the case comprehended in Article 616 (Code Civil Procedure) only when the requirements of Articles 1, 2, 3, 4, and 5 of the present law are fulfilled.

Article 14. The foreign minor, or the foreigner under interdiction, who dwells in Haiti shall enjoy the benefit of a legal mortgage on the property of his Haitian or foreign guardian or trustee where the guardianship or trusteeship has been established in Haiti and in accordance with the Haitian law. The same benefit is accorded the foreign owner's wife who resides in Haiti.

Article 15. Every act of acquisition of real property by a foreigner or foreign society must contain justification that the acquisition is made in conformity with Article 5 of the Constitution. For this purpose the act must bear: (1) designation of residence in Haiti; (2) a declaration concerning the profession, or civil capacity of the grantee, and the purpose of the acquisition; (3) mention of the number of its licence if the grantee has to have one. The purpose set forth in the act will not prevent a foreigner or foreign society from using the property for one of the other purposes prescribed in the Constitution.

Article 18. The present law abrogates all laws or provisions of law contrary thereto, especially Articles 479, 587, and 740 of the Civil Code and the law of July 16, 1920, and will be executed at the diligence of the Secretary of State for Justice.—*Given at the National Palace, February 13, 1925.*

CHAPTER V

1. That the *corvée* was an established institution prior to the inauguration of the Haitian Republic is shown by the following

NOTES

quotation from Moreau de St.-Mery, the historian of the French colonial period:

> There was, in 1717, a road from the Cape Leogane which passed through the Sainte-Rose gorge, picturesque Trou, and the Spanish territory along which one could travel as far as Mirebalais.
>
> In 1719 there were some footpaths opened which ran from the North to the West, without leaving French territory, but with incredible difficulties. It was not until the end of the month of August, 1750, that Mr. de Vaudreuil, commander-in-chief of the colony, by means of a *corvée* in which one hundred Negroes took part, opened the road that was in use until 1787.

2. In connexion with the abuse of the *corvée* system, Dr. Carl Kelsey stated in his testimony before the Senate Committee:

> I am very glad to comment [on the *corvée*], asking you to remember one thing, that I can pass no judgment as to the extent of the necessity leading to the introduction of the *corvée*. That is a very important modification. In other words, I might have done the same thing had I been put in the position of the man who made that decision. He had certain things that were of paramount importance, in his opinion. I have the feeling personally that the *corvée* was the biggest blunder we have made in Haiti. Perhaps we could not have known that in advance, but I suspect we should have known it, and I have the feeling we were told definitely, in fact, that it would have this bad result, so that we should have been warned by the advice given us.
>
> The fundamental trouble with the *corvée* was the way it was executed, not with the thing itself. There were individual men, under the *corvée*, handling large groups of men, who had their enthusiastic support all the way through, and under whom the men wanted to remain and continue the work after it was ordered discontinued. But a very unfortunate situation developed in two ways: first, the American officers at first did not seem to realize that the money they gave the native subordinates to be spent for food, etc., for the natives went largely into the pockets of the men to whom it was given—they did not realize that the local chief of section was perhaps tearing up the work cards of men who had served one or two periods on the *corvée,* and was sending them back into the *corvée* again. In that way he was able to punish those who would not pay bribes, or punish his enemies and reward his friends, so that some men were kept at work for several months. Of course, the average officer seeing the great mass

of peasants would not know one from the other. He would not recognize the fact that John Jones had been sent in two or three times. He was utterly ignorant. That gave the agitator the opportunity to say to those natives: "You see what the Americans are doing. They are planning to enslave you once more." I can give you later on, if the question arises, the same illustration from Santo Domingo.

3. The Major-General Commandant reported in October, 1920, that the marine-corps records at head-quarters show that of those "armed bandits" who actively oppose the government of Haiti in field operations, approximately 2,250 were killed, either by marines or *gendarmes,* during the first five and one-half years. The yearly record is as follows:

1915	212	*1918*	35
1916	50	*1919*	1,861
1917	2	*1920*	90

As indicated by the above figures, the actual field operations, from a military standpoint, were divided into two periods: the first, 1915–16, when the marines were first landed in Haiti and until the then existing state of anarchy had been overcome; the second period, 1918–20, the so-called caco uprising. During both these periods a state of actual war existed in certain parts of Haiti.

During this period one marine officer was killed in action and two wounded, twelve enlisted men were killed or died of wounds received in action, and twenty-six were wounded in action.

4. Dr. Kelsey, in his testimony at the Senate inquiry, said.:

> The marines themselves are to blame for some of the criticism heaped upon them. A certain type of man likes to brag of his exploits and of his wickedness. There has been a lot of this kind of thing where the basis of fact was extremely small. Certain investigators have been deceived in similar fashion. Some ex-service men seem to have tried to capitalize their alleged repentance. As I went about the country I tried to observe the attitude of the natives toward the marines. Nowhere did I detect signs of fear or of desire for revenge. On the contrary, there was a feeling of respect, often of friendliness. On the whole I feel that the men in the marine corps deserve our respect. We are too ready to believe that they change their character when away from home and among people of different colour. I am not trying to dodge responsibility or shield crooks, but to keep a balance in my verdict.

NOTES

We did much for the boys in France but absolutely nothing for those in Haiti. The fact is that there were many more acts of kindness than of cruelty. The good things have not been advertised to the world. Day after day I have talked with officers and men who are bending all their energies toward helping the Haitians. I have seen peasants going out of their way to call on and bring presents to men who had been stationed in their communities. The opposition to the marines is not all genuine and disinterested. The thief and grafter do not like interference. I suspect that behind all surface explanations lies the resentment against the uniform, the symbol of an outside force preserving order, the reflection upon the inability to control self, which hurts the Haitian's self-esteem. Here is the crux of the situation.

CHAPTER VI

1. In connexion with the participation of the common people in the government, the following extract from the testimony of Dr. Kelsey (Senate inquiry) is pertinent:

THE CHAIRMAN: "Was there ever a time, in your judgment, when the mass of the people were politically conscious and deliberately chose their governors?"

PROFESSOR KELSEY: "No; there has never been anything but a very small minority even voting, according to their own statements. I have one record of a brother of a provisional president who said in one of the communes just outside of Port-au-Prince that the delegates would be appointed militarily and summarily. That was his summing-up of an election."

SENATOR POMERENE: "You say that was under one of the provisional presidents?"

PROFESSOR KELSEY: "Yes; that was before we went in there. There never has been any election in Haiti. There never has been any democracy in Haiti. It is a perfectly foolish use of language to talk as if there had been. Haiti traded a slave system under white slaveowners for a slave system under mulatto owners, and they have run under a slave régime from the first up to the present time."

SENATOR POMERENE: "Do you think that is a condition of any substantial part of the peasantry in the country?"

PROFESSOR KELSEY: "Do you mean slavery?"

SENATOR POMERENE: "Yes."

PROFESSOR KELSEY: "Not under that name. Theoretically, any individual in Haiti may become president if he has military force and personal strength. Practically, the overwhelming mass of them are condemned to the direst poverty, with no hope of any way out."

2. At Marion, Ohio, in August, 1920, Mr. Harding stated: "If I should be elected President . . . I will not empower an Assistant Secretary of the Navy to draft a constitution for helpless neighbours in the West Indies and jam it down their throats at the points of bayonets borne by United States marines, nor will I misuse the power of the Executive to cover with a veil of secrecy repeated acts of unwarranted interference in the domestic affairs of the little republics of the Western hemisphere, such as in the last few years have not only made enemies of those who should be our friends but have rightly discredited our country as a trusted neighbour." *

The election of President Harding did not, however, alter the situation in Haiti, nor has there been any material change in policy under his successor.

CHAPTER VII

1. *Cash Position of the Government, September, 1927.*

At the close of the past fiscal year the treasury found itself in an exceptionally strong position. Because of substantial expenditures of the balance from the Series "A" loan, total assets declined from *Gdes.* 30,308,000 on September 30, 1926, to *Gdes.* 26,143,000 one year later. This diminution of total assets was inevitable and indeed desirable. No government should maintain excessive treasury assets in idleness, and in fact the Series "A" loan contract provides that balances should be expended for public works and for supplementary debt retirement as soon as the financial requirements of the Claims Commission had been determined.—*Report of Financial Adviser-General Receiver.*

2. *Extract from Monthly Bulletin of the Financial Adviser-General Receiver, Port-au-Prince, September, 1927.*

Certain commentators have recently seemed to take great comfort in a statement of this office that little progress has been made in the last twelve years toward the development of Haitian exports. The statement is true, but apparently they do not realize that it is necessarily an indictment of the Haitian business community. The cordial co-operation existing between the treaty departments and the Haitian

* *New York Times,* August 31, 1920.

NOTES

government, combined with the enlightened leadership of President Borno, has supplied Haiti with facilities for doing business which were hitherto unknown. Improvements of roads and trails, construction of bridges, availability of potable water, adequate telephone and telegraph service, medical attention, and added facilities for shipping have all been furnished to the Haitian producer and merchant. The rural community has demonstrated its appreciation of the benefits which have been accorded in the form of protection from disturbance and freedom to live peaceably as well as bestowal of many of the comforts of modern existence. It is unfortunate to have to record, however, that a large element in the urban community which should take the lead in supporting the progressive administration from which Haiti is now benefiting seems to take pleasure in embarrassing the government at home and in misrepresenting it abroad. This phenomenon is believed to be peculiar to Haiti. The citizens of most other countries are proud to see their country go forward in material progress and in the respect with which it is regarded by foreign nations.

Neither the Haitian government nor American officers employed by that government in several of its departments can directly increase the exports of Haiti. All that they can be expected to do is to furnish facilities which enlightened self-interest would seem to commend to the Haitian business community. Thus far there has been an apathetic indifference if not hostility to the forward steps inaugurated by President Borno.

EXHIBITS
and
BIBLIOGRAPHY

BLACK DEMOCRACY

EXHIBIT A

RULERS OF HAITI

Jean Jacques Dessalines, Jan. 1, 1804–Oct. 17, 1806; (Dictator) Birthplace, Grande Rivière;

Henri Christophe, Feb. 17, 1807–Oct. 8, 1820; President; "State Henri 1st; Birthplace, Isle of St.

PRESIDENTS OF THE REPUBLIC

NAME	TERM OF OFFICE
1. Alexandre Pétion	March 9, 1807–March 29, 1818
2. Jean Pierre Boyer	March 30, 1818–March 13, 1843
3. Charles Herard	December 30, 1843–May 3, 1844
4. Philippe Guerrier	May 3, 1844–April 15, 1845
5. Jean Louis Pierrot	April 16, 1845–March 1, 1846
6. Jean Baptiste Riche	March 1, 1846–February 27, 1847
7. Faustin Soulouque	March 1, 1847–January 15, 1859
8. Fabre Geffrard	December 23, 1858–March 13, 1867
9. Sylvain Salnave	June 14, 1867–December 19, 1869
10. Nissage-Saget	March 19, 1870–May 13, 1874
11. Michel Domingue	June 11, 1874–April 15, 1876
12. Boisronde-Canal	July 17, 1876–July 17, 1879
13. Etienne Félicité Salomon	October 23, 1879–August 10, 1888
14. F. Deus Légitime	December 16, 1888–August 22, 1889
15. F. M. Florvil Hippolyte	October 9, 1889–March 24, 1896
16. P. A. Tirésias Simon Sam	March 31, 1896–May 12, 1902
17. Nord Alexis	December 21, 1902–December 2, 1908
18. F. Antoine Simon	December 17, 1908–August 2, 1911
19. Michel Cincinnatus Leconte	August 14, 1911–August 8, 1912
20. Tancrede Auguste	August 8, 1912–May 2, 1913
21. Michel Oreste	May 4, 1913–January 27, 1914
22. Oreste Zamor	February 8, 1914–October 29, 1914
23. Joseph Davilmar Theodore	November 7, 1914–February 22, 1915
24. Jean Vilbrun Guillaume Sam	March 4, 1915–July 28, 1915
25. Philippe Sudre Dartiguenave	August 12, 1915–May 15, 1922
26. Joseph Louis Borno	May 15, 1922–
Re-elected	May 15, 1926–

* *Griffe.*—Black with very small proportion of white blood.
[1] Emperor Aug., 1849–Jan., 1859.   [2] Shot by revolutionary tribunal.

In one hundred and eight years, 1807–1915, twenty-four executives held office.

Seventeen of the twenty-four were deposed by revolutions, two of whom were murdered.

Five of the twenty-four died in office, one at least by poison, one in the explosion of his palace, one on the eve of his overthrow by revolutionists.

Two only of the twenty-four were allowed to retire peaceably from office; eleven of the twenty-four served for less than one year each. The six predecessors of President Dartiguenave averaged only a little more than eight months each. Eight only succeeded in maintaining themselves in office for a period equal to their elected terms.

[338]

EXHIBITS AND BIBLIOGRAPHY

1804–1807

Governor General for life Oct. 8, 1804. Emperor Jacques 1st, Black; Assassinated.

of Haiti" (the North of Haiti) June 2, 1811; King of Haiti, Christopher; Black; Shot himself.

OF HAITI—1807–1928

HELD OFFICE Yr. Mo. Days			BIRTHPLACE	COLOUR	REMARKS
11	—	20	Port-au-Prince	Mulatto	Died in Office
25	less	17	Port-au-Prince	Mulatto	Deposed by Revolution
—	4	3	Port Salut	Mulatto	Deposed by Revolution
—	11	12	Marmelade	Black	Died in Office
—	10	12	Cap Haitien	Black	Deposed by Revolution
—	11	26	Grande Rivière	Black	Died in Office
11	10	15	Petit-Goave	Black	President to Aug. 1849.
8	2	20	Anse-à-Veau	Griffe *	Deposed by Revolution [1]
2	6	4	Cap Haitien	Griffe *	Deposed by Revolution [2]
4	1	24	St.-Marc	Mulatto	Retired at end of term
1	10	4	Aux Cayes	Griffe *	Deposed by Revolution
3	—	—	Aux Cayes	Mulatto	Deposed by Revolution
8	9	18	Aux Cayes	Black	Deposed by Revolution
—	8	7	Jérémie	Black	Deposed by Revolution
6	5	14	Cap Haitien	Black	Died in Office
6	1	15	Grande Rivière	Black	Retired
5	11	12	Cap Haitien	Black	Deposed by Revolution
2	7	16	Aux Cayes	Black	Deposed by Revolution
—	11	24	Cap Haitien	Griffe *	Blown up in his Palace
—	8	24	Cap Haitien	Mulatto	Died by poison
—	8	23	Jacmel	Griffe *	Deposed by Revolution
—	8	20	Gonaives	Griffe *	Deposed by Revolution [3]
—	3	15	Fort Liberté	Black	Deposed by Revolution
—	4	23	Cap Haitien	Black	Murdered by mob
6	9	4	Anse-à-Veau	Mulatto	Retired at end of term [4]
4	—	—	Port-au-Prince	Mulatto	Served first term and re-elected

[3] Later murdered in prison.   [4] Elected after the intervention.

The presidential term has varied from 4 to 7 years. Antoine Simon, elected for seven years in 1908, would have normally retired in 1915. In this period seven presidents were "elected" and deposed; Simon by a revolution; Leconte killed by an explosion in his palace; Auguste died, it is said, by poison; Oreste was deposed and exiled; Zamor deposed and later murdered; Theodore deposed and exiled; and Sam dragged from the French Legation and murdered by a mob. Dartiguenave, the first president elected after the intervention, served his full term of seven years, a period equal to the combined terms of his seven immediate predecessors.

Louis Borno, who succeeded Dartiguenave in 1922, served four years and was re-elected in 1926. His term expires on May 15, 1930.

BLACK DEMOCRACY

EXHIBIT B

TREATY BETWEEN THE UNITED STATES AND HAITI

FINANCES, ECONOMIC DEVELOPMENT AND TRANQUILLITY OF HAITI

Ratification Advised by the Senate, February 28, 1916
Signed at Port-au-Prince, September 16, 1915
Ratified by the President, March 20, 1916
Ratified by Haiti, September 17, 1915
Ratifications Exchanged at Washington, May 3, 1916
Proclaimed, May 3, 1916

Whereas a Treaty between the United States of America and the Republic of Haiti having for its objects the strengthening of the amity existing between the two countries, the remedying of the present condition of the revenues and finances of Haiti, the maintenance of the tranquillity of that Republic, and the carrying out of plans for its economic development and prosperity, was concluded and signed by their respective Plenipotentiaries at Port-au-Prince, on the sixteenth day of September, one thousand nine hundred and fifteen, the original of which Treaty, being in the English and French languages, is word for word as follows:

TREATY BETWEEN THE UNITED STATES
AND THE REPUBLIC OF HAITI

PREAMBLE

The United States and the Republic of Haiti desiring to confirm and strengthen the amity existing between them by the most cordial co-operation in measures for their common advantage;

And the Republic of Haiti desiring to remedy the present condition of its revenues and finances, to maintain the tranquillity of the Republic, to carry out plans for the economic development and prosperity of the Republic and its people;

And the United States being in full sympathy with all of these aims and objects and desiring to contribute in all proper ways to their accomplishment;

The United States and the Republic of Haiti have resolved to conclude a Convention with these objects in view, and have appointed for that purpose, Plenipotentiaries,

EXHIBITS AND BIBLIOGRAPHY

The President of the United States, Robert Beale Davis, Junior, *Chargé d'Affaires* of the United States;

And the President of the Republic of Haiti, Louis Borno, Secretary of State for Foreign Affairs and Public Instruction, who, having exhibited to each other their respective powers, which are seen to be full in good and true form, have agreed as follows:

Article I

The Government of the United States will, by its good offices, aid the Haitian Government in the proper and efficient development of its agricultural, mineral and commercial resources and in the establishment of the finances of Haiti on a firm and solid basis.

Article II

The President of Haiti shall appoint, upon nomination by the President of the United States, a General Receiver and such aids and employees as may be necessary, who shall collect, receive and apply all customs duties on imports and exports accruing at the several custom houses and ports of entry of the Republic of Haiti.

The President of Haiti shall appoint, upon nomination by the President of the United States, a Financial Adviser, who shall be an officer attached to the Ministry of Finance, to give effect to whose proposals and labours the Minister will lend efficient aid. The Financial Adviser shall devise an adequate system of public accounting, aid in increasing the revenues and adjusting them to the expenses, inquire into the validity of the debts of the Republic, enlighten both Governments with reference to all eventual debts, recommend improved methods of collecting and applying the revenues, and make such other recommendations to the Minister of Finance as may be deemed necessary for the welfare and prosperity of Haiti.

Article III

The Government of the Republic of Haiti will provide by law or appropriate decrees for the payment of all customs duties to the General Receiver, and will extend to the Receivership, and to the Financial Adviser, all needful aid and full protection in the execution of the powers conferred and duties imposed herein; and the United States on its part will extend like aid and protection.

Article IV

Upon the appointment of the Financial Adviser, the Government of the Republic of Haiti, in co-operation with the Financial Adviser, shall collate, classify, arrange and make full statement of all the debts of the Republic, the amounts, character, maturity and condition thereof, and the interest accruing and the sinking fund requisite to their final discharge.

Article V

All sums collected and received by the General Receiver shall be applied, first, to the payment of the salaries and allowances of the General Receiver, his assistants and employees and expenses of the Receivership, including the salary and expenses of the Financial Adviser, which salaries will be determined by previous agreement; second, to the interest and sinking fund of the public debt of the Republic of Haiti; and, third, to the maintenance of the constabulary referred to in Article X, and then the remainder to the Haitian Government for purposes of current expenses.

In making these applications the General Receiver will proceed to pay salaries and allowances monthly and expenses as they arise, and on the first of each calendar month, will set aside in a separate fund the quantum of the collection and receipts of the previous month.

Article VI

The expenses of the Receivership, including salaries and allowances of the General Receiver, his assistants and employees, and the salary and expenses of the Financial Adviser, shall not exceed five per centum of the collections and receipts from customs duties, unless by agreement by the two Governments.

Article VII

The General Receiver shall make monthly reports of all collections, receipts and disbursements to the appropriate officer of the Republic of Haiti and to the Department of State of the United States, which reports shall be open to inspection and verification at all times by the appropriate authorities of each of the said Governments.

EXHIBITS AND BIBLIOGRAPHY

Article VIII

The Republic of Haiti shall not increase its public debt except by previous agreement with the President of the United States, and shall not contract any debt or assume any financial obligation unless the ordinary revenues of the Republic available for that purpose, after defraying the expenses of the Government, shall be adequate to pay the interest and provide a sinking fund for the final discharge of such debt.

Article IX

The Republic of Haiti will not without a previous agreement with the President of the United States, modify the customs duties in a manner to reduce the revenues therefrom; and in order that the revenues of the Republic may be adequate to meet the public debt and the expenses of the Government, to preserve tranquillity and to promote material prosperity, the Republic of Haiti will co-operate with the Financial Adviser in his recommendations for improvement in the methods of collecting and disbursing the revenues and for new sources of needed income.

Article X

The Haitian Government obligates itself, for the preservation of domestic peace, the security of individual rights and full observance of the provisions of this treaty, to create without delay an efficient constabulary, urban and rural, composed of native Haitians. This constabulary shall be organized and officered by Americans, appointed by the President of Haiti, upon nomination by the President of the United States. The Haitian Government shall clothe these officers with the proper and necessary authority and uphold them in the performance of their functions. These officers will be replaced by Haitians as they, by examination, conducted under direction of a board to be selected by the senior American officer of this constabulary and in the presence of a representative of the Haitian Government, are found to be qualified to assume such duties. The constabulary herein provided for, shall, under the direction of the Haitian Government, have supervision and control of arms and ammunition, military supplies, and traffic therein, throughout the country. The high contracting parties agree that the stipulations in this Article are necessary to prevent factional strife and disturbances.

Article XI

The Government of Haiti agrees not to surrender any of the territory of the Republic of Haiti by sale, lease or otherwise, or jurisdiction over such territory, to any foreign government or power, not to enter into any treaty or contract with any foreign power or powers that will impair or tend to impair the independence of Haiti.

Article XII

The Haitian Government agrees to execute with the United States a protocol for the settlement, by arbitration or otherwise, of all pending pecuniary claims of foreign corporations, companies, citizens or subjects against Haiti.

Article XIII

The Republic of Haiti, being desirous to further the development of its natural resources, agrees to undertake and execute such measures as in the opinion of the high contracting parties may be necessary for the sanitation and public improvement of the Republic, under the supervision and direction of an engineer or engineers, to be appointed by the President of Haiti upon nomination by the President of the United States, and authorized for that purpose by the Government of Haiti.

Article XIV

The high contracting parties shall have authority to take such steps as may be necessary to insure the complete attainment of any of the objects comprehended in this treaty; and, should the necessity occur, the United States will lend an efficient aid for the preservation of Haitian Independence and the maintenance of a Government adequate for the protection of life, property and individual liberty.

Article XV

The present treaty shall be approved and ratified by the high contracting parties in conformity with their respective laws, and the ratifications thereof shall be exchanged in the City of Washington as soon as may be possible.

Article XVI

The present treaty shall remain in full force and virtue for the term of ten years, to be counted from the day of exchange of ratifications, and further for another term of ten years if, for specific reasons presented by either of the high contracting parties, the purpose of this treaty has not been fully accomplished.

In faith whereof, the respective Plenipotentiaries have signed the present Convention in duplicate, in the English and French languages, and have thereunto affixed their seals.

Done at Port-au-Prince, Haiti, the 16th day of September in the year of our Lord one thousand nine hundred and fifteen.

>ROBERT BEALE DAVIS, JR. [SEAL.]
>*Chargé d'Affaires of the United States*
>LOUIS BORNO [SEAL.]
>*Secrétaire d'Etat des Relations Extérieures et de l'Instruction Publique*

And whereas, the said Treaty has been duly ratified on both parts, and the ratifications of the two governments were exchanged in the City of Washington, on the third day of May, one thousand nine hundred and sixteen;

Now, therefore, be it known that I, Woodrow Wilson, President of the United States of America, have caused the said Treaty to be made public, to the end that the same and every article and clause thereof may be observed and fulfilled with good faith by the United States and the citizens thereof.

In testimony whereof, I have hereunto set my hand and caused the seal of the United States to be affixed.

Done at the City of Washington this third day of May in the year of our Lord one thousand nine hundred and sixteen, [SEAL.] and of the Independence of the United States of America the one hundred and fortieth.

>WOODROW WILSON

By the President:
>ROBERT LANSING,
>*Secretary of State*

BLACK DEMOCRACY

EXHIBIT C

ADDITIONAL ACT BETWEEN THE UNITED STATES
AND HAITI

EXTENDING THE DURATION OF THE TREATY OF
SEPTEMBER 16, 1915

Signed at Port-au-Prince, March 28, 1917

The Republic of Haiti having recognized as urgent the necessity of a loan for a term of more than ten years destined for the amelioration of its financial and economic situation, considering from now this necessity as a specific reason susceptible of giving to the Convention of September 16, 1915, a duration of twenty years and desiring in consequence to exercise the right which it holds from Article XVI of this Convention;

And the United States of America, conforming itself to Article first of the said Convention and assuring its good offices for the full accomplishment of its aims and objects,

Have decided to conclude an additional act to this Convention, with a view to facilitating a prompt realization of the loan and to offer to the capitalists the serious guarantee which they claim of an uninterrupted stability indispensable to the development of the wealth of the Republic of Haiti;

And have been appointed as Plenipotentiaries,

By the President of the United States of America,

Mr. Arthur Bailly-Blanchard, Envoy Extraordinary and Minister Plenipotentiary of the United States of America,

By the President of the Republic of Haiti,

Mr. Louis Borno, Secretary of State of Foreign Affairs and Public Worship,

Who having exhibited to each other their respective full powers found to be in good and true form, have agreed as follows:

Article 1. The two High Contracting Parties declare to admit the urgent necessity for a loan for a period of more than ten years for the benefit of the Republic of Haiti as one of the specific reasons indicated in Article XVI of the Convention of September 16, 1915, and agree to fix at twenty years the life of the said Convention.

Article 2. The present act shall be approved by the High Con-

EXHIBITS AND BIBLIOGRAPHY

tracting Parties in conformity with their respective established procedures and the approvals thereof shall be exchanged in the city of Port-au-Prince as soon as may be possible.

Signed and sealed in duplicate in the English and French languages, at Port-au-Prince, Haiti, the 28th day of March, 1917.

[SEAL.]   A. BAILLY-BLANCHARD
[SEAL.]   LOUIS BORNO

EXHIBIT D

THE CONSTITUTION: ELECTORAL PROVISIONS

Article 107 provides: "The primary assemblies meet in the manner prescribed by the law without previous convocation, in each commune, on the tenth of January of even-numbered years. Their object is to elect, at the periods fixed by the Constitution, the Deputies of the people, the Senators of the Republic . . ."

Article 40 provides: "The attributes of the National Assembly are, first, to elect the President of the Republic . . ."

Article 45 provides: "In years of regular Presidential elections the National Assembly shall proceed to the business of electing the President on the 2nd Monday in April."

Had it not been for transitory provisions of the Constitution, it would follow that on January 10, 1922, the primary assemblies would have met *without previous convocation* and elected thirty-eight Deputies and fifteen Senators. These two bodies, so elected, would have met and constituted the National Assembly on the first Monday of April, 1922, and would have proceeded to the election of a President of the Republic for a term of 4 years from May 15, 1922.

However, under transitory provisions of the Constitution this procedure is suspended as follows:

Article C. "The first election for membership of the Legislative Body, after the adoption of this Constitution, shall be held on January 10th of an *even-numbered year.*

"*The year shall be fixed by decree of the President,* published at least three months before the meeting of the primary assemblies. . . ."

Article D. "A Council of State, instituted according to the same principles as those of the decree of April 15, 1916, consisting of

BLACK DEMOCRACY

twenty-one members apportioned among the different departments, shall exercise the Legislative Power until a duly elected Legislative Body shall have been constituted, at which epoch the Council of State shall cease to exist."

EXHIBIT E

Mémoire of the Union Patriotique d'Haïti *

On May 9, 1921, a committee representing the Union Patriotique d'Haïti presented to the Department of State and the Senate Foreign Relations Committee a mémoire the conclusions of which read as follows:

"The Haitian Republic was the second nation of the New World —second only to the United States—to conquer its national independence. We have our own history, our own traditions, customs, and national spirit, our own institutions, laws, and social and political organization, our own culture, our own literature (French language), and our own religion. For 111 years the little Haitian nation has managed its own affairs; for 111 years it has made the necessary effort for its material, intellectual, and moral development as well as any other nation—better than any other nation, because it has been from the start absolutely alone in its difficult task, without any aid from the outside, bearing with it along the harsh road of civilization the glorious misery of its beginning. And then, one fine day under the merest pretext, without any possible explanation or justification on the grounds of violation of any American right or interest, American forces landed on our national territory and actually abolished the sovereignty and independence of the Haitian Republic.

"We have just given an account of the chief aspects of the American military occupation in our country since July 28, 1915.

"It is the most terrible régime of military autocracy which has ever been carried on in the name of the great American democracy.

"The Haitian people, during these past five years, has passed through such sacrifices, tortures, destructions, humiliations, and misery as have never before been known in the course of its unhappy history.

"The American Government, in spite of the attitude of wisdom, moderation, and even submission which it has always found in dealing with the Haitian Government, has never lived up to any of

* The Mémoire was printed in full in the *Nation*, New York, May 25, 1921.

the agreements which it has solemnly entered into with regard to the Haitian people.

"The Haitian people is entitled to reparations for the wrongs and injuries committed against it.

"The great American people can only honour themselves and rise in universal esteem by hastening the restoration of justice—of all the justice due a weak and friendly nation which the agents of its Government have systematically abused.

"Reparations are due for the human lives that have been taken and for the property that has been destroyed or abstracted. An impartial investigation will provide the necessary statements and supply the basis for the estimates to be determined.

"The present political aspirations of the Haitian nation have been formulated by the Union Patriotique, a comprehensive national association which, through its numerous branches throughout the country and in all levels of society, includes virtually all the Haitian people. The undersigned have been sent to the United States by this association to make the will of the country clearly known.

"The Haitian people are filled with peaceful sentiments, but there is no doubt that they intend to recover definitely the administration of their own affairs and to resume under their own responsibility the entire life of the country, with full sovereignty and independence. They will never rest until they have obtained them.

"The salient aspirations of the Haitian people are summarized as follows:

"1. Immediate abolition of martial law and courts martial.

"2. Immediate reorganization of the Haitian police and military forces, and withdrawal within a short period of the United States military occupation.

"3. Abrogation of the convention of 1915.

"4. Convocation within a short period of a constituent assembly, with all the guarantees of electoral liberty.

"But the Haitian people desire too strongly the friendship of the great American people, and are too anxious for their own material, intellectual, and moral development not to wish and bespeak for themselves the impartial and altruistic aid of the United States Government. They have urgent needs, vital to the development of the natural resources of the country and essential to the full expansion of its agricultural, industrial, and commercial activity. The satisfying of these needs is absolutely necessary for the continued progress of the Haitian community.

BLACK DEMOCRACY

"Nothing would serve better to bring about the speedy re-establishment of normal relations between the two countries than the friendly aid of the United States Government in the economic prosperity and social progress of the Haitian Republic."

Note.—This mémoire was at least partly responsible for the Senatorial Investigation and incidentally for numerous reports and statements which were prepared by the Navy Department and the Marine Corps.

EXHIBIT F

EXTRACTS FROM REPORT OF DR. CARL KELSEY TO THE AMERICAN ACADEMY OF POLITICAL AND SOCIAL SCIENCE, 1922

The most enlightening analysis of the American Intervention in Haiti is the report of Dr. Carl Kelsey, of the University of Pennsylvania, to the American Academy of Political and Social Science, printed in the annals of this Society in March, 1922.

Dr. Kelsey spent nine months in Haiti and Santo Domingo in a searching analysis of the situation. It is regretted that lack of space prohibits the inclusion of his complete report, which should be carefully read by everyone who is interested in this subject.

Under the heading, "Some Reflections on Our Policy," Dr. Kelsey says in part:

"In so far as I can see there are but three general policies which might be adopted by the United States with reference to Haiti and the Dominican Republic:

"(1) Withdraw and refuse to accept any responsibility for what happens in either country; refuse to intervene again and refuse to let any other country intervene.

"(2) Withdraw and refuse to intervene again, but let other countries do as they please in regard to the collection of debts or the establishment of naval bases.

"(3) Continue the intervention, promising to withdraw as soon as conditions make possible the restoration of autonomy.

"When I went to Haiti I was inclined to feel that the first course was the best but I left convinced that it was not. There are many who believe that it is, but they have often weakened their case by impugning the motives of those who differ from them. They are in-

EXHIBITS AND BIBLIOGRAPHY

clined to claim that everything done by our government is done for selfish reasons and dominated by deceit and cruelty, while accepting all claims of other nations at their face value.

"The fundamental cause of the muddle in which we find ourselves in Haiti and the Dominican Republic is a lack of a clear understanding of the problem and our relation thereto. The older concept of the Monroe Doctrine was negative. We said to Europe 'hands off' but accepted no definite responsibility ourselves. This attitude on our part was, and is, a guaranty of independence to the two other countries without which it is doubtful if they could have maintained themselves. More recently we have encountered a rising insistence in Europe that we should assume responsibility or else permit other countries to intervene as they might deem best. Under this pressure we have intervened in a half-hearted sort of way. Unless we are prepared to surrender the Monroe Doctrine, and of this I see no sign, the time has come for us to assume definitely the responsibility it entails and to work out some definite policy.

"A century ago men, sensing an idea a little beyond their powers of expression, spoke glowingly of 'individual rights' as if they arose and existed apart from society. We know to-day that rights flow from society and are determined by it. To society the individual is responsible, and when the commands of society are violated, the individual is punished; that is, his rights are limited. Society judges the individual by his actions and not by his size. It recognizes that individuals differ and that the rights granted must be proportionate to the sense of responsibility developed by the individual. The insane man must have a guardian. When we deal with defective persons we do so not to punish them but to assist them and to protect others, that is, society."

And again Dr. Kelsey says:

"If the outside world is to intervene the questions of when, where, how, will have to be settled. The individual is most affected by the actions of his neighbours. If a man on the adjoining place begins to shoot indiscriminately with a high-powered rifle I am immediately involved regardless of whether he intends to do me harm or not. In an organized society I invoke the law. Under frontier conditions I handle the problem myself. In the present state of world organization we must follow the program of the frontier. The important thing is the clear recognition that each community must so conduct itself as to offer no threat to the safety of others. The large groups have rights as well as the small. Those societies which desire to be considered as nations must show themselves able to maintain the responsibilities of nations.

"I hear my Haitian friends say, 'But we have long been recognized as a free and independent nation by the United States.' True. The whale was long considered a fish, but its real nature was not changed by the mistaken classification of men. The difference between you and the whale is that you can become really free and independent if you will, and that is what we should like you to do. We are not outsiders. You are a part of our problem because of your location. We have been confused in our attitude towards you, as is shown by our indecision whether to call your island Haiti or Santo Domingo. We have neglected you in the past and for this we accept our full measure of blame but we are determined that the future shall tell another story. Your old programs of revolutions and indiscriminate borrowing of money must stop, not only because it checks your development, but because it has become a source of danger to us. Just now, to be sure, there is little danger of interference by another nation but we do not know what fifty years may bring forth and we have decided that it is easier to keep other nations out than to put them out.

"Every American with whom I have talked would prefer to let the island go its way without interference. I have never met anyone who desires to destroy the sovereignty of either government and no one ever suggests that the island should be absorbed into the United States. America is ready to continue its guaranty of independence but it seems ready also to insist on certain reforms. Now, if we may grant the sincerity of the government at Washington, and I see no reason to question it, what shall we do? For it is evident that we will not let other nations intervene."

EXHIBIT G

THE SEIZURE OF HAITI BY THE UNITED STATES

In the spring of 1922, twenty-four American lawyers presented to the Secretary of State of the United States a report entitled *The Seizure of Haiti by the United States*,* the introduction and conclusions of which read as follows:

* Published in full by The Foreign Policy Association of New York and distributed by the National Popular Government League of Washington.

EXHIBITS AND BIBLIOGRAPHY

Introduction

"Every material statement made in this document is derived from the official report of the hearings before a select committee of the United States Senate pursuant to Senate Resolution 112 authorizing an inquiry into the occupation and administration of the territories of the Republic of Haiti and the Dominican Republic. These hearings took place from October 4 to November 16, 1921. The official record of the proceedings has been published by the Government Printing Office. The facts disclosed are not only a part of the history of Haiti but most of them are established by testimony, by public documents, and official communications and reports passing between the Secretary of the Navy, the Hon. Josephus Daniels, Rear-Admiral William B. Caperton, United States Navy, and other officials. It is intended that the facts recited shall supply their own commentary. It is hoped that a recognition of the truth will lead to the adoption of the logical remedy."

Conclusions

"From the foregoing summary of the salient facts as to our intervention in Haiti and descriptive of the present status of the Haitian Government we deduce these general and specific conclusions:

"1. The presence of our military forces in Haiti after the disturbances of July 27–28, 1915, had quieted down was violative of well recognized American principles.

"2. The seizure and withholding by our forces in 1915 of Haitian national funds was a violation of international law and of the repeated professions by responsible American Government officials of our position and attitude toward Latin-American Republics and weaker governments.

"3. The imposition and enforcement of martial law without a declaration of war by our Congress and the conduct of offensive operations in Haiti by Admiral Caperton prior to the acceptance of the treaty by Haiti were equally clear violations of international law and of our own constitution.

"4. The methods employed by the United States in Haiti to force acceptance and ratification of the treaty framed by the United States, namely, the direct use of military, financial, and political pressure, violate every canon of fair and equal dealing between independent sovereign nations and of American professions of international good faith.

"5. The maintenance in Haiti of any United States military force or of the control exercised by treaty officials under cover of the treaty of September, 1915, amounts to a conscious and intentional participation in the wrong of the original aggression and coercion.

"6. The present native Government of Haiti, chosen in 1915, unsupported by any elected representatives since 1917, being now at the end of its term of office, no negotiations should take place with such Government which involve the future of Haiti or which can in any material respect affect its future.

"7. The functions of a department of colonies and dependencies assumed by the Navy Department and conferred on it by mere executive action are unauthorized by Congress or by other sanction of law, and should be condemned as essentially illegal and as a usurpation of power.

"8. We declare, without qualification, that the honour and good name of the United States, the preservation of the sovereignty and the cherished liberty of Haiti and her right to fair dealing on the part of the United States, as well as the possibility of assuring the continuance in the future of honourable and amicable relations between our country and Latin America, based on trust and confidence, all require:

"(a) The immediate abrogation by the United States of the treaty of 1915, unconditionally and without qualification.

"(b) The holding of elections of representatives to the legislative bodies of Haiti and of a President by the free will of the people at an early day.

"(c) The negotiation of a new treaty with a new Haitian administration for friendly co-operation between the United States and Haiti upon such terms as shall be mutually satisfactory to both countries and by the methods that obtain between free and independent sovereign States."

EXHIBIT H

"Occupied Haiti"

Under the auspices of the Woman's International League for Peace and Freedom, a committee of six, representatives of the United States Section of the W. I. L. P. F., two representatives coloured

EXHIBITS AND BIBLIOGRAPHY

women, a professor of economics and a representative of the Fellowship of Reconciliation, made a short visit to Haiti in 1926, and later published their report. As frankly stated in the introduction to this report, it is obvious that so brief a stay in Haiti was quite inadequate for anything like a thorough study of Haitian problems. But it is equally obvious that the committee had previously made a study of these problems and that its conclusions were based on an honest and unbiassed, if somewhat inadequate, investigation. It is certain that no fair-minded person can take exception to the following:

> They believe that their report shows the need for a well-considered and carefully planned program of progressive steps towards self-government, and especially for the re-establishment of an elected legislature, so that Haiti may be as well prepared as possible to stand on her own feet.
> They believe that they are suggesting something obviously reasonable, therefore, when they urge that an official committee be sent to Haiti to study the transition arrangements *in conference with the men who must work there; that is, with the leading Haitians and American officials,* and that this should be completed later, after an elected legislature is at work, by the final arrangements under which Haiti will begin the second chapter of her independence.

CONCLUSIONS AND RECOMMENDATIONS

EXTRACTS FROM THE REPORT OF THE COMMITTEE OF SIX

"Haiti constitutes a clear challenge to all who believe in the fundamental principle upon which the United States is founded, that government should rest upon the consent of the governed.

"The United States is at the parting of the roads. There has been for some time a drift towards imperialism, a movement veiled and therefore the more dangerous, dangerous to the liberty of our neighbours, dangerous to our own democracy.

"Our relations with Latin America are poisoned by the feelings roused by several instances of this imperialistic tendency on the part of the United States, and of all these instances our actions in Haiti are perhaps the most flagrant.

"Is it possible to give fair and dispassionate attention to the facts in regard to Haiti set forth, not merely in this and other unofficial reports, but in official publications, and not feel that the restoration of the independence of Haiti is binding on the United States, as both a moral and a legal obligation?

"From the point of view of United States interests, in the most 'hard-boiled' sense, there is little to be said for the continuance of our Occupation of Haiti. American investments there have in general not proved a source of legitimate profits, but of loss, and there is now nothing to justify, from the selfish point of view, the continued expenditure of United States money in administering the country.

"From the point of view of Haiti's interests, it is not true that we are in Haiti solely as disinterested benefactors, nor that we can show clean hands in our business dealings there. If our officials have tried to benefit the people of Haiti (as we believe they have), it is also true that the Occupation has cared for American financial interests there, of a none too creditable sort, at the expense of our poor and weak neighbours.

"Happily it is not the case that the United States is confined to the alternative of either occupying Haiti, or else regarding her necessities with indifference and unconcern. It is perfectly possible to be a good neighbour and help Haiti to attain health, education, public improvements and public order, by other less drastic, and ultimately more effective methods than military control.

"The authors of this report believe that the Occupation should be ended for the sake of Haiti, for the sake of the United States, and especially for the sake of good relations among all American republics, and finally because it is in itself an unjustified use of power. . . .

"To sum up the conclusions of the authors of this report, their impression of the present American administration is that its directing officials are honest, able and aiming to serve the people of Haiti, and that cruelty, abuse of personal power and violence seem to have substantially stopped, and the whole tone of the administration immensely improved over what it was at certain periods since 1915.

"The determining element in the situation, however, is the fact that it rests on force. This affects its character throughout. It tends to make the Occupation officials high-handed, careless of the law and, above all, contemptuous. It makes American rule deeply repugnant to all Haitians that still prize the independence that they have suffered so much to win and maintain.

"Although the maintenance of the Occupation is constantly excused on the ground that its object is to help Haitians in the funda-

EXHIBITS AND BIBLIOGRAPHY

mental matter of self-government, it is at best doubtful whether it is not doing quite the opposite.

"Our officials are setting up elaborate financial and administrative mechanisms which Haitians are not yet sufficiently advanced to manage by themselves. We are training them to subordinate themselves, and work under others, who take the responsibility. We are teaching them to accept military control as the supreme law, and to acquiesce in the arbitrary use of superior power. They are not permitted to elect representatives, nor to convene a National Assembly.

"Haïtians themselves complain that a generation is growing up without any political experience or habit of political responsibility or initiative, and that the government was never so militarized.

"Certain specific recommendations follow: . . ." *

EXHIBIT I

COUNCIL OF STATE

EXTRACTS FROM "DICTIONNAIRE DE LÉGISLATION ADMINISTRATIVE HAÏTIENNE," BY HANNIBAL PRICE

"At present the Legislative authority is exercised by a Council of State which provisionally represents the Legislative body, according to Article D of the Constitution. . . .

"The Council of State is the dean of our political bodies. It may be said it is as old as the proclamation of the National Independence. Were they not Councillors of State, the officers of the army who elected J. J. Dessalines Governor for life on January 1, 1804?

"Later, this title was officially given to them by Article 38 of the Imperial Constitution of May 20, 1805, which established a Council of State.

"We could cite many Councils of State in addition to the one of 1804, those of 1805, 1807, and April 25, 1844 (elected by the inhabitants of Cap Haiti and composed of 13 members), that of November 29, 1844 (appointed by Guerrier after dissolution of the preceding one and suspension of the Constitution of 1843); this Council took oath on March 6, 1845, at Saint Marc before Guerrier, who was dying, and convened the next day at Port-au-Prince; finally the Council of State of September 10, 1874.

"The following Chiefs of State were elected by Councils of State:

---

* The complete report was published in *Occupied Haiti*. (Writers Publishing Company, Inc., New York, 1927.)

Dessalines, Pierrot, and Riche; the two first were acclaimed by the army and the Council of State did nothing but ratify.

"The following Constitutions have been drafted by a Council of State: those of 1805, 1807, and 1811.

"We may add that the Council of State of 1916 has, if it did not draft, at least assisted in drafting the Constitution of 1918. It has also elected the present President of Haiti, Mr. Louis Borno."

BIBLIOGRAPHY

This bibliography is compiled for readers who may wish to study in more detail the history of Haiti and the Haitians. It is in no sense complete. No mention is made of the original documents and pamphlets in the collection of the author which have contributed to the historical accuracy of Black Democracy. Nor have the great number of magazine articles which have been written since the American intervention been completely listed.

Anthologie d'un Siècle de Poésie Haïtienne (1817–1925), by Louis Morpeau. Paris, 1926. (A study of the Haitian muse in the French and Creole, with bibliographical, critical, and biographical notes.)
Ardouin, B., *Etudes sur l'Histoire d'Haïti*, Paris, 1861.
Baker, C. S., *Some Colourful Haitian History*. Menasha, Wis., 1924.
Balch, E. G. (and others), *Occupied Haiti: being the report of a committee of six disinterested Americans representing organizations exclusively American, who, having personally studied conditions in Haiti in 1926, favour the restoration of the independence of the Negro Republic.* New York, 1927.
Barbe de Marbois, *Etat des Finances de Saint-Domingue.* Paris, 1790.
Bausman, F. (and others), *The Seizure of Haiti by the United States.* Foreign Policy Association, 1922.
Beard, J. R., *The Life of Toussaint l'Ouverture.* London, 1853.
Bellegarde, D., *Haiti and Its People.* Washington, 1922.
Bellin, N., *Description Géographique des Débouquements qui sont au Nord de l'Isle de Saint-Domingue.* Versailles, 1773.
Berlioz d'Auriac, J., *La Guerre Noire, Souvenirs de Saint-Domingue.* Paris, 1862.
Bird, M. B., *The Black Man; or Haytian Independence, deduced from historical notes.* London, 1869.
Brown, Dr. J., *The History and Present Condition of St. Domingo.* Philadelphia, 1837.
Cestero, T. M., *La Tragedia Haitiana.* New York, 1918.

BLACK DEMOCRACY

Charlevoix, Père P. F. X., *Histoire de l'Ile Espagnol ou St.-Domingue.* Amsterdam, 1733.
Coffey, R. B., *A Brief History of the Intervention in Haiti.* Annapolis, 1922.
D'Alaux, *Soulouque et Son Empire.* Paris, 1856.
Dalmas, A., *Histoire de la Révolution de St.-Domingue.* Paris, 1814.
Davies, John.—*See* de Rochfort.
Davis, H. P., "Notes on Haiti and San Domingo," *Pan-American Magazine*, 1917.—*Monthly Bulletin American Chamber of Commerce of Haiti*, 1823–1927. (Facts about Haiti, world's markets, February, 1924, etc., etc.)
Descourtilz, *Guide Sanitaire des Voyageurs aux Colonies, ou Conseils Hygiéniques des Européens destinés à passer aux Isles.* Paris, 1816.
Dorsainvil, J. C., *Manuel d'Histoire d'Haïti, par le Docteur Dorsainvil avec la collaboration des Frères de l'Instruction Chrétienne, ouvrage approuvé par le Conseil de l'Instruction Publique d'Haïti, le 29 mars, 1924.* Port-au-Prince, 1925.
Douglas, P. H., "The American Occupation of Haiti," *Political Science Quarterly*, New York, June and September, 1927.— Also *Occupied Haiti* (see Balch).
Du Cœur Joly, S. G., *Manuel des Habitants de Saint-Domingue.* Paris, 1802.
Edwards, Bryan, *An Historical Survey of the Island of Saint Domingo, an Account of the Revolt of the Negroes in 1791, and a Detail of the Military Transactions of the British Army in That Island in 1793 and 1794.* London, 1796.
Garan Coulon, J. Ph., *Rapport sur les Troubles de Saint-Domingue.* Paris, 1792.—Also *An Inquiry into the Causes of the Insurrection of Saint Domingo.* London, 1792.
Gruening, E. H., *Haïti y San Domingo.* Havana, 1922.
Haiti and San Domingo.—Cf. *List of References, Library of Congress, Division of Bibliography, August 15, 1921.*
Hakluyt, R., *Voyages; History of the West Indies.* London, 1812.
Hanna, Rev. W. S., *Notes of a Visit to Some Parts of Hayti.* London, 1836.
Hardy, C. O., *The Negro Question in the French Revolution.* Menasha, Wis., 1919.
Harvey, W. W., *Sketches of Hayti from the Expulsion of the French to the Death of Christophe.* London, 1827.
Hassall, Miss, *Secret History, or the Horrors of St. Domingo, in a*

EXHIBITS AND BIBLIOGRAPHY

series of letters, written by a lady at Cape François to Colonel Burr, late Vice-President of the United States, principally during the Command of General Rochambeau. Philadelphia, 1802.

Hazard, Samuel, *Santo Domingo, Past and Present; with a Glance at Haiti.* New York, 1873.

Inman, Samuel Guy, *Through Santo Domingo and Haiti.* New York, 1919.

Irving, Washington, *History of the Life and Voyages of Columbus.* London, 1828.

Johnson, James W., "Self-determining Haiti," New York, *Nation*, Aug. 25, 28–Sept. 4, 11, 25, 1920.

Kelsey, Carl, "The American Intervention in Haiti and the Dominican Republic," *Annals of American Academy of Political and Social Science.* 1922.

Kuser, John Dryden, *Haiti.* Boston, 1921.

Labat, R. P., *Nouveau Voyage aux Iles de l'Amérique*, 8 vols. Paris, 1742.

La Croix, Lieut.-Gen. Barno Pamphile, *Mémoires pour Servir à l'Histoire de la Révolution de St.-Domingue*, 2 vols. Paris, 1819.

Las Cases. *Relation des Voyages et des Découvertes que les Espagnols ont fait dans les Indes Occidentales, avec le Relation Curieuse des Voyages de Sieur Monteauban, Capitain des Flibustiers.* Amsterdam, 1698.

Léger, J. N., *Haiti, Her History and Her Detractors.* New York, 1907.

Mackenzie, C. (British Consul), *Notes on Haiti during a Residence in That Republic*, 2 vols. London, 1830.

Madiou, Thomas, fils, *Histoire d'Haiti*, 3 vols. Port-au-Prince, 1847.

Malenfant, Colonel, *Des Colonies, et particulièrement de St.-Domingue.* Paris, 1844.

Métral, Antoine, *Histoire de l'Exposition des Français à Saint-Domingue.* Paris, 1844.

Métral, Antoine, *Histoire de l'Exposition Militaire des Français à Saint Domingue*, with notes by Isaac, the son of Pierre Toussaint. 1841.

Mills, H. E., *The Early Years of the French Revolution in San Domingo.* Poughkeepsie, N. Y., 1892.

Moniteur, Le (Official Journal of the Republic of Haiti).

Moreau de Saint Méry, *Description Topographique, Physique*, etc., *de le Partie Française de l'Ile de St.-Domingue*, 2 vols. Philadelphia, 1798.

Moreau de Saint Méry, *Partie Espagnole*, 2 vols. 1796.

Nation (New York).—See Johnson; also many articles on the American intervention in Haiti.

Nau, E., *Histoire des Caciques d'Haïti*. Paris, 1894.

Niles, Blair, *Black Haiti*. New York, 1926.

Occupied Haiti.—See Balch.

Placide, Justin, *Histoire de l'Ile de Hayti, Ecrite sur les Documents Officiels et des Notes Communiques par Sir James Baskeet*. Paris, 1826.

Prichard, Hesketh, *Where Black Rules White*. New York, 1900.

Rainsford, Marcus, *Historical Account of the Black Empire of Hayti*. London, 1805.

Raynal, G. T., *Histoire Philosophique et Politique des Etablissements et du Commerce des Européens dans les Deux Indes*. Paris, 1820.

Redpath, James, *A Guide to Haiti*. Boston, 1861.

Rémy, Saint, *Solution de la Question Haïtienne*. Paris, 1854.

Rémy, Saint, *Petion et Haïti, Mémoires pour Servir à l'Histoire de Haïti*. Paris, 1851.

Rémy, Saint, *L'Ouverture, Chef des Noirs Insurgés à St.-Domingue*. Paris, 1850.

Report to the Secretary of the Navy by Brigadier General George Barnett, covering period June, 1915, to June, 1920.

Reports, "Relations with Haiti," issued by Office of American High Commissioner. Port-au-Prince, 1926.

Reports, Annual of American High Commissioner.

Reports, Annual, of the Financial Adviser-General Receiver.

Reports, Monthly, of the Financial Adviser-General Receiver.

Reports, Annual, of the Engineer-in-Chief (*Direction Générale*) Department of Public Works.

Reports, Annual, of the Chief Sanitary Engineer.

Reports, Annual, of the *Gendarmerie* of Haiti.

Reports, Annual, of the Agricultural Engineer (*Service Technique*).

Rochfort, Charles de, *A History of the Carriby Islands* (translated by John Davies). London, 1660.

Schoelcher, M. V., *Des Colonies Françaises*. Paris, 1842.

Schoenrich, Otto, *Santo Domingo, a Country with a Future*. New York, 1918.

EXHIBITS AND BIBLIOGRAPHY

Schomburgh, "Notes on St. Domingo," *Proceedings of British Association* for 1851.
Senate, U. S., *Hearings before a Select Committee on Haiti and Santo Domingo, United States Senate, Sixty-seventh Congress, Persuant to S. Res. 112, authorizing a special committee to inquire into the occupation and administration of the territories of the Republic of Haiti and the Dominican Republic.* Washington, 1922.
St. John, Sir Spencer, *Haiti, or The Black Republic.* London, 1889.
Steward, T. G., *The Haitian Revolution, 1791 to 1804.* New York, 1914.
Stoddard, T. Lothrop, *The French Revolution in San Domingo.* New York, 1914.
Tippenhauer, *Die Insel Haiti.* Leipzig, 1893.
Trollope, Anthony, *The West Indies.* London, 1860.
Union Patriotique, Mémoire of, published in the *Nation,* New York, May 25, 1921.
Vandercook, John W., *Black Majesty.* New York, 1828.
Vastey, Baron de, *Essai sur les Causes des Révolutions et des Guerres Civiles de Haiti.* Sans Souci, 1819.
Vastey, Baron de, *Réflexions Politiques sur les Noirs et les Blancs,* etc. Sans Souci, 1817.
Vincent and Bellegarde, *L'Année Enfantine d'Histoire et Géographie d'Haïti.* Brussels, 1924.
Weatherly, U. G., "Haiti: An Experiment in Pragmatism," *American Journal of Sociology.* Chicago, 1926.
Wimpfen, Baron de, *Reisen nach St. Doming.* Erfurt, 1798.

INDEX

A

Aborigines, 8-11, 14
Africans, (see Negroes)
Agriculture, 15, 90, 101, 105, 117, 212, 213; education, 260; Department of, 260, 268, 284-287
Alexis, Nord, President, 137, 138
American Chargé d'Affaires, (see American Legation)
American Interests (see also National City Bank and National Railroad), 142, 144, 200
American Legation, 132, 152, 153, 156, 159, 161, 176, 180, 181, 182, 183, 192, 199, 205, 214
American Minister (see American Legation)
Amis des Noirs, 30, 31, 34, 40
Artibonite Valley, 32, 72, 98, 100, 104, 275, 286
Atrocities, Spanish, 10-13. Colonial period, 36, 37, 42, 55, 56, 69; Haitian, 95, 120, 164; charges of, 219, 224-226, 232
Auguste, 138; President, 147
Automobiles, 275
Aux Cayes, 45, 127

B

Bank Nationale, 137, 142, 143
Bank, National City of New York, (see also Bank National of the Republic of Haïti), 144, 154
Bank, National of the Republic of Haiti, (Banque Nationale de la République d'Haïti), (see also Bank, National City), 143, 144, 145, 151, 152, 153, 154, 181, 273
Barnett, George. Brig. Gen. U.S. M.C., 225
Beach, Captain, U.S.N., 170
Benoit, (Battraville), 220, 222, 223
Biassou, 36, 37, 42, 44, 48
Blacks, (see Negroes)

Bobo, Dr. Rosalvo, 157, 159, 161, 162, 169, 173, 176, 177, 178, 179
Boisrond-Canal, 127, 132; President, 133, 134
Bolivar, 107, 108
Bonaparte, Napoleon, 57, 58, 59, 60, 61, 62, 70, 73, 86
Borno, Louis, 184; President, 244-251, 256, 259, 263, 271, 272
Boucaniers, 16-20
Boukmann, 36, 37
Boyer, President, 109-118
British, (see English)
Bureau Technique (see Public Works)
Button, Lieutenant, 221, 222

C

Caco, 145, 146, 148, 149, 150, 153, 155, 157, 169, 178, 188, 189, 218-224
Caperton, Admiral William B., U.S.N., 155-160, 167-179, 181, 202-204
Cap Francais, 21, 22, 33, 38, 39, 42, 44, 48, 51, 53, 54, 67, 69, 74, 84, 95. (see Cap Haïtien)
Cap Haïtien, 102, 109, 118, 125, 126, 146, 154, 155, 158, 162, 182, 216, 303
Caribs, 9, 10
Charlemagne, (Peralte), 218-222
Christophe, 4, 62, 64, 65, 66-72, 78, 81, 88, 91, 92, 99-102. President 103-109; King 109-113, 115
Citadel, 92, 110, 111
Civil strife, preceding Intervention, (see also Cacos), 143, 148-150, 155, 157, 161, 171
Civil War (see also revolutions), 105, 119, 125, 127, 128, 134
Claims Commission, 165, 199, 273
Claims, foreign, 133, 134, 143, 144, 151, 199, 273
Clervaux, 62, 65, 78, 81, 88

[365]

INDEX

Climate, effects of, 11, 23, 46, 72, 73, 74, 75, 77-79
Cocoa, 22, 24, 212, 286
Coffee, 24, 25, 97, 212, 266, 285, 286
Cole, Eli K., Colonel U.S.M.C., 205, 208
Colonial Assemblies, 32, 33, 34, 40
Columbus, Bartolomé, 11
Columbus, Christopher, 3, 6, 8-12, 14
Columbus, Diego, 12
Commissioners, French, 21, 23, 29, 38-45, 51
Committee of Safety, 179, 182
Communication, means of, 128, 134, 135, 197, 274, 275
Congress, U. S., 188, 192, 290, 299, 300
Conquistadores, 8
Consolidation scandal, 137, 143, 146
Constabulary, (*see Gendarmerie*)
Constitutions, of Haiti, 55, 57, 96, 101, 102, 103, 106, 109, 118, 130, 133, 134, 135, 209, 210, 211, 212
Constitution, (1918) amendments, (1928), 250-264
Constitution, (1918), provisions of, 210-214, 240, 241, 249
Constitution, revision of, 201-210
Constitution, (1918), transitory provisions, 211, 241, 249
Corvée, 216; abuse of, 217, 218, 234
Cotton, 21, 25, 212, 286
Creoles, 24, 26, 28, 29, 41
Council of State, 127, 203, 207, 211, 241, 242, 243, 244, 248, 251, 268
Crête-à-Pierrot, 72
Cul-de-Sac, 24, 223
Customs control, American, 152, 153, 182, 185, 195, 200
Customs duties, 116, 150, 151
Customs duties, hypothecation of, 153, 199
Customs houses, seizure of, 181, 182, 190
Customs, Receiver General, 187, 195, 196, 268, 271-274

D

Daniels, Secretary, 186
Dartiguenave, Philip Sudre, 173, 174, 176, 177, 178. President, 179, 180-190, 201, 207, 208; 214, 242, 244, 245

Davis, Robert Beal, Jr., 184
Debts (see also loans), 133, 137, 141, 143, 144, 150, 198, 199, 273
Delva, Charles de, 162
Deputies, Chamber of, 185, 202, 206, 240, 248, 299
Dessalines, 4, 55, 56, 61, 62, 64, 65, 70, 71, 73, 75, 76, 78, 79, 80, 81, 82, Liberator, 88; Governor General, 91-95; Emperor 96-98
Dissolution of Legislature, 202-209
Division, North from South, 104, 105
Domingue, 127; President, 131, 133
Dominican Republic,
Douglass, Frederick, 3
Dutch, 16, 18, 20
Economic conditions, Spanish colony, 12; French colony, 19, 21-26, 29, 56, 86; Free Haiti, 89, 97, 105, 108, 109, 115, 128, 189, 275, 284

E

Education, Haitian, 110, 125, 128, 146, 148, 238, 260, 266, 275, 284-287, 296
Edwards, Bryan, 36, 86, 305
Elections, Legislative, 203, 205, 242, 244, 245, 248, 250, 252, 299
Elections, Presidential, 148, 173, 176, 178, 207, 245, 249, 252
"Elite," 90, 97, 183, 191, 238, 241, 266, 292, 293, 294, 296, 298
Elizabeth, Queen, 14
Emancipation, 31, 39, 43, 46, 48
Empire, of Dessalines, 96-98; of Soulouque, 121-125
Engineers, (see Public Works)
English, 14, 16, 17, 20, 22, 45-47, 53, 59, 84-86, 115, 123, 126, 151, 167, 172
"Ephemeral governments," 141, 143-160, 293
Estates-General, 29, 30, 31
Exports, (see foreign trade)

F

Faustin I, (see Soulouque)
Filibusters, (see *Boucaniers*)
Finances, 144, 152-154, 170, 184, 193, 198, 292, (see also Financial Adviser)

[366]

INDEX

Financial Adviser, 188, 195, 196, 198, 214, 261, 268; and General Receiver, 271-274
Firmin, A., 136, 137, 243
Forced labour, (see *Corvée*)
Foreigners, (see Land ownership, foreign)
Foreign Recognition, 115, 180
Foreign Relations, 107, 115, 123, 129
Foreign trade, 25, 28, 115, 117
Forestry, 286
Fort Dauphin, (Fort Liberty), 61
Fort-Smith Commission, (negotiations for treaty), 157
France (see also French colony of St.-Domingue and French Legation), 16, 18, 20, 40, 46, 50, 59, 89, 91, 93, 94, 115, 116, 117, 118, 123, 141, 144, 151, 157, 172
French attempt to regain Colony, 106, 107, 108
French Colony of St.-Domingue, 4, 19-35, 38, 42, 44-47, 49-53, 55-57, 59-62, 64, 68, 74, 75, 79, 90
French Legation, 158, 159, 163, 164, 166, 167, 168, 173
French, Minister, (see French Legation)
French West India Company, 18-21
Fuller Commission, (negotiations for treaty), 157

G

Galbaud, 41
Geffrard, General, 124; President, 125, 126
Gendarmerie d'Haïti, 188, 194, 195, 202, 209, 216, 217, 219-223, 233, 237, 254, 263, 268, 269, 279-283
Germany, 136, 137, 141, 144, 150, 151, 158, 172
Gold, 15
Gonaives, 75, 90, 124, 135, 137, 146, 156, 266
Government, present organization of, 240, 267-269
Graft, government, 150, 207, 265, 274, 280, 288
Grant, U. S., President of the U. S. A., 128, 131
Guerrier, President, 119
Guillaume, Vilbrun, (see Sam)

H

Haitian Army, 194 (see *Gendarmerie*)
Haiti, area of, 105
Haiti, free, 91
Haiti, Republic of, 16, 25, 103, 104
Haiti, State of, 103, 104, 109; Kingdom of, 110
Haiti, united with Santo Domingo, 55, 115
Hanneken, Captain, 221, 222
Hazard, Samuel, 128
Health, (see public health)
Hédouville, General, 53, 54, 59
Herard, President, 118, 119
High Commissioner, American, 231, 269-271, 298
Hippolyte, 134; President, 135, 136
Hispaniola, 3, 6, 8, 10, 14
Hospitals, (see also Public Health), 276, 281
Hughes, Charles E., Secretary, 291, 296

I

Illiteracy, 25, 79, 110, 120, 209, 247, 285, 286, 294
Indemnity to France, 115, 116, 117, 118
Independence, Declaration of, 91
Indigo, 21, 24, 25
Industries, (see economic conditions)
Intervention, American, (see also United States relations with Haiti), 151, 155, 159, 167-179 (see treaty Haitian-American)
Intervention, American, achievements and failures, 236, 245, 267, 287, 292
Intervention, American, hostility to, 152, 182, 185, 191, 196-198, 201-209, 218-224, 229, 256, 259, 262, 268, 272, 281, 296
Intervention, American, policy, forecast of, 169-172; policy, 170, 171, 174, 175, 201, 210, 234, 237, 267, 297
Irrigation, 97, 197, 274, 275, 286
Isabella, town of, 11; Queen 8, 13

[367]

INDEX

J
Jean-François, 36, 37, 39, 42, 44, 48
Judiciary, 27; Haitian, 101, 106, 118, 202, 250, 252-264

K
Kelsey, Dr. Carl, 292, 295, 296
Killick, Admiral, 137

L
Labour, 25, 56, 97, 118 (see corvée)
La Navidad, 9, 10
Land ownership by foreigners, 96, 201, 202, 205, 208-215
Lansing, Robert, 171
La Plume, 69, 75, 78
Las Casas, Father, 13
Lasalle, 43
Laveaux, General, 46, 47, 49, 50, 51, 52
Lawyers, Haitian, 261
Leconte, 138, 145; President, 146, 147
Leclerc, Captain-General, 60-65, 66-82
Léger, J. N., 98, 124, 126, 133, 141, 176
Legislative bodies (see also Deputies, National Assembly, Senate) 100, 101, 103, 106, 116, 118, 131, 180, 240, 244
Légitime, 134; President, 135, 176, 203
Letters, Columbus, 8; Madame Junot, 60; Leclerc, 66, 75, 77-79, 80, 81; Christophe 67; Bonaparte, 68; President Sam (Guillaume), 163
Life Incumbency, 57, 91, 106, 118, 126
Lighthouses, 275
Livestock, 285
Loan, American, 193, 198, 200
Loans, domestic, 117, 144, 146, 147, 149, 153
Loans, foreign, (see debts), 117, 131, 136, 144, 145, 152, 153, 198, 199

M
Marines, U.S., 154, 159, 168, 169, 189, 194, 195, 219-223, 224, 226, 228, 236, 280, 295, 299
Martial Law, 184, 237

Massacres (see atrocities)
Massacre of Political Prisoners, 164, 165, 166
Maurepas, General, 62, 65, 70, 71, 72, 78
Medical School, 278
Menos, Salon, 173, 176
Metallus, General, 155, 162
Military expeditions, French, 40, 61, 65, 69, 73, 77, 86, 116
Military Occupation, U. S., (see also Intervention), 168-179, 182, 183, 210, 219, 225, 234, 237, 256, 269, 299
Minerals, 11, 15
Mocaya, 44
Modus vivendi, 188
Monroe Doctrine, 171, 172
Moyse, 61, 62, 64
Mulattoes, (see also racial relations) 15, 19, 27, 28, 29, 31, 32, 34, 37, 38, 45, 55, 73, 89, 97, 100, 108, 116, 118, 120

N
National Assembly of France, 31-34, 37, 38, 46, 53
National Assembly, Haiti, 131, 136, 149, 156, 192, 240, 244, 253, (see also dissolution of legislature)
National Bank (see Bank Nationale)
National City Bank of New York (see Bank, National City)
National Railroad, 142
Naval Court of Inquiry, 224-226, 227, 230
Natural resources, development of, 141, 171, 200, 213, 227
Navy Department, U.S., 154, 168, 169, 170, 173, 174, 175, 183, 186, 194, 198, 228, 233, 268, 269, 295
Negroes, 13, 19, 23, 25, 26, 28, 36, 37, 42, 48, 56, 69, 73, 76, 81, 89, 100
Nissage-Saget, 127; President, 128, 131

O
Ogé, Vincent, 34
Ogeron, Bertrand d', 19, 21, 22
Oreste, President, 148
Oscar, (Charles Oscar Etienne) 163, 164, 165, 166

INDEX

Ovando, 12
Ouverture, Paul L', 65, 69, 79
Ouverture, Toussaint l', (see Toussaint

P

Pauline, (Leclerc), 60, 61, 110
Peasant class, 97, 105, 212, 213, 216, 224, 239, 241, 247, 265, 266, 287, 294
Personnel, replacement of American by Haitian, 191, 235, 238, 268, 278, 281, 282, 283, 286, 288, 289, 290, 299
Pétion, 4, 55, 61, 79, 80, 81, 91, 92, 98, 99-102; President, 103-109
Pierrot, President, 119
Pirates, (see *Boucaniers*)
Plebiscite, 209 (see also elections)
Plaine-du-Nord, 24, 36, 54
Poincy, Chevalier de, 18
Political conditions in French Colony, 29, 31, 32, 33, 37, 40, 53, 89
Political parties, 133, 134, 247, 250
Polverel, 40, 43, 45, 47
Polynice, General, 165, 173
Police, (see *Gendarmerie*)
Population, aborigines, 13; Spanish Colony, 15; French colony, 23, 24, 26; Free Haiti, 105, 284, 303
Port-au-Prince, 43, 45, 46, 53, 61, 69, 90, 100, 102, 121, 126, 137, 147, 151, 156, 161, 162, 167, 176, 222, 223, 228, 275
Port-de-Paix, 22, 47, 49, 65, 72
President of U.S., 194, 260, 267, 268, 288
Press, Haitian, 236, 237, 246, 252, 255, 256, 257, 258
Prison, massacre in, 164; prisons, 280, 281
Proclamations and Orders, 49, 62, 66, 67, 68, 83, 85, 87, 88, 93, 168, 187
Public Health, Department of, 197, 198, 266, 267, 268, 269, 276-279
Public Works, Department of, 195, 197, 238, 267, 268, 269, 273, 274-276

R

Racial antagonism Haitian-American, 190, 191, 235, 256, 257, 296

Racial relations, 15, 19, 20, 23-26, 34, 43, 46
Rameau, Septimus, 131, 132, 133
Raymond, 34, 52, 63
Receiver General of Customs (see Customs)
Red Cross, American, 278
Removal of gold reserve, 154
Revolutions, Haitian, 98, 109, 112, 118, 119, 124, 161, 242
Revolt of Mulattoes, 32, 38, 46
Revolt of the Blacks, 36, 54, 76
Riche, President, 119
Rigaud, 45, 47, 52, 53, 54, 55, 61, 104, 105, 114
"Rights of Man," 31
Roads, 216, 217, 274
Rochambeau, Major-General, 52, 61, 62, 65, 82-84, 95
Rockefeller Foundation, 277, 278
Roume, 55, 59
Rulers of Haiti, 388, 389
Russell, John H., Colonel U.S.M.C., 225; Brig. Gen., 256. High Commissioner, 270, 271
Ryswick, Treaty of, 22

S

St. Christopher, 16, 18, 22
St.-Domingue (see French Colony of)
St. Nicholas, Mole, 8, 45, 53, 86, 135, 172, 175
St. Marc, 102, 112, 127, 146, 156
Salnave, 125, 126; President 127, 128
Salomon, President, 133, 134
Sam, (Vilbrun Guillaume), 137, 154, 155; President, 156, 161-167
Sam, T. Simon, President, 136, 137
Sanitation, (see public health)
San Souci, palace of, 110, 111, 112
Santa Maria, 8, 9
Santo Domingo, City, 12, 14, 61, 96; colony, 12-16, 21, 40, 55, 65, 86; Republic, 119, 123, 128, 130
Santo Domingo, united with Haiti, 55, 115
Senate, U.S., Inquiry, 167, 223-230; summary, 231-238, 269, 270
Service Technique, (see Agriculture, Department of,)
Simon, 138; President, 143, 144, 145, 146
Sisal, 286

INDEX

Slavery, 13, 23, 24, 29, 30, 31, 37, 38, 46, 76, 90, 115
Slave trade, 4, 13, 22
Senate, Haitian, 116, 152, 186, 189, 202, 203, 241, 248, 252, 299
Sonthonax, 40, 41, 43, 44, 47, 48, 51, 52, 53
Soulouque, Faustin, 119; President, 120; Emperor, 121-125
Spain, 9, 14, 18, 21, 23, 115, 116
Spanish Colony, (see Santo Domingo)
State Department, U.S., (see also United States, relations with Haiti) 142, 154, 168, 171, 172, 180, 182, 227, 228, 237, 261, 263, 268, 297
Sufferage, 241-251, 252, 293
Sugar, 12, 15, 22, 23, 25, 26, 29, 97

T

Tariff, (see also customs), 195, 274
Theodore, 148, 149, 151; President, 152, 154, 156
Titles adopted by Blacks, 37, 48, 91, 96, 100, 109, 121, 122, 127, 133, 135, 143, 155, 179
Treaty, Haitian-American, 180-193, 200, 290; (full text exhibit B)
Tortuga, 16, (see also *Boucaniers*)
Toussaint, The first of the Blacks, 4, 42, 48-57, 58-65, 66-73, 74, 75, 89, 92, 97
Toussaint (sons of), 61, 70
Treaty, Dominican-American, 152, 159
Treaty, Haitian-American, extension of (Additional Act) 192, 193, 198, 199, 200; (text exhibit C)
Treaty, Haitian-American, negotiations for, 152, 157, 169, 170, 172, 180, 183-187
Treaty, Haitian-American, opposition to, 181, 182, 183, 185, 186
Treaty, Haitian-American, provisions of, 187, 188, 194, 196
Treaty Officials, 194-201, 249, 256, 259, 260, 261, 265, 267, 268, 287, 288

U

Union Patriotique d'Haïti, 226, 228, 229, 230
United States, relations with Haiti, 115, 123, 124, 125, 130, 135, 142, 145 (see Intervention American)

V

Vasseur, Captain Le, 18, 19
Vincent, 59
Violations of Legations, 126, 166, 167
Voodoo, 36

W

Waller, Littleton W.T., Major-General, U.S.M.C., 204
Washington U.S.S., 155, 156, 158, 162, 167
Whites, expulsion of, 41
Whites, supremacy of, 25, 26, 31, 34, 42, 52, 89
Willis, 17, 18

Z

Zamor, Charles, 149, 163, 166, 173
Zamor, Oreste, President, 149-151, 152, 164

For Product Safety Concerns and Information please contact our EU representative GPSR@taylorandfrancis.com
Taylor & Francis Verlag GmbH, Kaufingerstraße 24, 80331 München, Germany

www.ingramcontent.com/pod-product-compliance
Lightning Source LLC
Chambersburg PA
CBHW071141300426

44113CB00009B/1040